GENERAL HARRIET TUBMAN

Carter Godwin Woodson

THE WOODSON SERIES

GENERAL HARRIET TUBMAN

Earl Conrad

Black Classic Press
Baltimore

General Harriet Tubman

Earl Conrad
Copyright 1943 by The Associated Publishers
Copyright 1990 by Anna Alyse Conrad

Published 2019 by Black Classic Press

Library of Congress Control Number: 2019937602

Print book ISBN: 978-1-57478-168-7
E-book ISBN: 978-1-57478-169-4

Cover design by Mitchell & Sennaar Communications, Inc.

Printed by BCP Digital Printing (www.bcpdigital.com)
an affiliate company of Black Classic Press Inc.
For a virtual tour of our publishing and printing facility visit:
https://www.c-span.org/video/?441322-2/tour-black-classic-press

Purchase Black Classic Press books from your favorite book seller
or online at: www.blackclassicbooks.com

For inquiries or to request a list of titles, write:
Black Classic Press
P.O. Box 13414
Baltimore, MD 21203

Introduction to the Woodson Series

The Association for the Study of African American Life and History (ASALH) is pleased to partner with Black Classic Press to make available the works published by the Associated Publishers (AP). Founded by Carter G. Woodson in 1921, the Associated Publishers dedicated itself to bringing to the public works by and about Africans and people of African descent that could not find a home among mainstream publishers.

For decades, Black Classic Press has distinguished itself as a company dedicated to ensuring that important works remain before the reading public. Moreover, the proprietor, Paul Coates, has been a stalwart supporter of ASALH and an exemplar of Woodson's philosophy that important knowledge about Black people must be available.

When Carter G. Woodson passed away on April 3, 1950, the Association he founded became the majority stockholder of the publishing house and continued to carry the mission forward. Over the years, the press was run by the giants of the Association, including Benjamin Quarles and Edgar Toppin. Yet, Miss W. Leona Miles was the day-to-day presence. She labored alongside of Carter G. Woodson during his last years, and continued to manage the AP until her own death in the 1990s. By the late 1990s, the publishing agenda of the Association had waned and, in 2005, the corporation was dissolved. Since then, ASALH has published directly through its own imprint, the ASALH Press.

The partnership between ASALH and the Black Classic Press could not have come at a better time: the centennial of the founding of Woodson's Association in 1915. The works will appear as originally published in their final editions. The Woodson Series will not only bring "Black Classics" back to life but do so at the major milestone in the history of the study of Black life, history, and culture.

Daryl Michael Scott, President of ASALH, 2013-2014

To My Wife, Alyse

THIS IS THE BOOK YOU HELPED ME TO DO,—
THE ONE THAT THE WHITE PUBLISHERS WOULD
NOT ISSUE. THAT IS BECAUSE THIS IS OF THE PEO-
PLE THAT THE WHITE RULERS ARE SLOW TO FREE.
BUT FREE THEM THEY MUST OR CONFLICTS LIKE
THE PRESENT WILL GO ON UNTIL THIS MATTER IS
SETTLED RIGHT.

FOR YOUR PART WITH THE LIFE OF HARRIET
TUBMAN—MY GRATITUDE.

EARL

CONTENTS

PART ONE

YOUTH AND REVOLT OF HARRIET TUBMAN

PART TWO

FOLLOW THE NORTH STAR

PART THREE

CAPTAIN JOHN BROWN AND "THE WOMAN"

PART FOUR

"I KNOW THERE'S GOING TO BE WAR"

Contents — Continued

PART FIVE

The War Years of Harriet Tubman

PART SIX

The Neglect and Death of Harriet Tubman

FOREWORD

There is a historic background to the writing of the life of Harriet Tubman. For this book was written before the surge of the black liberation struggle took hold and became part of that history.

Earl Conrad, reared in the Judaic tradition, was witness to the stagnant period of Jim Crow and its paralysing effect on a helpless and despairing segment of American society. Raised in Auburn, where Harriet Tubman settled after her many flights on the Underground Railroad, he often saw her sitting on her verandah, an old woman wearing the white shawl that Queen Victoria had given her. She lived in a part of Auburn which was segregated and called New Guinea. This was one influence on Earl Conrad which he carried away with him when he left Auburn to become a roving newspaperman.

The second and perhaps more profound influence on him was that, no matter what city he worked, the same segregation existed. Jim Crow was a national institution and lynching, rapes and outright murder of blacks were not uncommon.

Earl Conrad recognized the plight of black people as one that had to be altered so that a decent and more equitable society America could become. As a victim himself of anti-Semitism he had early understood the struggle that would have to be made to achieve the kind of society he envisioned.

He became one of the few white spokesmen for black liberation before blacks were able to be their own spokesmen. As he wrote, and I quote from the autobiography he completed before his death on January 17th, 1986: "I became convinced that the source of the essential historical America was in the black and white dilemma and that here I could find myself as a modern Abolitionist. Free the black man and help free my country from it incubus of slavery and bigotry. Who to write about? Through what character could such a story be told?" He found that character in Harriet Tubman.

The book was written in a period when blacks could not easily speak for themselves, when the stranglehold of the white power structure almost or quite measurabley stifled black spokesmanship and made it inevitable for an Abolitinist-type white spokesmanship to emerge. Earl Conrad was that kind of spokesman and Dr. Martin Luther King put it succintly in his book *Where Do We Go From Here: Chaos or Community,* when he wrote: "When the Negro (his designation at the time) was completely an underdog, he needed white spokesmen. Liberals played their parts in this period exceedingly well. In assault after assault, they led the intellectual revolt against racism, and took the initiative in founding the civil rights organizations. But now that the Negro has rejected his role as the underdog, he has become more assertive in his search for identity and group solidarity: he wants to speak for himself."

This spokesmanship by the blacks has spurred the development of civil rights and the improved condition of blacks today. Not complete has been this development, but the evolution of ever increasing mobility and equity for the blacks will continue henceforth. What Earl Conrad envisioned will become a new reality.

I am speaking for my husband, Earl Conrad, because I believe it is time that it be known of the fifty years he devoted to the black struggle. *General Harriet Tubman* is only one of the books he wrote about the black condition. His others included *Jim Crow America, The Invention of the Negro, Scottsboro Boy* (with Haywood Patterson), *The Premier, Club, Rock Bottom,* and *Gulf Stream North* (the story of the black menhaden fishermen, sharecroppers of the sea). He also wrote two books about William Henry Seward (Lincoln's Secretary of State and a figure in the movement of the Underground Railroad). One of these books was *Mr. Seward for the Defense,* dealing with the imprisonment of William Freeman, a black man who was defended by Seward in the first acknowledged case of defense on grounds of insanity; and the other book was *The Governor and His Lady,* the political and personal story of the Sewards which also dealt with the slavery question.

Tubman, Seward and Conrad all lived in Auburn.

When Earl Conrad wrote *General Harriet Tubman* the white publishers didn't want to publish a book about a black person, particularly a black woman. White editors remarked that there was no interest in such a subject, but Dr. Carter Woodson had the perception and wisdom to undertake to publish this biography.

If Earl Conrad were alive today he would feel that he was well rewarded to have this biography of Harriet Tubman reissued.

Anna Alyse Conrad
Coronado, California
1989

ACKNOWLEDGMENTS

Scores of persons have contributed the information, the understanding and diverse other assistance that has been necessary in effecting this completed life of Harriet Tubman. I could not possibly call it my own. It is as much the property of others, and of the Negroes in particular, as Harriet herself was the claim of her people and her country. Men and women from all walks of life, Negro and white, have lent their bit to *Harriet Tubman.*

Harriet's living relatives, Harkless Bowley of Baltimore, Mrs. Carroll Johnson of Auburn and Mrs. A. J. Brickler of Wilberforce, Ohio, have provided interesting memoirs of the liberator's life and have verified the biography of Sarah H. Bradford. This does not include all of Harriet's relatives but lists those rather that have offered material used in the book.

Perhaps if I had not heard Richard B. Moore speak on the life and work of Frederick Douglass, stimulating me to an interest in the Negro question, although I had been approaching it before, I might not have entered upon this study.

Mrs. Helen Woodruff Tatlock of Maplewood, New Jersey, was very helpful in granting a long interview in which she provided valuable reminiscences.

Without the constant aid of Boyd B. Stutler of New York and Charleston, West Virginia, whose expert knowledge on the John Brown affair has been at my service, the portion devoted to Harriet's relationship to the Old Man of Harper's Ferry, would be sadly deficient. Mr. Stutler aided, edited, encouraged and watched over the unfoldment of the whole story.

For assistance in the form of correspondence, for information, suggestions and diverse aids I owe thanks to a long list and I place it here in the unalphabetical manner in which I happen to take up letters and notes:

Mrs. Florence Carter of New York; Samuel Hopkins Adams of Auburn, New York; Oswald Garrison Villard of New York; Angelo Herndon of New York; Alice Stone Blackwell of Cambridge, Massachusetts; Elizabeth Lawson, George Murphy, Philip Van Doren Stern, John Garay, Leonard Ehrlich, Isabel Walker Soule, Cyril Briggs, Hildegarde Hoyt Swift and Herbert Aptheker of New York; Carter Godwin Woodson of Washington; Wilbur H. Siebert of Ohio State University; Miss Katherine S. Day of the Stowe House, Hartford, Connecticut; Mrs. Fannie Lonon of the Harriet Tubman House, Boston; Helen Storrow of Cornish Point, Buzzards Bay, Massachusetts; J. M. Pollard Sr. of Buffalo and Auburn, New York; Rufus Gibson of the Schomburg Collection in the 135th Street Branch Public Library, Harlem, New York; Sarah Bard Field of Los Gatos, California; Katherine Rose Foster of Baltimore; Eleanor Roosevelt; Mrs. Louise Bradford Varnum of Rochester; George S. Schuyler, Elmer Carter, Ella Reeve Bloor, Lawrence Levy, Theodore Bassett, Congressman Sol Bloom, all of New York; the Reverend James E. Mason of Salisbury, North Carolina; Sven Skaar of Los Angeles, California; and Harriet Stanton Blatch.

Claude A. Barnett of Chicago; Dr. Alden M. Squires of Brookline, Massachusetts; Carl Murphy of Baltimore; Lucy E. Anthony of Moylan, Pennsylvania; Professor W. F. Galpin of Syracuse University; Lillian W. Balcom of Boston; Julia V. Davis of Washington, D. C.; the Reverend A. Clayton Powell of New York; U. S. Bassett of New Haven, Connecticut; Wilbur G. Lewis of the Rochester *Democrat & Chronicle;* Albert DeLeon of Boston; June Purcell Guild of Seattle, Washington; Mrs. Nicholas Shaw Fraser of Geneseo, New York, and the following of Auburn, New York: Henry B. Johnson, Mrs. Frances Smith, Mrs. H. D. Noble, Charles D. Osborne, Henry M. Allen, Richard C. S. Drummond and Mrs. Ralph R. Keeler.

Also Dr. J. Dellinger Barney of Boston; Rose Karen Nelson of

New York; Isabel Howland of Paris, France; Hilda E. Higginbotham, Newton, Massachusetts; Dorothy Kurtz of New Rochelle; Olive Tryon Drummond, Oneida, New York; Mrs. M. E. C. Shimer of Cortland, New York; Edward T. Sherwood of Brooklyn; Dr. L. D. Reddick of New York; Emma B. Sweet of Rochester; Jerome B. Peterson of Brooklyn; Robert S. Ross, Mamaroneck, New York; Francis Payne, Newton, Connecticut; Reverend B. C. Robeson of New York; the Reverend Lorenzo King of New York; and Arthur B. Spingarn of New York.

Many Government officials have assisted me in tracing records relating to Harriet's work: Mr. Roy I. Melvin, clerk of the Circuit Court of Dorchester County, Maryland; Alvin P. Tisdel, superintendent of documents of the United States Printing Office; P. M. Hamer, chief of the Division of Reference of the National Archives, Washington, D. C.; George J. Olszewski of the Office of the Clerk, House of Representatives; James F. Rich, clerk of the Surrogate's Court, Auburn, New York; Stanley Guppey of County Clerk's office, Auburn, New York; County Clerk J. D. Shayler of Cayuga County, Auburn, New York; Major General E. S. Adams of the War Department; W. C. Black of the Veterans Administration, Washington, D. C.; W. H. McCrillis of the office of the Secretary of the Interior; E. L. Bailey of the Veterans Administration, Washington, D. C.; Burton S. Heal, Recorder of New Castle County, Wilmington, Delaware; Arthur Trader, Land Commissioner's Office, Annapolis, Maryland; Porter B. Chase, Military Department of the Adjutant General's Office, Boston; and Governor Payne Ratner of Kansas.

Libraries are famous for their clock-like work with biographers and historians, and the response to queries for information on Harriet Tubman has been no exception to this rule. I am grateful to the executives and the staffs of all libraries, and to the workers of the New York Public Library especially. The Library of Congress, including Louise G. Caton, Anne L. Baden, A. H. Leech, St. George Sioussat; and Fred Landon of the University of Western Ontario, London, Canada; James W. Foster, Enoch Pratt Library, Baltimore; William W. Bishop, University of Michigan; Helen B. Allen, Har-

ACKNOWLEDGMENTS

vard College Library; Arthur L. Bailey, the Wilmington Institute Free Library; Wallace H. Cathcart, the Western Reserve Historical Society, Cleveland; and of the Boston Public Library, Richard G. Hensley, Emily Nelson Hewins, Zoltan Haraszti, Elizabeth R. Adams and Jean Ehrenfield; Mrs. Harriet Teter, the Newberry Library, Chicago; Rossa B. Cooley, Penn Normal Industrial and Agricultural School, St. Helena Island, South Carolina; Mabel Runnette and Miss Polite of the Beaufort Township Library, Beaufort, South Carolina; Dr. Morris L. Radoff, archivist, Hall of Records, State of Maryland; Elizabeth W. Meade, Hall of Records, Maryland; Hugh M. Flick, supervisor of public records, the University of the State of New York, Albany; Sarah R. Bartlett, Concord, Massachusetts; M. McE. Murray, Ontario Historical Society, Toronto, Canada; Frances M. Staton, the Public Library of Toronto, Canada; Helen M. McFarland, Kansas State Historical Society; Kirke Mechem, secretary of the Kansas State Historical Society; Blake McKelvey, Rochester Historical Society; Luther P. Jackson, Virginia State College; J. Alvin Russell, St. Paul Normal and Industrial School, Lawrenceville, Virginia; W. J. Elliott, the St. Catherines Public Library, St. Catharines, Ontario, Canada; Charles H. Wesley, Howard University and Frances B. Wells, State Library, Annapolis, Maryland.

To all of these and to all others who have assisted me in the preparation of *Harriet Tubman* I express my deepest gratitude.

EARL CONRAD.

GENERAL
HARRIET TUBMAN

PART ONE

YOUTH AND REVOLT OF HARRIET TUBMAN

CHAPTER I

THE BREAD OF SERVICE

Although the time of Harriet Tubman's beginning as a slave is without certainty the *times* are not; and that is more important to the understanding of this woman than the detail of a date.

She was born during the dark and starless night of slavery,[1] probably in the year 1820. The place of origin was Bucktown, a village of a few hundred persons, in Dorchester County, Maryland. Harriet was the property of a plantation owner, Edward Brodas, who owned so many slaves that he hired out to other farmers those he did not need.[2]

Could we have the opinion of her master at this hour, he would perhaps date her birth even later, saying, "She was born about 1823 when she first began to run errands for me." Fortunately, a century or more afterward, the opinion of Brodas is not weighty, and although Harriet was certainly fetching things for her master in the middle of the third decade of the nineteenth century, she was breathing and bawling in a ramshackle cabin a few years earlier.

In a shack that was rain-soaked, discolored, without windows and almost airless, she took her place alongside an already large family. The slapdash framework leaned and it hung on as did most slave shanties. Somehow it weathered the storms, and its poor hungry boards rattled a raw kind of music when the wind blew.

Harriet's American ancestry traces back as far as 1725 or 1750, for it is known that her grandparents on both sides were full-blooded Negroes who came, shackled, from Africa. The wretched Middle Passage, with its torture and revolt, was the pioneer beginning of her forebears. These ancestors set foot deep into the earth, and they remained rooted to it for centuries. Lowliest of the lowly, earthiest of the earthy, Harriet's ancestry was of that period in the world's history when nations arose and expanded, cost what it might —for the Negro in particular. In the America of Harriet's grandparents, the Underground Railroad, of which Harriet became the guiding genius, was already taking root. On to the North, on to Canada. This became the primary thought of the blacks, uniting them, giving them a common aspiration. And at night, over special paths and with secret aid, they went. By 1750 there had been thirty slave revolts in the United States area and the legend of these had spread among the Negroes, giving impetus to the development of new underground courses to the North. In spite of repression and denial of education, the black people were finding a way, even in the time of Harriet's grandparents. When she was born a vast network of underground channels leading to the "north star and freedom" had already spread over the continent. By word of mouth the news passed of a land of freedom up above, and songs of this country sprang into the Southern air. More than this, by the time Harriet was toddling about on the Brodas plantation the Negro people, from Delaware down through Texas, had become united by their tradition of revolt and escape, and more than one Negro was planning a black republic in the South.

So dissolute was the slave system that Harriet, like all chattel, was not entitled to a legal name upon birth. Since her parents, similarly, were not permitted a civil marriage, the girl inherited two sets of names: from her mother, Harriet Green, and from her father, Benjamin Ross. The new-born was called Harriet Ross, thus combining some identity from each parent. In accordance with Southern custom Harriet, when she worked out, was called Araminta, a name amiably conferred upon most slave girls. Likewise, Harriet, as a token of respect, had to refer to her mistress as Miss Susan. This was a kind of unwritten law, based upon the policy that familiarity was unwise, and it was wrong to grant a slave anything—

including a name of her own preference. So, variously as Harriet Ross and Araminta Ross, she plied her childhood on the Brodas plantation and in the service of others.

Scattered and fragmentary though the information may be on Harriet's kin, all accounts converge upon the point that she was an intermediate member of a family of eleven children. She had two sisters carried away in a chain gang, one of whom left two children.[3] There are accounts of six brothers, William, James, Benjamin, Robert, Henry and John, those she rescued by spiriting them off, under cover, to safety in the North; and a sister Mary Ann; but the other sisters and brothers were sold into the slavery of the deep South.

Of Harriet's African ancestry there is a legend that it was of the Ashanti country. Harriet herself stated that in her youth the people about her said she was "one of those Ashantis."[4] That was a tribute to her early sense of rebellion, for the Ashanti leaders on the West Coast of Africa fought off Britain's invasions for four centuries, resisting bondage until they became a colonial possession of England in 1896. Ashanti courage became a legend throughout Africa, and it is still a reality on the Black Continent.

The Reverend Samuel Miles Hopkins of Auburn, New York, a student of African life and a profound anti-slaver, surmised that she descended from the Fellatas, another courageous African strain. It was the custom of scholarly whites at that time to theorize about possible origins of Negroes. These attempts to trace her lineage were tributes to her bravery, but her courage was due, not to the fauna or flora of the African jungle nor the tribal sociology of that continent, but to the purely American conditions of the time. The oppression of her people developed in her qualities of irrepressible spirit in the face of tyranny. Whatever her origin, she issued from the black race of old, that people which survived the perils of Africa for a million years, as it has survived the repression of the white man on a foreign soil. She was as black as the paint that any artist can squeeze from his tube: proudly, typically, symbolically black, so that all who beheld this woman, all who touched her, knew they touched upon the reality of the Negro people.

*   *   *   *   *

Half way up the Chesapeake Bay, large cruisers *en route* to

Baltimore passed Dorchester County in which Harriet lived for almost one-third of her life. In the center of the county was the drowsy hamlet of Bucktown, with no more than a dozen houses, and included in this number was the store, the church, and the postoffice. Behind the houses, and stretching in all directions, was the fertile country itself, and in remote corners of this landscape there moved, dot-like, the figures of black men and women as they nursed the soil's abundance. Just southwest of the town the Brodas plantation opened up, the home itself large and squat at the edge of a county road, the slave cabins a hundred yards behind, and the fertile acres rolling southeasterly toward the Big Buckwater River. Here was a background, idyllic and blooming, and Harriet, had she only been free, would have been content to live out her life there.

Once or twice she had been taken for a wagon ride six or seven miles off to the west to the shore of Mother Chesapeake, the region that was ripest with life, for the bay was stored with terrapin and the shore waters seethed with trout and bass hungry for worms. There were oysters and crabs to the point of industry, and the wild fowl spread upon the waters with primitive calls. A few times, as early as her fifth or sixth year, she went on long errands, miles to the east, where the slim line of the Transquaking River ran straight up the State, and she stopped and ached at the beauty of its tributary, the Chicacomico that stretched, thread-like, off toward the Atlantic.

An old and a rich country, Maryland—fit for kings, and slaves. Indeed, Charles I of England had named this region after his wife, Queen Henrietta Marie, and from then, 1632, to the time of Harriet, the lush riches of the country had been owned by almost regal wealth and worked by a subject people. For a century and a half tobacco planters had lived luxuriously here on the labor of their slaves, and this tobacco earth was the soil of Harriet's grandparents. Then came revolution in 1776, and tobacco sales to England fell to zero. The Dorchester farm land took on a new dress. There followed the tall stalk of corn, the waving yellow of the wheat field, acres of rye, and some areas became pastoral, with cows and sheep feeding, and snorting pigs trying to jump the fences that hemmed them in. So the centuries had rolled over in the central part of the Eastern Shore, with the black man rooting himself to this soft earth, the generations coming and going, and now Harriet, a small thin one, stood in the sun, wearing a tattered cloth that she called a dress, and wondered at the gulf between slaveholder and slave.

*   *   *   *   *

From the time when Harriet first toddled out of the cabin at her mother's skirts and looked up the dirt pathway at the large mansion that was known as "the big house" she had wondered about this place and compared it with the shack in which she and her folks were housed.   Soon she learned that the abundant orchards of apple and pear trees, the laden peach and plum trees, were not for her, nor for Rit, as her mother was called, nor for Ben, as her father was known.   Forbidden fruit stretched away endlessly across the fields. She could feed the chickens but only the Brodas family knew the taste of the fowl.   The crowing of the rooster, the bleating sheep and the lowing of the cattle were in her ears always, reminding her only of the things that she and her family could tend but not own, listen to but not feed upon.

She was a vital child, even though the coarse hands of her masters and mistresses tried often enough to beat the strength and spirit out of her.   Harriet herself has told of a childhood when the rebellion in her heart took the form of mischief and disobedience toward her owners.   Reacting against the sharp contrast of "the big house" that loomed up above, like an evil god, she acquired a deep family sense, and made the cares of her parents and her brothers and sisters her chief concern.   She merged into their lives pivotally, loving them the deeper for her early discovery of life's injustice. Sometimes she frolicked with her small brothers and sisters outside in the weeds and trampled grass, but these moments were few.   At night when Ben came home from his work in the nearby forests where he supervised the cutting and hauling of great quantities of timber for the Baltimore shipyards, she ran to him, eager to take a lift skyward in his strong, lumberjack arms.   There was little warmth in her childhood other than what she found in her own cabin.

Harriet never had a day of schooling.   She was suddenly ripped out of infancy and placed into slave labor.   At five she knew what it was to have a mistress, to keep house, to take care of a baby, to labor day and night, and to feel all of the callous injury that some indifferent white souls in the South of that time leveled upon their fellow humans.

One thing Harriet loved beside her family and her people, and this was the world of nature. The serenities of the field, the generosity of plant and animal life that made no distinction between black and white, the fundamental equity of wind, rain and earth before all men: that was an early discovery. The great changes of the season, she found, spared not the black man any more than the white, and the rain fell upon all colors.

The slaveholding system, or as it flatteringly called itself the Patriarchal Institution (only to be renamed the "peculiar institution" by the Abolitionists), never betrayed character as far as Harriet was concerned. The "patriarchs" attempted no subtlety in showing her "her place." She never, from the outset, had anything in her make-up of the "faithful" or "loyal" slave. She was, from the first, without trust, presenting her hardness of spirit in direct contraposition to the lordly offensive of her overseers. Her earliest conflict with the social setup was as violent as most subsequent engagements.

Her first mistress believed that a slave could be taught to do nothing and would do nothing but under the sting of the whip.[5] Harriet, fresh from a fleeting childhood in the cabin, the orchard and the field, was placed at housework without any directions as to how to proceed. It was the first time she had even been in a then modern white home. Her failure to satisfy on that bright morning, when she was not more than five or six, brought on the wrath of an intemperate "Miss Susan." She was lashed about the face and neck with a whip four times before breakfast.[6]

The next labor that the child performed has been described by Franklin B. Sanborn, an anti-slavery historian. "When Harriet was six years old, she was taken from her mother and carried ten miles to live with James Cook, whose wife was a weaver, to learn the trade of weaving. While still a mere child, Cook set her to watching his muskrat traps, which compelled her to wade through the water. It happened that she was once sent when she was ill with measles, and taking cold from wading in the water in this condition, she grew very sick, and her mother persuaded her master to take her away from Cook's until she could get well.

"Another attempt was made to teach her weaving, but she would not learn, for she hated her mistress, and did not want to live at home, as she would have done as a weaver, for it was the custom then to weave the cloth for the family, or part of it in the house." [7]

Harriet was resisting, hardening herself for a later, more definitive engagement with her masters. She did not want to work inside a home. Often when she was sent to a bedroom to beat up the feather beds she pretended that she was working hard, but when she had blown them up she would resentfully throw herself into the middle of them.[8] She wanted labor in the field and the comparative freedom of, at least, the fresh air and the sight of clouds moving happily northward. She was already determined upon the belief that her resistance could influence those who insisted upon her bondage. It would have been a miracle if this child had not ultimately become a rebel after such baptism in the slaveholding Christianity.

Harriet has related an incident of the following year. "I was only seven years old when I was sent away to take care of a baby," she said. "I was so little I had to sit on the floor and have the baby put in my lap. And that baby was always in my lap except when it was asleep or its mother was feeding it.

"One morning, after breakfast, she had the baby, and I stood by the table waiting until I was to take it; near me was a bowl of lumps of white sugar. My mistress got into a great quarrel with her husband; she had an awful temper, and she would scold and storm and call him all kinds of names. Now you know, I never had anything good, no sweet, no sugar; and that sugar, right by me, did look so nice, and my mistress' back was turned to me while she was fighting with her husband, so I just put my fingers in the sugar bowl to take one lump and maybe she heard me for she turned and saw me. The next minute she had the rawhide down. I gave one jump out of the door and I saw that they came after me, but I just flew and they didn't catch me. I ran and I ran and I passed many a house, but I didn't dare to stop for they all knew my mistress and they would send me back.

"By and by when I was almost tuckered out, I came to a great big pig-pen. There was an old sow there, and perhaps eight or ten little pigs. I was too little to climb into it, but I tumbled over the high part and fell in on the ground; I was so beaten out that I could not stir.

"And there I stayed from Friday until the next Tuesday, fighting with those little pigs for the potato peelings and the other scraps that came down in the trough. The old sow would push me away when I tried to get her children's food, and I was awfully afraid of her. By Tuesday I was so starved I knew I had to go back to my mistress. I didn't have anywhere else to go, even though I knew what was coming. So I went back." [9]

Harriet was given a flogging by the master of the house; and yet she said of this and other subsequent experiences that she did not blame the slaveholders for their cruelty. She understood their upbringing; she blamed the slave-system itself. "They don't know any better," Harriet explained, "it's the way they were brought up. 'Make the little slaves mind you, or flog them,' was what they said to their children, and they were brought up with the whip in their hands. Now that wasn't the way on all plantations; there were good masters and mistresses, as I've heard tell, but I didn't happen to come across any of them."

*   *   *   *   *

The seasons turned slowly for her, almost as imperceptibly as the annular rings appear in a growing tree. She worked here and there; now for someone living near Cambridge, on the gently elevated shore of the Choptank River; and again she toiled farther to the north, in the deeper recesses of Dorchester County where forests and hills wound from the Chesapeake easterly across the State. Then she would be hired out to someone whose plantation stretched along the bay, and she looked from the house on the hilltop down into the cove, her eye sweeping the shell-covered shore.

Harriet, at the age of nine, for example, was hired out as a nurse and general houseworker. After slaving all day she was required to attend the baby at night. Her mistress was particularly cruel and whipped her as often as five or six times a day. When

Harriet was nearly starved to death and unable to perform her tasks she was sent home to her master.[10]

It was on these trips home when she was rebuilt into health by her patient and understanding mother that she had the only touches of human warmth that she knew. Most of this was extended to her by her mother, a nervously sensitive woman who forgot slavery—as much as one could ever forget it—in ministering to the needs of her growing family. If mother could not give them freedom and material things, and not even enough food, she could and did give a love that loosed no harsh words upon her brood. There was enough fighting out there beyond, and no need for it in the cabin. Upon Harriet more than the others she showered this affection, for she perceived that the child's rebellious ways brought her into difficulties. So often now Harriet had come home beaten up, whimpering, muttering her hate and vengeance, praying, showing too much wisdom for one who was not yet in her teens. And all that she could do was to go to her mother's shoulder, or her father's arms, asking, "Why?" Harriet Green held back her tears, or rushed about the cabin in some flurry of labor to keep hidden her emotions; and Ben Ross, not a large but a strong man, with a stable quality his wife lacked, and a hopeful, religious sense, would say, "Child, don't fret so about it all. Heed God and be as good as you best know how to be." But Mother Green did not hide her feelings from her husband. She was a complaining sort—to him—and often spoke of Harriet as a special problem. Ben would look downward helplessly; he was as much a slave as their daughter.

There was not even much of this, the brooding and contemplating. Master Brodas never allowed much time for recovery. As soon as the little body was fattened up a bit, she was rushed off to some new station. When she recovered from the abuse of her latest employer she was hired to a master who required her to do the work of an able-bodied man, hauling wood, splitting rails, and other kinds of laborious work. Failing in any task given, she was shamefully beaten.[11]

A man's work was her lot even before she entered her teens. Her arms were becoming fibrous, her hands strong and calloused. Her eyes were becoming sullen, and the lids hung heavily, in a way that remained with her throughout life. Her features were forming prematurely; and even this early in life her lower lip protruded heavily, as though thoughtfully. She had not much pride of dress for she had never had a new one, and would not have known how to feel about a pretty article of clothing. She was unwashed and not considered attractive at all; she was just a *thing,* to be taught how to push and pull, to sew and cook—and then be compelled to do these things. During this period her muscles were moulded into the hard lines that were useful later to Abolition. Her own master, Brodas, she said, was never unnecessarily cruel, but some of those to whom she was hired out proved to be tyrannical and brutal to the utmost limit of their power. But as a field hand she was preparing for the life of hardship and endurance that lay before her.[12]

*   *   *   *   *   *

By the time she was twelve or thirteen she had won a victory for she no longer had to work indoors. During the remainder of her slavery she farmed, wearing a bandana to protect her head from the sun; and her skirts, getting longer, brushed against the upturned earth. In the neighboring fields were her brothers and she could wave to them, or sing a song and hear an answering chant a moment later. She could go down to the cabin and get a drink and say a kind word to her mother or one of her little sisters, and if when she returned to her post in the field the overseer objected she jarred him with her defiance. By now, among all the Brodas slaves, and among the Negroes on the Hughes, the Meredith and the Ross farms nearby, they talked of the young spitfire who defied and laughed at overseers.

Harriet had long since turned her ears Christward. When she decided that book-learning might forever be inaccessible to her, she began to pay closer heed to the biblical quotations that she heard from her mother and father. Ben and Rit were regular church attendants; the Bible was the one thing for which they had much respect. There was good in this book and its idea, they averred, and if only the white man practised what he said he believed, everything would be fine. It is not strange then that the lines which reached Harriet most deeply were the ringing ones that had to do with man's advance, with a slave's right to deliverance. When she learned that some Negro had been seen or heard of on his escape toward the North, the line ran through her mind, "Hide the outcast; betray him not that wandereth," and she prayed that the white folks would respond to her inner thought.

Working in the field, Harriet had picked up much of the folk-thinking that was prevalent. Such legend was centuries old, introduced here by the early colonial settlers, and passed on to all classes at that time by reason of the indentured servants, the Negroes and the children of masters, all living in the same household. The colored people gave the greatest impetus to such lore. Folk-thinking, superstition and religion often became an inextricable intermingling, but she was questing and trying to unravel the knots in her understanding. She could not yet distinguish between the kind of religion she wanted, that which could be useful to her for her own salvation, here on earth, and the whole web of myth and superstition with which she was surrounded.

END CHAPTER I

CHAPTER II

A BLOW FOR FREEDOM

"Soon after she entered her teens she was hired out as a field hand, and it was while thus employed that she received a wound which nearly proved fatal, from the effects of which she still suffers. In the fall of the year, the slaves there work in the evening, cleaning up wheat, husking corn, etc. On this occasion, one of the slaves of a farmer named Barrett, left his work, and went to the village store in the evening. The overseer followed him and so did Harriet. When the slave was found, the overseer swore he should be whipped, and called on Harriet, among others, to help tie him. She refused, and as the man ran away, she placed herself in the door to stop pursuit. The overseer caught up a two-pound weight from the counter, and threw it at the fugitive, but it fell short and struck Harriet a stunning blow on the head. It was long before she recovered from this. . . ." [12]

This is the key to the later Harriet Tubman: for if a woman's life ever contained a youthful episode which was a lever to unlock all of the other facets of her being, that incident was such a one.

With this, the seal of bondage was literally stamped upon her head, as though life must give this prisoner a number in the way that men brand cattle. But because Harriet was sensitive, and already possessed of instincts broader than those necessary for merely her own preservation, this imprint upon the head was destined to become her revolutionary badge of faith. She had been baptized in fire: the overseer had ground a symbol upon her which was as clear an impress as that which the Abolitionist printing press was already making upon its own pamphlet. Harriet's consecration to Negro liberation distinctly originated in that raw drama which occurred when she was not more than fifteen or sixteen years old. And so her childhood—if it can be said that she ever had any—came to a sad end, quite in accordance with its whole tragic development.

It was not alone the maltreatment to which she had been subject that caused Harriet to strike out in sympathy with the other. There were other, powerful factors at work at this time, both in Harriet's region and throughout the South, and it was out of these forces that the girl drew the strength to champion another.

Harriet, like many slaves in Dorchester County, had been influenced by Nat Turner's revolt in Virginia a few years earlier. The daring Turner had in 1831 delivered his fierce blow at the slaveholders, he and about seventy others striking up an insurrection that covered a twenty-mile bloody swath through hilly Virginia. They had killed sixty whites before Federal troops arrived, whereupon the militia and native whites, in an indiscriminate massacre of reprisal, killed about one hundred and twenty Negroes. For weeks Nat Turner cleverly eluded the white posses that hunted him but at last he was discovered, and he too took his turn upon the gallows.

Nat Turner had stirred up a hornet's nest. Perhaps this was largely because he had struck at an opportune time. For ten years there had been a sore depression in the United States; cotton and slaves brought less to the slaveholders in this period than they would at any time again until the Civil War. Mexico had just abolished slavery and was making a mighty effort to have the institution abolished in Cuba and Puerto Rico. In the colonial islands of the world and in many Southern slave states there had been sporadic outbursts of revolt by large and small groups of blacks . . . and the meaning of it all was that the Negro was beginning to move, that forces were at work inside the white population to derrick the Negro out of his trapped condition.

In Dorchester County, Harriet, then a growing girl driving oxen in the field and carting heavy produce, was exultant over the bravery of her fallen slave brothers in the State across the Chesapeake Bay. She hung upon every bit of information that trickled into Bucktown about Nat Turner's exploit. One or two of the free Negroes who knew how to read gathered slave groups about them at night, in the quiet of the cabins, and read to them the grim dispatches from stricken Virginia, and the controversial reactions that raged throughout America.

Harriet listened, nourished, not seeing Turner nor his confederates upon the gallows, but beholding only the enormity of the attempt, perceiving only how Nat's plan, begun by a half dozen men, had spread and infected dozens in twenty-four hours. It was the sign of it all that she studied. It was the power of men working and fighting together. It was the meaning of the black man advancing to his own nationhood.

There had been other sharp outbreaks that had left their mark on the South, on Dorchester County, on Harriet herself. In 1822 Denmark Vesey organized an insurrection in the region of South Carolina and involved thousands of Negroes in a plot that was smashed. Long before the Denmark Vesey outbreak, in the year 1800 the six-foot-two giant, Gabriel Prosser, planned an uprising in nearby Virginia. One thousand were to take part in that campaign and its repercussions continued up to the time of Harriet's adolescence. By the time she was fifteen, the Gabriel, Vesey and Turner traditions, and the legend of a dozen smaller upsurges in that generation, penetrated the whole South, and the black people were actively smouldering against the concentration-camp life of the plantations.

These were the influences that had given Harriet the courage to strike a blow.

*   *   *   *   *

Back on the plantation she passed the remainder of the fall in her parents' cabin. She was disabled and sick, her flesh all wasted away.[2] She lay on a pallet, or more correctly a bundle of rags in a corner of the room, and through dulled eyes she watched the movements of her family about the small, box-like place. She tried not to cry out her pain for fear of disturbing her small sisters and brothers, Benjamin, Mary Ann, and the others, but sometimes the anguish could not be borne. The child talked to herself and slept mostly, dreaming much, and in this way escaping from the plantation and the squalor of the dark dwelling.

No sooner did Harriet emerge from her crisis than her owner tried to sell her. Brodas guided one party after another down the narrow, dirt pathway that led to the shanty; arriving, he would bang on the door as a warning, push open the creaking boards as he might some dog kennel or cowshed, then usher within the prospective buyers. They wasted not much time here: through slit eyes they quickly noted the face grown scrawny, the dented head with its wound still alive, and the dulled, disinterested eyes. Their examination of the livestock complete, they invariably turned away, shaking their heads vigorously. And the more the prospective buyers rejected Harriet, the more exasperated became Brodas, and the more determined to sell her. As Harriet herself stated later, "They wouldn't give a sixpense for me." That is the best medical estimate of how critically ill she had been and how weakened she had emerged, for in the Dorchester County of that time probably any Negro with breath in his or her body could be bought at some price —all, it seemed, but Harriet.

She had sustained a convex dent in the skull, a mark which always remained. This has been referred to as a fracture of the skull. Whether or not this was so, Harriet had become only a wasted, sorrowing bundle of anguish that whimpered and moaned through the cold nights. Naturally, there was a response for her all through the Green-Ross household. They rallied around her, the brothers, sisters and parents, like any brood does toward a newborn. Harriet, the maimed, was born unto them.

The Negroes in the other shanties came to the Ross cabin from time to time, looked in, and greeted the girl casually, as though they did not want her to know how hopeless they really felt about her prospects of a good recovery. The region still rang with the story of her daring intervention in behalf of a fellow Negro, for although slaves were injured daily, not all bore the scars of a bold self-defense; and such a brand as Harriet had, that of taking another's blow, was almost unknown. Although they could see her physical helplessness, they could not know that there had occurred a sharp stimulus in the girl's thinking. This she did not even know herself, but it was there.

That went on until about Christmas of that year, which was probably 1835. By now she was able to emerge from the cabin and move around a little, and with this improvement she tried to help her mother. But she worked in a disabled fashion; she was silent and the songs were wanting that once had arisen throughout the day from her easy throat. She would plod for awhile, and then tearfully she would turn toward the soiled rags that passed as a mattress, and hurl herself ino their miserable refuge.

Harriet, desperate, turned to prayer. The significance in this development lay, not in the fact that she took up prayer, but rather, in the *kind* of prayer, for she prayed that her master be changed, softened, *converted!* Naturally such a prayer was no more realizable than if Lincoln had merely prayed for the slavemasters to give up their slaves, but her hope for a changed master was a step in the direction of the dream that all mastery might change, and that one day the whole system of slavery might be abolished.

Simultaneous with this advance in her understanding, a precisely opposite impression of her developed among the Brodas people. As a worker, of course, Harriet was still "not worth a sixpence." In fact, her masters, glancing at the enfeebled girl, perceiving the horrible injury done to her head and hearing now that she had "spells of sleep" that descended suddenly as she moved about in her daily tasks, shook their heads with the same wisdom as that which they might apply to an ailing cow or mare, and they decided that she was "half-witted." These periods of somnolence were a residue of the blow that she received. The injury had left her subject to a sort of stupor or lethargy. In the midst of conversation or some household task she would suddenly halt and fall into a deep slumber. This might happen three or four times a day. Presently she roused herself and resumed her conversation or work directly from the point where she had left off.[3]

Harriet's owners speedily interpreted this malaise as a calamitous blow to her senses. To begin with, they had never known what she was thinking, as indeed they knew little of the thinking of most Negroes, and now, when they came near to her, she was completely uncommunicative. As her views at this time indicate, she was really thinking twice as rapidly and clearly as before, but her silence, together with her weakened condition and the seizures of somnolence, conspired to present her to them as one who was now hopelessly useless and wrecked; and hence, dull-brained. Could her owners have known her prayer for a changed master, could they have discerned within this the germ of her later realization that *slavery must change,* they would not have been so quick to regard her as blunt-witted, and they might have sensed how really damaging that blow had been! Frank C. Drake, a newspaperman, writing upon this phase of her life, reported that "the white people on the plantation thought she was half-witted—*a theory she did not seek to disturb.*" [4] Far from seeking to upset this conception, Harriet learned to utilize it; for, it was just at the time when Mr. Brodas passed his opinion upon her that Harriet appraised him for what he was; that is when her intellectual faculties deepened, that is when she concluded upon the hopelessness of slavery, and at the same time embarked upon her own quest for freedom.

Her prayer at that time is one of the most revealing in the annals of religion, or more correctly, in the history of practical revolutionary thinking.

"And so," she said, "from Christmas until March (probably of the years 1835-1836) I worked as I could, and I prayed through all the long nights—I groaned and prayed for old master.

"Oh Lord, convert master! Oh Lord, change that man's heart!"

She prayed always, about her work, everywhere. When she went to the horse-trough to wash her face she took up the water in her hands and said, "Oh Lord, wash me, make me clean!" Lifting the cloth to dry her face, she implored that all of her sins be wiped away. Taking the broom to sweep, she entreated with the same kind of symbolism, "Oh Lord, whatsoever sin there be in my heart, sweep it out, Lord, clear and clean."

In March a new, a decisive factor entered into the situation, resulting in such a sharpening in her prayer as to represent the birth of a new, a fiery will. Rumor reached the Ross cabin that she and many others of her family might be sold South, or go with the chain gang down to the cotton and rice fields.

"Then," said Harriet, "I changed my prayer. I began to pray, *'Oh Lord, if you aren't ever going to change that man's heart, kill him Lord, and take him out of the way!'*" [5]

It had happened! The mighty religion of that time had struck root in her, as in thousands of other Negroes. In the North John Brown was acquiring a similar vision at about the same time; in New England hundreds of Abolitionists were bent by the same furious zeal. Harriet had sought out a god that might help her and she found one—with a hammerlock, for that was the kind that a slave needed!

*   *   *   *   *

Edward Brodas died within a year or two of the time that Harriet had been injured. The girl's serious illness had saved her from being sold South: no buyer wanted someone who might die, who might be an unprofitable laborer. Although Harriet had been anxious for her master's death, even to praying for it, she declared later that she sorrowed much upon the death of this man: "Oh then, it appeared as if I'd give the whole world full of gold, if I had it to bring that soul back."

Before Edward Brodas died he managed to sell some of Harriet's family to the South. Little is known of those dispatched to the South except that they retained the name of Ross, while those who later went North bore the name of Stewart.[6] When Brodas died the slaves were told that their master's will provided that none of them should be sold out of the State.[7] That information was received by the slaves with jubilation.

The death of Brodas was accompanied by a change of masters which was no improvement upon the old situation. The estate passed to an heir who was too young to administer the plantation, and the active mastery fell into the hands of his guardian, a man who, in all accounts, bears a most dignified "Doctor" before his name. Doctor Anthony Thompson was a preacher about Bucktown, apparently one of those abounding in the South at that time, of whom it has been said, they never delivered a sermon but that it was taken up with the obligations and duties of slaves to their masters.[8] In spite of Doctor Thompson's ministrations in the sphere of the divine he stinted his slaves on food and clothing and "led them a rough life generally." He has been described as a spare-built man, bald-headed, and wearing a wig.[9] A striking resemblance to the mature William Lloyd Garrison—minus the wig and the anti-slavery fervor!

There was at work the large, lumberjack hand of Ben Ross in the next stage of Harriet's life.

The thickly wooded Eastern Shore was naturally a lumbering

center and a major source of revenue for the slaveholders. One of these timber operators was the builder, John Stewart. He had hired Ben Ross from Dr. Thompson and made Ben the inspector of his lumbering gang. This was a responsible job, one that meant the supervision of the cutting and hauling of large quantities of wood to be sent to the Baltimore ship-yards. Ben, being a superior workman,[10] was worth five dollars a day to Stewart: and that was regarded as a sizable sum.

A valuable worker such as Ben might have gained the ear of his employer and confided the problem of his daughter who had been sick, who was still not altogether well, and in need of a decent place in which to work. Something of the sort happened, for Harriet soon started working for Stewart. John Stewart was a more lenient man than Brodas, Doctor Thompson, or the others, for long after Harriet's family escaped to the North many of them continued to bear his name. The steady period of employment with him and the fact that there is no record of any sharp incident taking place in connection with the service proves that here there was something of a moral breathing spell. She lived for five or six years with Stewart. At first she worked in the house. Later she labored in the open field, in the man-sized jobs that she liked best; she drove oxen, carted, and plowed, sometimes earning money enough in a year, beyond what she paid her master, to buy a pair of steers.[11]

* * * * * *

She recovered strength while she was still in her teens. The sunshine and the open air, the green fields and her own will to live —these were the medicines. Hard work put flesh upon her body, and she filled out and became womanly.

She attracted both Negro and white mainly for her typical qualities. There were already signs of that later magnetic appearance described in terms ranging from "magnificent" to "fierce." Her mouth was large and the cast of it was loose, with lips everted. Her eyes were heavy-lidded and appraising. A round, receding chin was set, rock-like; and her hair was short and crinkly. By now too she was almost as tall as she ever would be, which was about five feet; and her limbs had become strong. Labor in the field required nothing more for dress than that her body be covered, no matter with what, and so she wore the ill-fitting, rough, cast-off dresses discarded by the women of the Big House.   Pins held up her skirts and blouses; she went stockingless, and even walked shoeless across the paths, the fields and roads of the region.   She could not have gloried in her appearance, made formless by such apparel, but there was one item of dress that she did prefer: this was the colorful bandana, sultanic in effect, that always circled her head.   She wore such a headgear almost all of the days of her life.   The bandana gave to her a hardy, peasant-like appearance that no other style could achieve.

Her self-respect was in other things, like her running speed and the lithe freedom that was hers in a dash across a field or down a country road.   She took delight in her singing voice, for she sang whenever she could, and especially in the field it was good to lift the voice.   She caroled soft Methodist hymns, and already she, like many slaves, composed her own verses.   But her deepest emotion was the feeling that there was essentially no rank in this life, that she was as good as any white master or mistress.

"As Harriet grew older she became a marvellous specimen of physical womanhood, and before she was nineteen years old she was a match for the strongest man on the plantation of the new master to whom she now belonged.   He would often exhibit her feats of strength to his friends as one of the sights of his place.   She could lift huge barrels of produce and draw a loaded stone boat like an ox." [12]

That is an almost legendary strength.   It is the power that has been related of John Henry, the steel-driving Negro whose might was that of a giant.   Another report has it that her naturally remarkable power of muscle was so developed that her feats of strength often called forth the wonder of strong laboring men.[13] And John Brown was so astounded at the physical impression of this woman, together with the knowledge of her achievements, that he could only convey his regard for her by applying masculine terms to describe her.

Harriet, like her people, was gaining strength.   If her new-found force was not calculated, if it was not deliberately acquired by her own knowledge that she might need it in her future contests, then it was nature at work, subtly giving her a defense which her independent nature required. At all events she made a remarkable recovery from the critical encounter with the overseer. The period of labor in the fields developed in her those sinews which she later employed in the travails of Abolition and the Civil War. These were the earth years when her feet plunged deeply into the furrowed soil and when her mind extracted from the experience of slave labor patience and wisdom, vision and a supreme fearlessness.

END CHAPTER II

CHAPTER III

ESCAPE

The 1830's advanced grimly, with the black man snapping his chains here and there, while Abolitionists fired their guns in a hard, steady attack.

There were deep currents abroad in the land, and hardy spirits, white and black, preparing to unite these forces into one mighty flood of national feeling. Quakers and Puritans; refugees from revolutionary Europe; black men from Haiti who could tell how Toussaint Louverture had done it and how it might be done here; free blacks from Canada; new arrivals from far away Louisiana. They were on the march definitely, finding their way to New England and to Canada, there to enter into the wide network of the Northern radical movement, and from there to strike daggers into "the meanest and most shameless form of man's enslaving in the annals of history." [1]

Harriet caught glimpses of all this as she pushed her way over the rich sod of Dorchester. Rumors came to her ears of the white friends in the North, of the Negroes who were already there and doing things, of the black men who edited newspapers that actually attacked the slaveholding rule, and she had dreams of going to all of that. Years later she said, "I seemed to see a line, and on the other side of the line were green fields, and lovely flowers, and beautiful white ladies, who stretched out their arms to me over the line, but I couldn't reach them. I always fell before I got to the line." [2]

The line that Harriet dreamed of was no more or less than the Mason-Dixon border, and what went on above was the great movement for freedom: and it beckoned to her. The rumor, the word, and the legend came and fell upon her ears, as upon the senses of all blacks, almost incredulously. White men helping them? Yet it was true, and who was the Negro that had not heard of Garrison? The "beautiful white ladies" were no dream at all, but a very real group, at work mostly in New England, and in spirit holding out

24

their arms toward Harriet in the South. Elizabeth Cady Stanton and Susan B. Anthony had long since rebelled at the straitened conditions of women in all ranks of life. Lucy Stone, "a delightful young creature with voice of gold," had already spoken out against the major injustices of the time. Abby Kelly Foster was known to Abolition audiences far and wide. There were Sallie Holley, Lydia Maria Child, Lucretia Mott, and many others. Their words were heard throughout America and their influence had swept into Maryland.

But these women were white, with the white woman's increasing opportunities for education, career, money and public audience. It was more remarkable that Sojourner Truth, the first Negro woman orator in the land and one of the earliest suffragists, was already nationally known for her evangelical work, for her anti-slavery pronouncements, for her militant role among the white women suffragists. Sojourner was in her prime now, a tall, graceful woman, slim and strong, as hard work sometimes makes one; and the novelty of an ex-slave vying with polished and cultured white women for public leadership was a fact that hammered at the smug senses of those thousands of whites who believed in their own superiority.

Another was coming up, the most articulate colored woman of the century: this was Frances Ellen Watkins Harper, whose prose and poetry graced the most important Abolition journals, whose lecture campaigns drew hundreds to any hall in which she spoke. There were others, Sarah Douglass, Mary Cary, Grace Mapps, Mary Bibb, Frances Coppin: they were a solid corps of active Negro women who were growing up to speak and write and fight in various cities of the North and West.

Indeed, by now almost every Negro in the free states found *something* to do for freedom: they aided on the Underground Railroad with money and time and energy; they attended the white and Negro meeting halls and lent name and voice and appearance to their protests; they organized and signed petitions. In short, it was an age of genius, and a revolutionary movement, black and white in content, was crystallizing. For the first time in American history an understanding was growing up between a handful of whites and Negroes. There in the North they were finding their way to each

other, joining forces in the cause, training and strengthening each
other, and calling down to the South for more men like Douglass,
and women like Harriet, to *do* something; revolt, or come North,
but hurry!

The movement for freedom was many-sided by now, to the
point where there was much inner-feuding over questions of policy.
Abolitionists denounced Colonizationists, and the other way about:
the radicals split hairs over whether the Constitution was a pro-
slavery or an anti-slavery document, for momentous meanings hinged
upon the truth or falsity of this interpretation . . . until one day
Frederick Douglass would come along to study these matters and
formulate a policy by which men could fight.   The leaders of labor
made clear to the working people that there could never be a flourishing trade union movement or an independent political movement
of labor until slavery was abolished.   Colonel Thomas W. Higginson, the best historian of Abolition, wrote later that anti-slavery was
a people's movement, that it was stronger for a long time in the
factories and shoe shops than in the pulpits and colleges.   One wing
of the labor ranks raised the slogan, "Down with all slavery, both
chattel and wages."   Simultaneous with the mushroom growth of
the Abolition societies and the forward march of white labor in the
North, there sprang up regional farming cooperatives.   Inside these
cooperatives the anti-slavery question took hold and these reformers
too threw their full influence onto the side of the Negro.

The Negro drive toward leadership and culture was as irrepressible as the Civil War itself.   Black men appeared on the social
scene out of all proportion to the enslaved condition of the Negro
mass.   No place in the North, no meeting hall, no underground den
where policies were formed, but had its Negro actives, leading and
doing the strenuous work.   Fugitives hastened to educate themselves
to become more effective in the work of capturing the white North
for the sentiment of freedom.   The free Negroes perfected themselves in oratory, literature, the sciences and arts.   But it was the
slaves who leaped the highest, as soon as the most elementary opportunities presented themselves.

In Philadelphia black William Still, a prominent Abolitionist,
was already operating one of the busiest stations on the railroad to

freedom. Scores of other Negroes, too, were functioning in this act of the revolution, running back and forth from North to South, guiding off escaping slaves to the free states. Samuel R. Ward preached to a white congregation in the North. Richard Allen founded the African Methodist Church, although he died before the organization really took form. The Massachusetts Negro, David Walker, had sometime earlier published his Appeal, calling on the Negroes to unite and the slaves to arise, and that exercised a profound influence. Kentucky-born William Wells Brown was fighting on all fronts, organizing, writing, shuttling on the Underground, and speaking publicly. Negro contributors were coming to the fore in such numbers that the whole myth of white superiority was delivered a shattering blow. Martin R. Delany was in the very forefront as a physician, an agitator and editor; Robert Purvis' clear political thinking was the talk of the Abolitionist world; Lunsford Lane, who had come up from North Carolina, took to the rostrum, poised his good right arm and let them have it on the whole question; and until the rise of Frederick Douglass there was that small, but dynamic Charles L. Remond, employed as a lecturer by the Anti-Slavery Society. There were dozens of others, educators, mathematicians, poets, lawyers, ministers. It was a list for enumeration in a book-length chronology, and several such books did appear in subsequent years.

Harriet's region must have been very oppressive for it produced many of the foremost Negro revolutionaries. From here came the Abolitionists S. R. Ward, H. H. Garnet, and J. W. C. Pennington. In 1830, Hezekiah Grice of Maryland called the first Negro convention in American history. In Baltimore a whole corps of freed Negroes were busy aiding the Underground Railroad. Frederick Douglass had been praying for years, but at last, in 1838, he decided to pray with his heels—and that he did in an escape, which was and event in American history. Before long New England and the entire North would know of him.

In Boston William C. Nell was studying American history and discovering that the first man to fall in the American Revolution was the Negro, Crispus Attucks, and Nell was preparing for issuance on a later day his invaluable study, *Colored Patriots of the*

American Revolution. Negro-edited periodicals like *The Anti-Slavery Record* and Samuel Cornish's *The Weekly Advocate,* were carefully pointing out that the American Negro actor, Ira Aldridge, was the rage of England as early as the 1830's; that in Russia the Negro poet, Pushkin, dominated that muse even in this decade; that in France the Negro novelist Dumas was hailed as the greatest of the Old World; and Cuba's colored Placido was now her promising poet. And this when the mass of the Negroes, the world over, were still in chains.

Black-edited magazines and newspapers went into the progressive homes. Black folk music inspired the composers, the poets and the artists. Color had passed into the Anglo-American bloodstream, changing the hue of the skin of whole portions of the country's population: brown skins and mulatto colorings spread widely in the Virginia country and down in New Orleans, and indeed, wherever Negro and white were for long in association. Black labor was making the wealthy wealthier and slave labor was angering the slaves to ever greater anger. The color question had already split the Government and populations of the North and South into huge, conflicting forces, and some statesmen were trying mightily by every ruse of law and logic, religion and morals, to keep the Union intact —and others, by the same means, to split it. The Websters and the Calhouns were sparring with each other, smoothing over the disputes about Western territories, compromising, cheating. And all this time the blacks around Harriet watched nightly a tiny sky-point known as the North Star—and now and then a party stole away to follow it.

It was the fighting age, when reform was the outlook and those democratic seeds were planted which would later sprout and grow into the leaves of grass that Walt Whitman talked about when he wrote of America and the people and "nature without check with original energy."

Those pivotal ten years closed on the *Amistad* case, when Joseph Cinque became a remembered name. The nation rang with the alarm in 1839 when a ship floated in on the Long Island shore, with fifty-four Negroes aboard, three of them young girls. They had been seized and chained on the African coast by Spanish slavers, even though Spain had outlawed slave-trading; and when the blacks could no longer stand the crouching and retching in the hot confines, Cinque led them: they killed the captain, and four of the crew, and they took over the boat. Two white men were allowed to live—that they might steer the craft, and then the *Amistad* went on a ghostly, derelict ride through the seas till it reached the coast. The Negroes were jailed amid a great Abolitionist protest and as the two white navigators claimed the blacks as their slaves: then a long fight went on in the courts. The voice of the anti-slavers lifted in the streets; the protests were non-ending and the halls filled to overflowing, as the voice of a growing minority of strong-backed, strong-minded, free-thinking citizens demanded, "Let these people go!" And when the Supreme Court, obeying the voice of the people, decided that the Negroes had been seized contrary to Spanish law, they released them and the New England crowds greeted a half-hundred new free Negroes. Ten years of organizing had borne fruit in a great victory—and the noise of it all reverberated across the plains of America, and the plantations of Dorchester County too, saying, spiritually, "You have friends in the North: revolt!"

Yes, Harriet had friends, real ones, white and black, many of whom were willing and ready to lay down their lives for her and the black people. She did not know them as yet, and they did not know her, but she had heard of them. They, like Harriet, were still maturing, even as the anti-slavery question itself was growing in America. Now in the 1840's the time was moulding them, uniting them, black and white, into a significant political movement which was the talk of America and Europe. New England had produced such a corps of white leaders, Garrison, Phillips, Weld, Whittier and others, riding to fame and fortune and some to immortality upon the back of the slave, that critics referred to Boston as a modern Athens, as a place developing a "Golden Age of Genius." But a cause elicits the strongest stuff in men, and perhaps no age prior to that had produced a greater cause. Congressmen would soon lash out in the legislative halls: Charles Sumner of Massachusetts, Thaddeus Stevens of Pennsylvania, and Joshua Giddings of Ohio. The South had produced noted anti-slavery rebels, Cassius M. Clay, John G. Fee, and the Grimké sisters. Out in the West a young Abolitionist named Herndon was exerting an incisive influence upon his law associate, Abe Lincoln.

It was a young movement, too, in the main. John Brown, in 1840, was one of the "older" Abolitionists, and not very successful in business. Perhaps he reflected too much about his "greatest or principle object," that of working for freedom, and he was still haunted by the remembered sight of a Negro boy being beaten with a shovel. He was still beardless, prime and springy of step, and most of all he was busy spiriting off slaves to the North via that old locomotive that ran by night from darkness in the South to Northern light.

Harriet, chopping wood in the Dorchester forests, pushing the plow on the plantation, taking into her sinews the strength of the sap in the trees and the hardness of the rock underfoot, opened her mind to all of the inklings of activity that were going on up above and bided her time. To go North or to stay South, that was the question. To live here and to marry here, to slave, or to escape—these were her thoughts. To risk the dangers of escape or to face the humiliation of slavery, which? To desert her mother and father and their love, or to save herself? Over and over these thoughts raced through her mind, month in and out, year upon year.

It was marriage that decided her upon remaining still longer in the South. John Tubman was her last major experience in slavery.

*   *   *   *   *

Harriet was always notably silent about the matrimonial phase of her life, and it is the only chapter upon which, apparently, she was hesitant to speak. But there is sufficient information to reconstruct at least the outline of their life together, and to discern a conflict.

Harriet married late. It would have been late even for a white woman of that time, and it was especially so for a Negro mating because the people of color were nearly always married in their teens. She was married somewhere about 1844 to a free Negro named John Tubman, which means that she was about twenty-four years old at the time.

She could not have considered "taking a husband" in the sense that we understand it today. As a slave she would ordinarily have to live with the husband *selected for her* by her master. In her case, whether from the question of her health or other reasons, she was exempt from this procedure. That she married a free Negro proves inordinate factors operated in her marriage. In a region and a time of slave-breeding, she was not considered a breeder type and she was left actually to choose a husband. In marrying John Tubman she was already in contact with, at least, a bit of freedom, that small measure which was allotted to free-born or manumitted Negroes in Maryland.

The husband bore the name of Tubman from the connection of himself or his father with the ancestral home of the Tubman family,[3] which reigned for centuries, like a dynasty in the "Glascow," at the western boundary of the town of Cambridge, overlooking the Choptank River. This estate contained about 265 acres and it was the principal part of what was known in the seventeenth century as "Lockerman's Manor." John Tubman's parents, grandparents, and perhaps great grandparents had ministered to the wants of the Tubmans inside the spacious mansion, with its large rooms, high ceilings, beautifully carved colonial mantels, open fireplaces, mahogany stair rails, walnut floors and deep window seats.[4] Whether John Tubman ever saw the inside of this place, or worked here, there is no means of knowing, but his forbears well knew this interior—as slaves.

Harriet's marriage to a free Negro did not exempt her from her slave labor in behalf of Doctor Thompson. It meant only that at night she could share the cabin of a free Negro. But whether by accident or irony, she had happened upon a slight advance in her social station, even if only that of association, for the marriage of a slave woman to a free Negro was unusual. She not only earned money for Doctor Thompson, but likely she also helped support John Tubman. He was not one to fret himself about his wife's overworking. He distinctly preferred her to remain satisfied with her lot as a slave; and he was reluctant to listen to her complaints about slavery and her now increasingly frequent threats of going to the North.

John Tubman not only did not trouble himself about Harriet's fears that she might be sold South, but he did his best to betray her after she escaped.[5] How he attempted betrayal is unknown, but that is the best clue to him. Any Negro who betrayed another in flight was an abject and extraordinary individual.

Prior to her escape she "never closed her eyes that she did not imagine she saw the horsemen coming and heard the screams of women and children as they were being dragged away to a far worse slavery than they were enduring there." [6] This was Harriet's major fear, and John Tubman made light of it. He chided her, called her a fool, and said that she was like old Cudjo (a mythical character) who, when a joke went around, never laughed till half an hour after everybody else got through.[7] By this analogy John Tubman meant that Harriet perceived dangers where none existed, or crossed bridges before she reached them.

It was not long after these two came together that mentally they began travelling different routes. Harriet continued in her fitful dreams of escape or local insurrection, being a moody and unconsolable mate, and John Tubman was ever trying to understand this woman who looked at life with such serious eyes.

Harriet loved John Tubman; and he was the only deeply physical love of her life. She lived with him for at least five years before her flight; and the proof of her affection is in the fact that two years after her escape she underwent all of the hazards of a journey back into the slave country to see him and bring him North. Then she discovered him married to another, and no longer caring to live with her.[8] Her return to take him to the North proves all that need be known of her love. Indeed, it may have been his hapless, unworried nature that she loved, for no doubt this was his character. In the cabin he had been a light-hearted fellow, providing relief to the long days beneath the hot sun and the bullet-like glances of military overseers. John Tubman was a Negro who whistled, and not long after Harriet left and after his first upset, he went whistling to another cabin. At any rate, soon after Harriet had flown from the South, he was married to a woman named Caroline.[9]

One of the influences of John Tubman was to arouse in Harriet a curiosity about legal questions. She inquired of him how he happened to be a free Negro. Out of this questioning she entered upon an investigation of her own background which produced an astounding discovery. She was in reality a free Negro!

Her own mother, Harriet Green, had been freed, but was never informed of her right!

Harriet consulted Dorchester County records in about the year 1845. She paid a lawyer five dollars to trace the will of her mother's first master. The examiner searched back as far as sixty-five years and he located a will giving Harriet's mother to an heir named Mary Patterson. Harriet's mother was to serve this person until the age of forty-five, but Mary Patterson died young, unmarried, and as there was no provision for Harriet Green in case of her owner's death, she was actually emancipated at that time.[10] But no one informed Harriet's mother of her rights and she and her children, including Harriet, remained in bondage.

Harriet's anti-slavery emotions deepened when she discovered this fact for she realized that there had been played upon her family and herself a typical, deliberate, slaveholding trick. She nursed this new injury to her heart, gave up all hope of ever becoming a manumitted Negro, and pledged herself to find a way out of this whole military and legal system, a way that brooked no dealing with "papers." Papers were part of a white man's civilization, and the whites could juggle them as they pleased. She had other plans.

John Tubman's most durable contribution to the partnership was that of his name. Harriet never ceased using it.

John Tubman influenced Harriet to appreciate all the more the need for freedom and its possible joys. Her escape was becoming more and more inevitable, and his resignation to the present scene more and more inviolate. It was now only a question of time . . . and the right situation.

*   *   *   *   *

The sleeping seizures continued throughout the years, attacking her daily, forcing her to suspend work for brief periods, and making it impossible for her to forget for a moment that slavery had maimed her. The sleep was of an amorphous type, not very deep, and it was troubled with dreams: she described these dreams to those about her.   She had heard many stories of the Middle Passage, the voyage of slaves from Africa to America, and her dreams often reflected this phase of slavery.   In one dream she saw a ship's deck with black men in revolt and white men lying in crimson stains upon the floor.[11]   This was about what had happened in the *Amistad* case, and in dozens of other voyages across the Atlantic.   Such stories had been told to Harriet by older slaves who themselves witnessed mutinies in the very ships that had brought them to these shores.   In another dream she was on a ship at night and a Negro woman clasping a child to her bosom crept from below and leaped into the sea.[12] Suicide had been responsible for a high toll of slave casualties, especially on board the terror-rife slave ships that crossed the seas.   And self-inflicted death still took a toll throughout the South.

The dreams revealed to her fellow blacks a restlessness which, they knew, was likely to burst forth one day in the form of escape or some other type of outbreak.   Her descriptions of them also indicated a naturally developing sense of poetry, an actual facility for composing it.   The world was in her mind, and if she could not get up in the public square and denounce it, she could express her criticism through relating these dreams of swift deliverance, martyrdom, bloodshed.   But the dreaming was parent to the later acts of disciplined revolt.

Finally, the turning years had deepened her religious sense and matured her early views.   Harriet, a born wrestler with ideas as well as with the physical tasks of the plantation, had only one recourse, and this was to transform the white man's religious conception to suit a black woman's purpose.   She did that without at all being aware of the process by which the change transpired.   For years she had been attentive to the quotations from scripture, and by now she had an arsenal of lines, all of which fitted the purposes of a slave.   Yet it went deeper than that.   Nat Turner, Denmark Vesey, Cato, and other Negro revolutionaries, all implicit religionists, had taught the black American *applied* religion.   It was this that Harriet acquired.   If once she had prayed for release from an individual master, now she was desirous of an end to all of slavery for all of her people.   It was no longer a personal matter between herself and a Brodas or a Thompson.   The question of her salvation, she understood, was tied up with the issue of emancipation for her entire people. Although she prayed and quoted extensively from liberal Scripture, she no longer required of the "Lord" to do any of the changing of masters or killing of them for her. By now she herself was ready to kill for freedom, if that was necessary, and defend the act as her moral, her religious right.

*　　*　　*　　*　　*

The spectre that had haunted Harriet for so long, the fear that she might be sold to a far more degrading slavery in the deep South appeared one day as an immediate threat and impelled her to leave at once. The escape was precipitated by the death of the young heir to the Brodas estate. Rumor reached the slaves that Doctor Thompson planned to sell them directly. Then it hit like a thunderbolt when, one Saturday, it was whispered in the quarters that two of Harriet's sisters had been sent off with the chain gang.[13]

Harriet's flight occurred in 1849.[14] She had been living with Doctor Thompson for two years, she and her husband occupying one of the many cabins in the "quarters." Her parents and several brothers and sisters still lived on this plantation, all in the service of Doctor Thompson, or hired out to other nearby users of slaves.

The accounts of Harriet's breakaway attest the immeasurable peril involved in forsaking a Southern plantation. For long she had been agitating among her brothers an escape to the free states, and at the present opportunity she persuaded three of them to accompany her. But the brothers did not go very far. They became frightened by the dangers of discovery and returned. In spite of Harriet's objections they brought her back with them.

It was no wonder that the brothers lost courage. Their course was across one of the most hazardous no-man's-lands in history, not less perilous than a field of battle—and hundreds of miles in depth! This became evident to Harriet's brothers from the minute they stole away. On all sides were whites and Negroes who knew them, who might suspect they were escaping, who might inform on them, prevent their even getting out of Dorchester County. If one person reported to Doctor Thompson that they were seen heading North, that news would be relayed speedily to the slaveholders and slave-catchers all through the region. Handbills announcing their escape could be spread far and wide overnight. Then, what men could not find, bloodhounds might.

Harriet remained over Sunday. On Monday night a Negro from another part of the plantation came privately to tell her that she and her brothers were to be carried off that night.

That was enough! Harriet decided to venture forth alone, and this time to make good the flight. She said of this moment that this was her thought:

> "There's two things I've got a right to and these are Death or Liberty. One or the other I mean to have. No one will take me back alive; I shall fight for my liberty, and when the time has come for me to go, the Lord will let them kill me."

Harriet's last contact with her mother was when old Rit was on her way to milk a cow. Harriet approached and said, "Here, mother, you go along; I'll do the milking tonight and bring it in." Whether or not she did the milking does not much matter, but the ruse to retire her parent to the cabin succeeded.

Only one further step remained: to notify someone, anyone whom she could trust, of her plan to start out at once, for if she suddenly disappeared with nobody knowing where she was they might believe she had been seized and shipped South.

Harriet went to the "big house" to find her sister Mary, but when she located her, in the kitchen, there were others about, which prevented Harriet from speaking. She resorted to some mild roughhouse with her sister in order to draw her away from the others and out of the house. The sister ran out, with Harriet trailing behind; but outside, still another barrier developed.

The master of the house came riding up on horseback, and as frolicking during working hours was forbidden or frowned upon, Mary had to dart back inside of the house without having learned Harriet's intention.

And now, for the dual purpose of notifying someone, anyone, of her intention to leave, and to allay any suspicion by the master, she broke into song. The melody was often used by escaping slaves but it was also sung in church. She advanced toward the doctor and sang as she passed him. Did he wonder if her song had a double

meaning?   He stopped his horse, turned around in the saddle and
stared at her as she burst forth with these verses:

> I'm sorry I'm going to leave you,
> Farewell, oh farewell,
> But I'll meet you in the morning,
> Farewell, oh farewell.

> I'll meet you in the morning,
> I'm bound for the promised land,
> On the other side of Jordan,
> Bound for the promised land.

> I'll meet you in the morning,
> Safe in the promised land,
> On the other side of Jordan,
> Bound for the promised land.[15]

Long before Harriet decided to leave she had found an ally
in a white woman who lived in this region, one who had vouchsafed
aid to the slave woman in case she ever wished to escape.   Such
allies were not unusual: white Southerners often helped slaves on to
the North, especially the Quakers and a few Southern Abolitionists.
Even slaveholders, if they were paid, were known to send on an occasional fugitive.   The story of this abettor has been recounted thus:

"Harriet had a bed quilt which she highly prized, a quilt she
had pieced together.   She gave this bed quilt to the white woman.
I recall that Harriet even told me this woman's name, but what it
was I do not remember.   The white woman gave her a paper with
two names upon it, and directions how she might get to the first
house where she would receive aid.

"Harriet reached this first house.   When she arrived and
showed the woman of the house the paper, Harriet was told to take
a broom and sweep the yard.   This surprised Harriet but she asked
no questions.   Perhaps she suspected camouflage.   Anyone passing
the house would not suspect the Negro girl working in the yard of
being a runaway slave.   The husband, who was a farmer, came
home in the early evening.   In the dark he loaded a wagon, put her
in it, well covered, and drove to the outskirts of another town.   Here
he told her to get out and directed her to a second station. . . ." [16]

Harriet followed the North Star until it led her to liberty. Cautiously and by night she traveled, carefully finding out who were her friends. Aided partially by the organization of the Underground Railroad but succeeding in her flight mainly because of her own initiative and resourcefulness, she at last crossed the "line" which then separated the land of bondage from the land of free men. Thus she completed a journey that was epochal in the life story of her people.

Early one morning she arrived on free soil in Pennsylvania. The ex-slave's exalted emotion upon this occasion is evident in her own unforgettable words:

"When I found I had crossed that line, I looked at my hands to see if I was the same person.   There was such a glory over everything; the sun came like gold through the trees, and over the fields, and I felt like I was in Heaven." [17]

END OF PART ONE

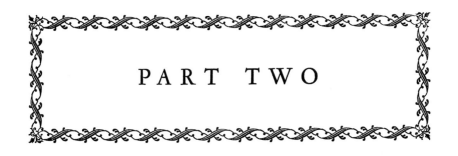

PART TWO

FOLLOW THE NORTH STAR!

"The romance of American history will, of course, be found by posterity, in the lives of fugitive slaves."—
Colonel Thomas W. Higginson in
The Liberty Bell *for* 1858, *p.* 47.

CHAPTER IV

THE BIRTH OF "MOSES"

"Rachel weeping for her children, and would not be comforted because they are not."
Matthew ii. 18; Jer. xxxi. 15

Once Harriet Tubman thrilled to the new-found emotion of freedom, there developed in her an urge toward championship of others which became the unceasing work of her life.

Harriet said that at this critical instant she "felt like a man who was put in State Prison for twenty-five years. All these twenty-five years he was thinking of his home, and longing for the time when he would see it again. At last the day comes—he leaves the prison gates—he makes his way to his old home, but his old home is not there. The house has been pulled down, and a new one has been put up in its place; his family and friends are gone nobody knows where; there is no one to take him by the hand, no one to welcome him.

"So it was with me. I had crossed the line. I was *free;* but there was no one to welcome me to the land of freedom. I was a stranger in a strange land; and my home, after all, was down in Maryland; because my father, my mother, my brothers, my sisters, and friends were there. But I was free and *they should be free!* I would make a home in the North and bring them there! . . .[1]

With this resolve in mind she set out for Philadelphia. That city was large enough to be protective; she could find work there, lose herself within its immensity, and remain beyond the grasp of the slaveholders or their agents. She gained employment at once, and denying herself all comforts, hoarded every cent.[2] It was the most menial work, domestic labor of the type to which she was accustomed, cooking, laundering, cleaning and scrubbing. She labored in hotels and clubhouses, changing employment as she improved her income or working conditions. From Philadelphia she switched to a place at Cape May, New Jersey. There was a good reason why she passed from one post to another. . . .

Harriet was undergoing her first major experience in the North, the supremely important one of free labor. She was joyous at the discovery that she could select her own employer, or change jobs when conditions were unsuitable, and above all, retain her earnings or dispose of them as she saw fit. This confirmed in her the realization of the next great advance which the three millions of her people needed. Meantime her own achievement of free-labor anticipated, by almost two decades, the Negro mass arrival at this economic stage.

Soon after her arrival in Philadelphia she made the acquaintance of a valuable Negro named William Still. He was the chief "brakeman" on the Underground Railroad in that city; this was an important post because the Quaker City was a veritable "Grand Central Station" on the Road. Still directed what was known as the Vigilance Committee (also called the Active Committee), which was a group of Negroes and whites who helped pass fugitives on to the North. Since 1847 he had clerked in the offices of the Pennsylvania Anti-Slavery Society, and by now he was known throughout that State for his Abolition labors. To him posterity owes a debt of thanks for the records he kept of so many of the slaves that Harriet carried to freedom.

Her eyes opened to the incessant sacrifice of the Quakers. She observed how they raised funds to advance the work of the Underground; employed colored help if and when they were in a position to hire; boycotted South-made products in order to weaken the slaveholders; wrote and purchased anti-slavery literature; and in diverse ways transformed their moral creed into a force for freedom. In this first contact with the anti-slavery movement she was most impressed when she learned that hundreds of blacks were passing back and forth, annually, between the North and South, steering groups of fugitives to safety. Not all escaped through Pennsylvania, however, and in fact the peak of such activity was then in the Middle West, in the region of Ohio, where Levi Coffin was King of the Road, but there was a heavy traffic hereabouts, and Harriet prepared to enter into this, the front line of the revolutionary anti-slavery movement. She familiarized herself with the anti-slavery influences that had matured in the non-slaveholding states. She watched, with vital interest, the struggle to establish the Fugitive Slave Law which, if it were enacted, would make possible her recapture and return to the slave-owners.

Unable to read and write, she was handicapped in understanding all of the influences at work. Mainly she concentrated on saving her money in order to plunge into the task of abducting her family and friends. When she communicated with her family she had to dictate her letters to others. The earliest letters that Harriet dictated were those directed to the sister whom she first brought to the North. Intermediaries conveyed the plan of escape to this sister. In December, 1850, she visited Baltimore and brought away her sister and two children. They had come up from Cambridge in a boat, under the protection of her sister's husband, a free black.[3]

A living relative, Harkless Bowley, the son of the sister aided by Harriet, has added a few words to this episode, as Harriet described to him the story of the flight. She had told him of her plan to get his mother away from Cambridge, Maryland. The breakaway occurred on the day his mother was to be sold at auction to another slave-owner. During the course of the sale, conducted at the courthouse, the auctioneer went to dinner. Meantime his mother was hidden in a house only a five minutes walk from the courthouse.

"When the auctioneer returned, mother was gone. My father, John Bowley, took mother and two children in a small boat to Baltimore. Aunt Harriet had a hiding place there for her. In a few days she took her and the children and several others aboard the Underground Railroad." [4]

Harriet ushered this company into the free states, but what happened to them thereafter is no more a matter of record than is the history of most slaves who fled the South. There is, of course, a general explanation: that the experiences of the escaped blacks, both on their way North and after achieving freedom, were not greatly different from Harriet's. All entered into the Northern free labor economy; many participated in the radical movement; they lived their personal lives, of course; and later, when the war broke out, they did their bit in behalf of the Federal Union. Thus, their histories, after freedom, were similar to Harriet's, hers differing only in its intensity, only in that she was immeasurably more the leader than any of those whom she rescued.

Much is concealed behind the rather innocent phrase, "she visited Baltimore and brought away her sister and two children." To look simply at this and not examine the drama that lies beneath, is to miss the story of "the true romance of America." Ignoring for the moment that Harriet and her companies had to journey hundreds of miles, with each step of the way a peril, we get a glimpse of the danger involved in the fact only of their having to be in Baltimore after escaping. A Baltimore writer, Katherine Rose Foster, white, discussing Harriet's work in that city, touched upon the proscription at that time. "This city used to be a difficult place for even free colored people to get away from, and much more so for slaves. A law forbade a Negro's leaving here by railroad or boat without being weighed, measured, and then given a bond signed by persons well-known locally." [5] Harriet had to know how to circumvent these and scores of other hazards.

It has often been said, "She made nineteen trips into the slave country," but the meaning of this enormous enterprise has been hidden in the lack of illustration. A trip into the slave territory and the "kidnapping" of a band of blacks was no less than a military campaign, a raid upon an entrenched and an armed enemy. If it was anything less than a military task then it would not have engaged the attention of such a martial figure as John Brown, as for many years it did. If conducting was not a military assignment then no men would have been hounded, harassed, jailed and wounded, and no lives would have been lost. The Underground Railroad era was one of prolonged, small-scale guerilla warfare between the North and the South, a campaign that, for its activities, was often violent and always perilous. It was so much like guerilla warfare that it influenced John Brown into the theory that a more extensive development of this type of conflict might be useful as a means of breaking the grip of the slaveholders upon the economy, the politics and the government of the nation; it was one of the longest campaigns of defiance in the nation's history. When it is remembered that the Underground was an institution in American life for at least a half century, that by 1850 it was an issue so much at the core of the American problem that it called forth an ignominious Fugitive Slave Law, and that it was one of the greatest forces which brought on the Civil War, and thus destroyed slavery,[6] then alone is it possible to comprehend its significance. Harriet Tubman's outstanding participation in the Underground in its last and most vigorous phase, from 1850 until the Civil War, must be approached in the light of such a far-reaching influence as that.

*   *   *   *   *

Almost from the start of her activity as a conductor on the railroad to life, she operated under the harassment of Senator Mason's Fugitive Slave Law. This bill, of the most repressive nature, took as its first toll the political reputation of Daniel Webster, who at the time was regarded as the nation's outstanding statesman. When, out of political opportunism, he sought to compromise the feud between the North and South by championing the view of the slaveholders that escaped Negroes must be returned to their owners, he pitched suddenly in the esteem of the North and never thereafter regained his prestige. This repercussion served to illustrate how much at the heart of the times was the fugitive slave question. Simultaneously, thousands of Northerners who had been passive to the question of slavery awakened, and resented the law that gouged their rights; and their anti-slavery mood became crystallized. A part of the North settled down to the business of openly defying the law. Of course, some officials here and there proceeded to enforce the act, but it quickly became the majority belief in the free states that there was more justice in the defiance of the law than in its observance.

Probably the most revolting stipulation of the act was that a man claimed as a fugitive was to have no right of trial by jury! This assumed guilt of the accused beforehand and thus flaunted all prior practice of Anglo-Saxon jurisprudence. An alleged fugitive was also denied his right of habeus corpus! On the contrary, the law specified that a special commissioner was to have sole power to decide the question of slavery or freedom for any fugitive, and this upon a warrant presented by any slave catcher. Most of all, this act, actually once a part of the Federal law, contained a bribe! The commissioner's fee was only five dollars if he freed the Negro, and ten if the fugitive were sent back to slavery. Add to that, and here was the catch that aroused even the most neutral to the question of slavery: all citizens could be called upon by the sheriff to help capture a wanted black man, and if they refused they were subject to legal penalties—fining and even imprisonment. Such an act, in its latitude of provisions for the repression of a people, white and black, made every Northerner a party to the question of slavery, and by its very nature it created anti-slavers ten times more rapidly than had the Abolitionists with their score of years of agitation!

Harriet intensified her operations just about when enforcement of the bill began, making her Underground efforts doubly dangerous.

*   *   *   *   *

Success with her first party emboldened a second return to the South a few months later, and this time she brought away her brother and two other men.[7]

Throughout this period she dreamed of returning to John Tubman in order to bring him North, but this was not until two years after her escape. She does not seem to have reached her old home in her first two expeditions.[8] When at last she ventured into Dorchester County to see him it was the Autumn of 1851, and then she found her husband and learned of his infidelity. At once she abandoned him forever and collected a party of fugitives and brought them safely to Philadelphia.[9] It was her third descent into slave country; for two years she had toiled incessantly, saved money, and spent it upon these bands of fleeing Negroes. Her efforts, almost from the start, extended beyond the rescue of her own immediate family; and indeed, in the third flight the party was composed of entirely unrelated fugitives.

With the enforcement of Mason's law, residence in the free states became unsafe for fugitives and their families, and there was an exodus of them to Canada. In Massachusetts alone, forty Negroes sped to Canada within thirty-six hours after the measure became law. Likewise in Pennsylvania and in New York State, in those cities and towns where there had been large settlements of escaped blacks, there was a "refugee march" to the North country. Here they were safe, for in 1833 Queen Victoria had proclaimed free all of the colored on Canadian soil. The earliest evidence of Harriet's arrival in Canada is in 1851, when she piloted a party of eleven to the town of St. Catharines. In this refuge, part of a territory known as Canada West, Harriet made her home for the next six or seven years—if it can be said that she, with her constant traveling in these years, regarded any spot as her home.

That was Harriet's fourth journey. Having learned that she could outwit the forces of the law, the agents, the bloodhounds and the press, she returned to Maryland in December of that year. In the party of eleven were her brother and his wife. For all she sought safety "under the paw of the British lion," as she described Canada. Frederick Douglass, living in Rochester, may have sheltered this entire party. He gave aid to the Underground, protecting fugitives who went through Rochester, while on their way to Canada. Writing of the Underground line, he referred to a party to which he was once host: "On one occasion I had eleven fugitives at the same time under my roof, and it was necessary for them to remain with me until I could collect sufficient money to get them to Canada. It was the largest number I ever had at any one time, and I had some difficulty in providing so many with food and shelter, but, as may well be imagined, they were not very fastidious in either direction, and were well content with very plain food, and a strip of carpet on the floor for a bed, or a place on the straw in the barn-loft." [10]

With her party of eleven Harriet undertook more than merely their removal to a free clime. It was a severe winter for the run-aways. They earned their bread by chopping wood in the snows of a Canadian forest; they were frost-bitten, hungry and naked. Harriet kept house for her brother, and the ex-slaves boarded with her. She worked for them, begged for them, encouraged them, and carried them through the hard winter. [11]

St. Catharines, the first point of arrival in the free climate, became one of the main centers of freedmen's activities in that decade. This place was the northernmost center of Harriet's activities for several years. St. Catharines' population was about six thousand. The Reverend Hiram Wilson presided over the Negro community, and it was to him that Harriet brought her parties of fugitives on her journeys thereafter. For the self-freed he found temporary shelter, employment, and permanent homes in one or another of the Canadian cities. It was here that Harriet had her first real taste of freedom and learned what it was to live, as a human, in a "modern" town. The Welland Canal went through St. Catharines, and the town was improved enough to have a telegraph and railway line; the populace lived in small, neat, wooden homes; there was no Jim Crow section, and Harriet, for the first time—like the other Negroes—felt herself belonging to a community. St. Catharines became a kind of experimental grounds; it was a bee-hive of interest for the Yankee anti-slavery movement, for here were the first Negroes on the American continent—on a large scale—with the opportunity of proving themselves as citizens. The colony plunged into the task, demonstrating its worth by working industriously, keeping up their homes carefully, buying property, convening to discuss the plight of themselves and their enslaved brothers, handling matters of their own civic relation to St. Catharines, and educating themselves as rapidly as possible. Harriet yearned for such a state of affairs as this for all of her people, and she could never for long remain in that flourishing atmosphere without making fresh plans to speed South and capture a few more "articles," as the slaves were called in their masters' ledgers.

By now she was passionately aware of the movement for freedom all through the North and among the Canadian fugitives. She realized that the anti-slavery struggle was a multi-sided affair. She learned of the Garrisonians, with their dis-unionist aim and their belief that the Constitution was essentially a pro-slavery document, and she heard others, political actionists, discuss Frederick Douglass' belief that the Constitution was an anti-slavery document, and that the Negro could go free within the framework of the present society, the present Constitution. She heard of the Colonizationists and their hope of building a Negro world in Africa, but this she scorned: she who had worked the United States soil knew that this land was hers and it must be made to serve her interests. She believed in the power of the Underground as the front line against slavery. She perceived in this more than the mere rescue of her fellows. She knew that each time a black left a plantation the slave-owner suffered a sharp economic setback. If the masters underwent large enough losses many would be ruined and slavery might become unprofitable and insecure. Harriet knew that each abduction from the South was a recruit to an anti-slavery organization in the North. Every time white sympathizers with the Road were brought into activity to help along fugitives, the Negro gained allies or strengthened those he already had. Harriet knew that the Underground was the immediate struggle. Emancipation might be the aim of Garrison, of Douglass, and of many others, and this indeed was her chief aim as well, but the Underground was a process that would develop the North, and organize and educate it for the time when it would have to face a belligerent South.

In the Spring she returned to the States. She earned money by cooking for families and working in hotels. From Cape May, in the Fall of 1852, she went back once more to Maryland, and brought away nine more fugitives.[12]

In five journeys Harriet had rescued a number totalling not less than thirty and probably not exceeding forty. Already they were calling her Moses, and talking of her bravery. Rapidly she was building a mansion for freedom, and her legend was growing. Like Paul Bunyan who swung an axe and felled a forest, and black John Henry who could outdrill the steam engine: such was Harriet, who, when she took one step, straddled all of the states and placed a foot in another country! Only she was real and no myth! And a *woman*, something new in the lore of giant life!

END CHAPTER IV

CHAPTER V

A CHRISTMAS GIFT FOR CANADA

"There is strength
And a fierce instinct, even in common souls."
Felicia D. Hemans

Harriet Tubman said that during the period when she regarded St. Catharines as her home, which was from 1851 to 1857, she made eleven journeys into the slave country. This meant that she operated regularly throughout those years, working in the Canadian town intermittently, but making about two trips a year, and managing to spend several months annually in the Maryland region. It was during the mid-fifties that some of her most important campaigns occurred, and in these years belong numerous fragments of adventures that cannot with certainty be dated. It was not until the close of 1854 that Harriet "stole" three of her brothers in one nip, walking off also with three other persons, all of whom hailed from the Bucktown-Cambridge zone. . . .

As was frequent in Harriet's campaigns, the groundwork was laid by the use of a code letter. In this instance Harriet engaged a Northern assistant to write to a free Negro in Dorchester County who could read and write, and who, from time to time, aided escaping slaves. This was Jacob Jackson, a fellow conspirator, whose job this time was to notify Harriet's brothers of her approach. The significant passage in the communication reveals the utilization of the biblical tradition: "Read my letter to the old folks, and give my love to them, and tell my brothers to be always *watching unto prayer,* and when the *good old ship of Zion comes along, to be ready to step aboard."*

The postal authorities, who examined all mail addressed to slaves, intercepted the note, suspected the religious wording and other dubious features of the letter, and they called in Jacob Jackson to ask him the meaning of its contents. The free Negro knew at once the importance of the communication, but he said, "That letter can't be meant for me. I can't make head or tail of it." Yet he immediately notified Harriet's brothers that she was coming, advising them that they must be ready to start for the North.

The abductor arrived barely in time, for her three brothers, Benjamin, Henry and Robert Ross, were under duress: they had been threatened with the danger of immediate transfer to the hated deep South. Their sale, to go down to the cotton and rice fields with the chain gang, had been set for Christmas Day, but as the holiday happened to fall on a Sunday, the sale was postponed until the next day, and this gave Harriet just time enough to perfect the escape. She established contact with them, and gave them secret notice to be ready to start immediately after dark, the first stopping-place to be their father's cabin, forty miles away.[1]

The cabin of their parents, Benjamin and Harriet Ross, was in Caroline County, conveniently north of Dorchester. There is the word of Ben Ross himself, in a statement several years later, that their master, Doctor Thompson, in addition to his slaveholding had been interested in real estate to the extent of a dozen farms, at least,[2] and on one of these, in the county north of Dorchester, they were located, and slaving through their declining years.

But an unforeseen circumstance prevented the perfect functioning of the flight.

Perhaps the most trying situation among slaves was that in which a husband or wife, rather than continue under the terror of a brutal overlord, took the road to freedom, leaving his or her mate behind in slavery. As it often happened, one might be suffering terribly while the other was in a situation which was, at least, tolerable. Then came a struggle between love of one's mate, or love of liberty. In many cases love of liberty prevailed—and such an instance occurred upon this very journey, involving Harriet Tubman's brother, Henry Ross.[3]

At the hour when Henry Ross was supposed to join with the others in a dash toward their parents' shack in the uplands, his wife took to bed with approaching childbirth, and he had to go for a midwife. With this development, Henry decided to remain—at least for a few hours.

But when Harriet was ready, she never waited for anyone, nor did she wait for Henry. She gave orders to the brothers Benjamin and Robert who were on hand, and to two other men and a woman who meant to escape, to start with her at once.

In most men's lives the fact of one's wife giving birth to an infant would delay plans of any type. But a slave's life was dislocated from reality; there was no sense or logic to slavery's processes, and inversely, this gave to its victims a rationale that also followed no normal precepts. The birth could not have taken long, and at once Henry Ross became desirous of flinging out for the North. If he didn't go now, he might not again have the opportunity for a long time.

It was difficult for Henry to leave his wife, who had just gone through such travail, and added to this, she suspected his design. He would start for the door and she would ask where he was going. Once he went out of the door, and stood by the corner of the house, near her bed, listening. At length he heard her sobbing and crying, and not being able to endure it, he went back.

The last words of the wife, Harriet Ann, to her husband, were, "You're going to leave me; but, wherever you go, remember me and the children."

Nor does there seem to have been in Harriet Ann's mind any further question, neither an issue such as forgiveness, nor a need for censure: there was only this grim and tortuous hour—atop the child-birth—an exclamation of despair, and then acceptance of a situation that was bred by the hopeless nature of their white-enshrouded environment.

Henry Ross broke away into the night at full speed for his father's cabin.[4]

Sometime during the middle of Christmas Eve the main party, exhausted and famished, arrived in the vicinity of the Ross Cabin in Caroline County. Harriet was accompanied by two men, John Chase and Peter Jackson, a girl named Jane Kane, and the Ross brothers, Benjamin and Robert. They headed for the fodder house, located near the cabin.

Harriet had not seen her mother ever since her escape in 1849, which was at least five years before. However, she and her brothers decided not to let the old woman know of their arrival in the neighborhood for fear that she would raise an uproar which might endanger them. To add irony to the situation, the old woman had been expecting the boys all day, to spend Christmas with her as usual. She had killed a pig, made all the other preparations that her means could afford and she sat watching for their arrival.

Here then were three of her children, and one of them the famous and long-absent "Moses," only a few yards away from her, and she was destined not to see any of them! It was a poignant moment all around. Harriet decided to send the two strange men to the cabin to arouse old Ben, to acquaint him with the presence of some of the family, to advise him of the plan of escape, and to warn him not to allow mother Rit to know what was going on.

John Chase and Peter Jackson advanced from the fodder house to the Ross cabin, and attracted the attention of the father; he came outside into the cold Yuletide night air, and he heard their story. Immediately he gathered provisions, and went to the hiding place, slipping the food within the door. But here is one of the few insights to the character of Harriet Tubman's father. . . .

Ben Ross knew that he must not see any of his children, no matter how he aided them. He knew that his sons' mistress, Eliza Ann Brodins, or one of her representatives, would arrive at the Ross cabin in a day or two and ask Ben if he had *seen* his children. He did not want to tell a lie; and therefore, he would have to help his children without looking at them—even though he knew Harriet was here—Harriet, whom he had not seen since her first flight!

Meanwhile, Henry Ross, hurrying through the night miles from Bucktown, arrived at daybreak and joined the group in the storage house.

The strange drama of old Ben coming to the hiding place several times, but not seeing his children, went on all through that woeful Christmas Day. It rained very hard all that day, and the party could do nothing other than to wait for nightfall. It was a forthright crew that hid in the fodder house, looked down at the old folks' cabin and discussed their escape. Benjamin Ross has been described as "twenty-eight years of age, chestnut color, medium size and shrewd." Robert Ross, aged thirty-five, the oldest member of the company "had hardly been treated as well as a gentleman would treat a dumb brute." John Chase and Peter Jackson were of like mould, and had rebelled from similar masters. Twenty-two-year-old Jane Kane declared that her master, Rash Jones, was "the worst man in the country." [5]

With desperation born of such a background it is possible to understand the discipline with which Harriet and her brothers looked at the parents' cabin, all day long, saw their mother moving about, and yet would not reveal their presence. That night, just before it was time to leave, Harriet and her brothers stole down to the cabin, looked in through the little window of the place and took a farewell view of their mother as she sat by a fire, with a pipe in her mouth and her head on her hand as she rocked back and forth in her chair, wondering what had happened to detain her sons from the Christmas dinner.

When the time came for the escape to resume, Old Ben went a short distance with the party, but in a strange manner. He tied a handkerchief tightly over his eyes so that he would not be able to see them! In this way he accompanied them for a time, until at last the father and his children bade farewell. They left him blindfolded, standing in the road, ready to turn back, as they went on to the North.

Nor is there anything incredible in this account of old Ben's preparation for the white lie he later had to tell the slave-hunters. He was religious and honest, and falsehood was alien to his nature. And when the "head hunters" came to his cabin a day or two later to ask whether the escaped sons had stopped here, the aged Rit said she hadn't seen her sons at all, not even for Christmas, and she was heartbroken over it. The report also went back to Doctor Thompson that Old Ben hadn't *seen* one of his children this Christmas,—and that was good enough for Doctor Thompson! [6]

*　　*　　*　　*　　*

It was several days before the party arrived at Wilmington, calling at the home of Thomas Garrett. The journey thus far was entirely on foot, for when they arrived, Harriet was almost barefoot, and one of the men was about shoeless too. They had gone by night through a gauntlet of towns, including Dover and Smyrna, said to be "the two worst places this side of Maryland line," [7] through Canterbury, Camden, Moreton, Middletown, Pleasant, St. George, French, Elkton, and at last arriving at the Quaker's house in Wilmington. It was cold traveling and food was not plentiful, but they cheered one another as Harriet, by all of the devices of her several years experience, took them, at last, to Garrett's welcome shelter.

It was the night of the 28th of December when Harriet and her company started away from the Quaker's place on the next important leg of their journey. The Wilmington Abolitionist wrote a letter the next day to J. Miller McKim, of the Vigilance Committee in Philadelphia. McKim was white and one of the most important anti-slavery men in Pennsylvania. He had been one of the earliest to raise his voice for freedom, being in the work as far back as 1832. Garrett wrote:

Wilmington, 12 mo. 29th, 1854

Esteemed Friend, J. Miller McKim:—We made arrangements last night, and sent away Harriet Tubman with six men and one woman to Allen Agnew's, to be forwarded across the country to the city. Harriet, and one of the men had worn their shoes off their feet and I gave them two dollars to help fit them out, and directed a carriage to be hired at my expense, to take them out, but do not yet know the expense . . .

THOMAS GARRETT [8]

McKim, William Still and the others of the Philadelphia Vigilance Committee received them at just about the time when Garrett's letter arrived. It was a group that much impressed the Philadelphians, for it gave them an opportunity to meet three of Harriet's brothers, and they were pleased to see more of Harriet's stock on their way to freedom. William Still wrote an interesting entry in his valuable chronicle upon this occasion. Of Harriet he said, among other things, that "she was a woman of no pretensions, indeed, a more ordinary specimen of humanity could hardly be found among the most unfortunate-looking farm hands of the South." [9]

And this "ordinary specimen of humanity" took them all forward, station by station, through the Underground networks, until at last, early in 1855, they reached St. Catharines—and freedom.

END CHAPTER V

CHAPTER VI

THROUGH THE UNDERGROUND NETWORK

Although the center of Harriet Tubman's Underground operations was in the region of her birth, Dorchester County, Maryland, and in neighboring counties, her abductions were carried on throughout the East, and even into the far South. She had heard of the high death rate in the rice swamps, and the labor in chains, and it was her very fear of being sold into this bondage that had finally motivated her to escape; yet when she entered into *conducting,* she ventured into that region. Once when Harriet was working as a cook in a large hotel in Philadelphia, the play, "Uncle Tom's Cabin," was being performed. Her fellow servants urged her to see it, but she refused, saying, "I haven't got the heart to go and see the sufferings of my people played upon the stage. I've heard "Uncle Tom's Cabin" read, and I tell you Mrs. Stowe's pen hasn't begun to paint what slavery is at the far South. I've seen the *real thing,* and I don't want to see it on any stage or in any theatre." [1] The Negro historian, William Wells Brown, also refers to Harriet's adventures into the most difficult parts of the Southern country.[2]

There has been some difference of opinion as to whether Harriet used the Appalachian route, this being one of the most important passages to the North. That route extended as far South as Georgia and Alabama, and although Harriet, John Brown, and a conductor named Dillingham are reported to have used it, another historian, Wilbur H. Siebert, states that Harriet told him that she did not travel by the mountain route.[3] There is no reason why she should have found it necessary to function in the Mid-West when there were so many thousands in the East who were always ready to flee with any responsible conductor undertaking to lead them. Most of the evidence of Harriet's action deals with her piloting from the Eastern Shore northward along the East Coast, and westward from Albany to Canada. In the Maryland-Delaware region she was thoroughly acquainted with the stations and hiding places: she knew the roads, the swamps, the forests and other out-of-door protections; and she learned to know scores of white and Negro friends who helped her along. It was natural then that she should function best in that environment. Proof of her operations primarily in the East is William Still's history of the Underground Railroad which is a veritable monument to Harriet's work.

Harriet's route from Maryland to Canada was a checkered one, even though she usually managed to reach Philadelphia and New York on her way to free soil. Her most favored passage was that which took her northward out of Dorchester County into the State of Delaware, then into New Jersey and Pennsylvania until she reached Philadelphia. This was regarded as the most difficult stage of the journey, as the travel was through slaveholding and pro-slavery country until Pennsylvania was reached. Once within that state there were very live dangers of recapture, for many citizens obeyed the Fugitive Slave Law implicitly and were always ready to claim a reward for nabbing a helpless slave on the move. Some of these rewards went into the thousands of dollars, and one report has it that the rewards for Harriet alone reached as high as forty thousand dollars (probably total rewards offered by various authorities); and each town had its special commissioners, many being anxious to earn ten dollars for returning a fugitive. Harriet made use of stations at Camden, Dover, Blackbird, Middletown and New Castle in the State of Delaware, on her way to Wilmington and Philadelphia.[4]

At Camden, for example, Harriet and her broods put up at the Cooper House, a regular stopover for fugitives. This gray-painted, brick house was near the north entrance of the village. Negroes were concealed in a small, bunk-lined room above the kitchen. This hide-out was entered by a ladder, and a round window near the peak of the roof admitted light and air. At Odessa, Delaware, the slaves often stayed at the Friends Meeting House, on the south side of the main street. It was a plain brick structure about twenty feet square, with a pitched roof and pent eaves across the gable ends. This roof covered a loft in which the blacks hid.

So on, through the towns of the border states, the fugitives found shelter in homes of all types, in buildings of all sizes, in infinite forms of concealment. They were hidden in chimneys, in barns, under hay and straw, and sometimes in "potato holes" which were board-lined dugouts in the ground ordinarily used to store produce.

Delaware's most important station was that of Harriet's good friend, the Quaker, Thomas Garrett, at Wilmington. He was the outstanding champion of the Negro in that state, and in the course of his career he aided about 2,700 fugitives on toward the North. He admired nobody more than he did Harriet whose caravans he constantly sheltered. An ample corps of station masters and local conductors operated around the Garrett region, most of them functioning in conjunction with him, and regarding him and his house as the center of the Delaware movement. Mostly these aides, if they were not colored, were, like Garrett, Quakers. Harriett came to know all of these allies intimately.

In Chester County, a hotbed of the Road, there were dozens of assistants, with John Hunn and Jacob Lindley as the leaders. Doctor R. C. Smedley, a historian of the Underground Railroad in that county says that Harriet sent on parties, unaccompanied by herself, but inspired by her encouragement and directions, and these passed through the Chester County stations regularly.[5]

In other nearby counties the work plunged ahead with the same zeal. William Rahenstraw and Day Wood of Lancaster County forwarded passengers on to James Taylor and Levi B. Ward in West Marlborough. All of this was in the very region of the Mason-Dixon line where the chase was hardest, the risks most severe. The Reverend James E. Mason, of Livingston College, a Negro educator who knew Harriet, wrote of her difficulties in this section where the slave chains were heaviest and where the "crack of the slaveholder's lash repeatedly resounded in her ears." [6]

From there they went to John Vickers, or William and Simon Barnard in Darby; or if not to them, then to John Jackson, also in Darby; and from here they were passed on to Philadelphia. Sometimes James Pugh went to Philadelphia and notified the Vigilance Committee of the arrival of a group in nearby Pennsbury. Then J. Miller McKim of the Quaker City abettors of the Underground, or one of his associates, proceeded to the outskirts of Philadelphia and met this latest incoming command. Philadelphia was a pivotal connection for escaping troups. Here the fugitives were "examined" by a committee; William Still recorded the slaves' experiences, and the organization helped them on to New York. Not all cities had, like Philadelphia, an actual organized group such as the Vigilance Committee. Harriet learned of these sympathisers very early in her work. Certainly she knew many of them by 1852. "These gave her money which she never spent for her own use, but laid up for the help of her people, and especially for her journeys back to the 'land of Egypt' as she called her home . . ." [7]

In New York she called with her groups at the offices of the Anti-Slavery Society where Oliver Johnson and others greeted her. From there Harriet and her gangs jumped to Albany. The travel between these two points was by a variety of means—foot, stagecoach, railroad and even boat ride up the Hudson River. This was the most eventless portion of the Underground of any of its lines in the nation. The sparsely settled banks of the Hudson, and the diverse means of travel available, made for relatively safe passage. Then, too, the New York office of the Anti-Slavery Society was a strong branch: when parties proceeded from New York they were financially secure, the "brakemen" were experienced, and the network was more securely organized than in the border states.

The Road had some of its staunchest supporters in New York State, especially from Albany across the breadth of the state. The Underground touched at Troy, Schenectady, Fonda, Little Falls, Peterboro, Canandaigua, Oneida and at last it reached another "junction" or station of importance, the Reverend J. W. Loguen's at Syracuse.

An interesting stop that usually preceded Harriet's arrival at Loguen's home was the famous Peterboro mansion of Gerrit Smith, the powerful political figure, reformer and philanthropist. According to his cousin, Elizabeth Cady Stanton, the Peterboro place was an important station on the Underground. The barn and the kitchen floor were utilized as chambers for the fugitives. And here Harriet met Smith's friends, described by Mrs. Stanton as "choice society from every part of the country." [8] Whenever she found herself among such groups she responded to their urgings to describe the

South and to relate her adventures. However, of this society, only the discerning Gerrit Smith possessed a real understanding of her value. He admired her military fibre and her organizational talents, and the least he could do in tribute he always did: before she left he pressed a few banknotes into her hands and commanded her to take good care of her charges.

Then to Syracuse, where Harriet and the black Reverend Mr. Loguen became fast friends, cooperating now in the fugitive work, and later joining with Captain John Brown in the matter of the uprising at Harper's Ferry. In Syracuse too, the Hazards, Garnets and Rowlands, Abolitionists, were her abettors and friends.

If Boston was the agitational center for New England, then Central New York was the stage for the Empire State. Abolition and woman suffrage thrived, as busy organizations raised their protests constantly and rooted the anti-slavery mood into the hearts of thousands. Auburn, the home of William H. Seward, was a hive for the Underground as well as a publishing center for Abolitionist literature; it was here that Frederick Douglass' celebrated autobiography was printed. Central New York was the sphere of Seward, Smith and Douglass, of Susan Anthony and Elizabeth Cady Stanton; and a rallying ground for the parliamentary struggle among Eastern anti-slavers.

And at last Rochester, home of Douglass, Susan Anthony, the Porters, the Holleys and other foes of slavery. Rochester was the last big stop on the Underground and from here Harriet and her companions could look back on the whole route. Frederick Douglass, writing about this same series of stations, on what might be called the Harriet Tubman route, has mentioned the names of the more important "forwarders" and it is significant that most of them were Negroes.[9] That is important to understand, for the history of that period, as it has been consciously distorted or incompetently miswritten, has pointed chiefly to white Abolitionists: and that is a one-sided emphasis, for who would have been the most serious workers for freedom if not the Negroes whose own salvation was at stake, and in particular, those developed and leading blacks who were fully aware of the historical importance of their nation in America? The Underground Railroad was the most dangerous front in the whole conflict, short of the Civil War itself. After all, the people who escaped over the Road, were black. If it is true, as it has been estimated, that more than 50,000 slaves fled from the South to the free states and Canada, then it has to be true that the Negro people, in this situation alone, produced at least 50,000 individual revolutionary acts. And what other people in America up to that time, yes, including even the founding fathers, in their great struggle against Britain, exceeded or equalled such a demonstration of illegal protest?

Sometimes Harriet and her slave collections took shelter inside a Rochester Church. That was the African Methodist Episcopal Zion Church at Spring and Favor Streets. Fugitives by the score hid in its pews. "Here also was her spiritual home while in Rochester." [10]

When she didn't put up with Douglass, or Susan Anthony or at the church, it was with the Porters. The Porter family had moved here from Philadelphia, bringing along a Unitarian and an Abolitionist influence. They were hosts to leading Abolitionists and they were also regular receivers of fugitives, including Harriet's groups. [11]

From Rochester the slaves pushed on through several small towns. At Parma they hid in the cellar of a store at Parma Center; they put up at the Milhan House in Williamson, and from here they were smuggled to the docks of the gristmilling town of Pultneyville, where lake captains aided in transporting them thence to Niagara Falls. At the Falls they crossed into Canada over the Suspension Bridge which connected the two countries.

Such was the devious route out of "Egypt" which Harriet traveled. It was a flexible arrangement, and the path she followed was likely to vary with each journey. Any means of locomotion that was available was used, but chiefly the travel was on foot.

*　　*　　*　　*　　*

How did Harriet plan her trips? What were her methods, and what kind of a discipline did she exact from her parties? Could anyone at all go north with her? What about her strategy of movement and the question of defensive arms?

Interesting questions, but vital to the safe conduct of her parties. There is a general answer: a situation of such widespread repression against the Negro and his allies naturally called forth a need for such a cautious advance and such a preparedness for defense as that employed in the methods of irregular warfare.

In addition to the fundamental requisites of travel on the Road, such as arming with a pistol or other firearm, and the possession of funds and a knowledge of routes to the North, there were countless tricks of travel, and Harriet was acquainted with most of them. The most elementary knowledge, of course, was to be able to recognize the North Star, for all travel was done at night, and this star was the main reliance. Most conductors knew the trick of looking for moss on the north side of trees, and by this being able to determine a northerly direction. That knowledge was applied on dark nights when the guiding star was beclouded. A favorite resort of Harriet was to arm herself with passes which others wrote out for her. There were escapes by men in female attire, and women dressed like men, and on at least one occasion such a ruse was adopted by Harriet. All of the resorts of an ingenious humanity were used, with no possible avenue and means of escape remaining unexplored.

The Reverend James Freeman Clarke, a white Unitarian minister of New England during that effervescent period when transcendentalism flourished alongside the anti-slavery movement, has related how Harriet planned her work. There were people in the slave states, even slaveholders, who were willing to secrete fugitives if paid enough for doing it, she told him. She once passed an evening at his house and gave an account of her methods. She said she first obtained enough money, then went to Maryland, where she privately collected a party of slaves, and got them ready to start. After satisfying herself that they had enough courage and firmness to run the risks, she next made arrangements so that they should set out on Saturday night, as there would be no opportunity on Sunday for advertising them, and they would thus have one day's start on their way North. Then she had places prepared where she knew they would be protected and taken care of, if she had the money to pay for that protection. Then, said Clarke, when she was at the North, she tried to raise funds until she got a certain amount, and then went

South to carry out this plan. She always paid some colored man to follow after the person who put up the posters advertising the run-aways, and pull them down as fast as they were put up, so that about five minutes after each was up it was taken away.[12]

That, of course, is quite general, but it indicates cautious planning.

Another, dramatizing her method, said: "On some darkly propitious night there would be breathed about the Negro quarters of a plantation word that she had come to lead them forth. At midnight she would stand waiting in the depths of woodland or timbered swamp, and stealthily, one by one, her fugitives would creep to the rendezvous. She entrusted her plans to but few of the party, confiding only in one or two of the more intelligent Negroes. She knew her path well by this time, and they followed her unerring guidance without question. She assumed the authority and enforced the discipline of a military despot."[13]

Harriet was the unquestioned leader of her escaping patrols. The attitude was martial, severe. "She could not read or write but she had military genius," it has been said of her.[14] Her sense of army discipline has been shown in the frequent references to her attitude toward traitors in her midst. She was ready to destroy anyone who might renounce or endanger her charges. "She was gentle, kind, and sympathetic, yet quick of action. Always ready to move on the appointed time. Once when she with 25 slaves had lain in a swamp all day until well in the night without food, when the hour came for her to move, one of the men became faint-hearted and wanted to go back, saying that they would die anyway, and he would take his chances back on the old plantation. The others used all their persuasions in their power to have him continue but of no avail. She stepped up to him and aimed a revolver at his head, saying, 'Move or die!' He went on with the rest and in a few days he was in Canada a free man."[15]

Sometimes members of the party became exhausted, footsore, and bleeding, and declared they could not go on; they must stay where they dropped down, and die; others thought a voluntary return to slavery better than being overtaken and carried back, and insisted upon returning. "Then there was no remedy but force; the revolver carried by this bold and daring pioneer would be pointed at their heads . . .; and so she compelled them to drag their weary limbs on their northward journey." [16]

William Still referred to her sleeping seizures which did not impede her course. The idea of being captured by slave-hunters or slaveholders seemed never to enter her mind, he said. While she manifested such utter personal indifference, she was much more watchful with regard to those she was piloting. Half of the time she had the appearance of one asleep, and would actually sit down by the road-side and go fast asleep when on her "errands of mercy" through the South. "Of course Harriet was supreme, and her followers generally had full faith in her, and would back up any words she might utter. . . . Therefore, none had to die as traitors on the 'middle passage.' " William Still attributed her success in going into Maryland as she did to her "adventurous spirit and utter disregard of consequences. Her like it is probable was never known before or since." [17]

Strong words, these, especially as they come from the man who has left to posterity the most important set of records pertaining to the Underground Railroad. After all, he was at the center of the work; he knew the conductors, the travellers and the station masters. Hundreds, perhaps thousands, of fleeing slaves passed through his hands. He was a Negro and he could understand his people better than could Thomas Garrett, Levi Coffin, Oliver Johnson, Gerrit Smith, or any of the other white allies of the fugitive. Finally, when William Still referred to the Underground as the "middle passage" he uttered something that was important in another way, for this phrase covered two centuries of Negro history in America. Originally the term "middle passage" meant the route of the slave by ship, in chains, across the Atlantic, from free Africa to slave America. Now as Still used the expression, it signified a transformation of the concept to mean a passage from Southern bondage to Northern freedom, reversing the old meaning, and representing the beginning of a process to set aright the question of man's subjection by man.

*   *   *   *   *

Harriet employed several stock techniques for various situations.

A few methods were more or less effectually employed on each trip. A favorite ruse, adopted only after several years of experience, was to escape on the first stage of the journey by horse and carriage. Usually this was the master's own property! This tack was sheer daring and was based upon the theory that slaves would not be so bold as to attempt such means. Negroes driving a horse and buggy must certainly be going on an errand for their masters. Usually they drove all night Saturday and all day Sunday before abandoning the horse and buggy. Harriet urged this procedure upon any escaping groups that could arrange to take off this way, pointing to it as an unsuspected means of gaining much distance before search began. "She would put them (the escapees) in a cart covering them with vegetables, and drive them to some hiding place.[18]

Infant fugitives were always handled in the same way—at least by Harriet. The number of children that escaped to the free states was surprisingly large. This is understandable when it is realized that many parents knew that their offspring might be sold as early as they became of use. The separation of parents from their young was one of the most constant crimes of slavery as well as one of its most heartless, and so couples with children invariably thought of escape. Harriet knew that these were the best material for flight: parents would sacrifice for their children and would not weaken.

"I have heard her tell how she carried a ticking bag around her waist," says Helen W. Tatlock who knew Harriet well. "If there were babies to be brought North as often there were she gave them paregoric to stop their crying, and put them in this bag, when near farms or towns, so they might not cry and so attract notice." [19]

Part of the strategy of conducting was, as in all battle-field operations, the knowledge of how and when to retreat. Numerous allusions have been made to her moves when she suspected that she was in danger. When she feared the party was closely pursued, she would take it for a time on a train southward bound. No one seeing Negroes going in this direction would for an instant suppose them to be fugitives.[20] Once on her return she was at a railroad station. She saw some men reading a poster and she heard one of them reading it aloud. It was a description of her, offering a reward for her capture. She took a southbound train to avert suspicion.[21] At another time when Harriet heard men talking about her, she pretended to read a book which she carried. One man remarked, "This can't be the woman. The one we want can't read or write." Harriet devoutly hoped the book was right side up.[22]

Legend has it that she was discovered by her friends asleep in a local park beneath a sign advertising a reward for her capture, which meant nothing to her, as she could not read.[23] There is an interesting recollection by the late Harriet Stanton Blatch, the white suffragist, which serves to verify this point. "She made my young blood tingle as she told how she sat right under a poster advertising a reward for her capture and return somewhere in the South." [24]

Once on the path, there began the contest between the fugitives and the law. The pursuers started after them. Advertisements were posted everywhere. There was one reward of $12,000 offered for the head of the woman who was constantly appearing and enticing away parties of slaves from their masters.[25]

In the last analysis, it was the exigency of the moment that determined the tactic. Each mile of a journey north presented its new situations, and called forth novel and experimental measures. Harriet and her parties encountered an infinite variety of difficulties and their adventures took ever-varying forms. A few of the fairly complete stories of whole journeys across the Mason-Dixon line show that the various trips differed in countless respects, save only that travel was by night, by guide of the North Star, and there was a general destination under Harriet's lead. That was the cloth, but each trip was woven in a different pattern. Disguise, concealment and maneuvering adapted itself only to the immediate sphere of movement. The blacks peered into the night as far as their eyes could see—and that was as far as they could dare their immediate move. No ruse was impossible if it might save one's life, and there is even related a story about Harriet having to hide fugitives in a manure pile with straws in their mouths to enable them to breathe.[26]

This is the most extreme mention of the defense and desperation related of Harriet's excursions. It sounds as though it is on the legendary side: but it is not impossible, and, however extreme, the very fact that such an episode can be told, serves to illustrate and symbolize how the "land of the free and the home of the brave" then treated its black Americans.

END CHAPTER VI

CHAPTER VII

GUERILLA WARFARE IN THE MID-'FIFTIES

"Go down, Moses."

The intensive work continued on into the mid-fifties, when men aided the slave or fought him. Who was the man, woman or child that had not a concern for the Negro? Either to defend or attack him? By now there were but few who were neutral. The profound historian, the giant poet, the schoolboy, the humble slave—all; and Harriet touched upon each.

It was about this time when Samuel J. May, white Abolitionist and historian, had need for the services of Harriet, but not knowing her as yet, his efforts to free a certain slave failed. The historian, in his volume published after the Civil War,[1] referred to a fugitive case that had much impressed him. He described how a colored man had appealed to him for help in bringing North his aged mother. May's attempts to achieve the woman's freedom by purchase, paying three hundred dollars, failed. He concluded his several-page account with the observation—a considerable tribute to Harriet, "I did not, until five years afterward, become acquainted with that remarkable woman, Harriet Tubman, or I might have engaged her services in the assurance that she would have brought off the old woman without *paying* for what belonged to her by an inalienable right—*her liberty*." It was in the very late fifties when May finally met the conductor.

The poet of democracy, Walt Whitman, was heart and soul with the fugitive, too, for the bard, as appears in his "Leaves of Grass" well understood the black man's plight. The runaway slave had come to his house "limpsy and weak" and he went where the Negro sat and led him in and assured him,

"And brought water and filled a tub for his sweated
body and bruis'd feet."

The fugitive stayed a week before he was recuperated and passed North, and meantime Whitman "had him sit next me at table, my fire-lock lean'd in the corner."

Whether truth or poetry, Whitman did not over-portray the "limpsy and weak" fugitive. The "bruis'd feet" were Harriet's *most* of the time. Usually Thomas Garrett, who was in the shoe business, provided her with footgear. She could wear out shoes in a single trip North, and she needed a new pair every few months. Once she was helped in this way by Gerrit Smith's son, Greene Smith. "I remember," she said, "once after I had brought some colored people from the South, I went up to Peterboro to the Big House. Gerrit Smith's son, Greene, was going hunting with his tutor and some other boys. I had no shoes. It was on Saturday afternoon and—would you believe it?—those boys went right off to the village and got me a pair of shoes so I could go with them." [2] Thus the spirit of Abolitionism had spread until "the schoolboy of twelve" in the North could delay even the joys of a hunting trip to help an ex-slave woman, and then to have her go with them.

That is one of the few glimpses of a light moment in Harriet's days in the pre-Civil War period. Harriet going hunting! She, who packed a gun on her night jaunts, must have been a good shot, able to teach Greene Smith and his friends a few things about how to stalk out in the open country.

But for one such incident as this there are a score of incidents more grim than happy. Sometime in this period Harriet and one of her parties were about thirty miles below Wilmington. This was in the rigorous Smyrna (Delaware) district, where white patrols were incessantly vigilant for fugitives. It was March and "she had two stout men with her." Harriet, sensing the possibility of danger on the road through which they were escaping, decided to veer her course. The party left the highway, and took off through an open field until they came to a small stream of water. It was probably a branch of the Chester River which flowed through this region; there was no bridge and no boat, and there was no alternative but to cross it.

". . . She went in," says Thomas Garrett, "the water came up to her armpits; the men refused to follow till they saw her safe on the opposite shore. Then they followed, and if I mistake not she had soon to wade a second stream; soon after which she came to a cabin of colored people, who took them all in, put them to bed, and dried their clothes, ready to proceed next night on their journey.

"Harriet had run out of money, and gave them some of her under-clothing to pay for their kindness. When she called on me two days after she.was so hoarse she could hardly speak, and was also suffering with violent toothache." [3]

If that was an example of Harriet's fortitude, there was another incident, belonging also to this period, when her resourcefulness was forcibly shown. In this incident there was revealed her mature talent for acting. Colonel Thomas Wentworth Higginson never ceased to marvel over her facility as an actress and an entertainer. In his famous letter in which he called Harriet "the greatest heroine of the age" [4] he mentioned her ability to act, and he spoke another time of her as a wonderful comedian.[5] Harriet was fonder of the present episode than most others which befell her. "One of her masterly accomplishments . . . was the impression of a decrepit old woman. On one of her expeditions . . . she had the incredible nerve to enter a village where lived one of her former masters. This was necessary for the carrying out of her plans for that trip. Her only disguise was a bodily assumption of age. To reinforce this her subtle foresight prompted her to buy some live chickens, which she carried suspended by the legs from a cord. As she turned a corner she saw coming toward her none other than her old master. Lest he might see through her impersonation and to make an excuse for flight, she loosed the cord that held the fowls and amid the laughter of the bystanders, gave chase to them as they flew squawking over a nearby fence." [6]

In the mid-'fifties there were a number of cases of escapes by women who disguised themselves as men. The most famous instance was the flight of Ellen Craft who dressed herself as a young master, (she was very light and could do this), and escaped with her husband who played the part of her body-servant. Maria Weems, a Negro girl, dressed like a man in 1855 and made good a flight. Perhaps it was these and other successes that prompted Harriet to allow her brother's sweetheart to escape in that manner. In any case, such a mask was adopted by a girl named Catherine, the friend of Harriet's brother, William Henry Ross. ". . . William Henry had long been attached to a girl named Catherine, who lived with another master; but her master would not let her marry him. When William Henry made up his mind to start with Harriet, he determined to bring Catherine with him. And so he went to a tailor's, and bought a new suit of men's clothes, and threw them over the garden fence of Catherine's master. The garden ran down to a run, and Catherine had been notified where to find the clothes.

"When the time had come to get ready, Catherine went to the foot of the garden and dressed herself in the suit of men's clothes. She was soon missed, and all the girls in the house were set to looking for Catherine. Presently they saw coming up through the garden, as if from the river, a well-dressed little Negro, and they all stopped looking for Catherine to stare at him. He walked directly by them round the house, and went out of the gate, without the slightest suspicion being as to who he was. In a fortnight from that time, the whole party was safe in Canada." [7]

*   *   *   *   *

Harriet first appeared in Boston in 1854, according to the Negro historian, William Wells Brown.[8] For some time she attended anti-slavery events without taking a prominent part in them, without yet making her appearance as a public speaker. "For eight or ten years previous to the breaking out of the Rebellion," Brown wrote, "all who frequented anti-slavery conventions, lectures, picnics, and fairs, could not fail to have seen a black woman of medium size, upper front teeth gone, smiling countenance, attired in coarse, but neat apparel, with an old-fashioned reticule or bag suspended by her side, and who, on taking her seat, would at once drop off into a sound sleep."

That is one of the few physical descriptions of Harriet during the middle period of the Underground years. Brown went on to say that she was soon a welcome visitor at the homes of the leading Abolitionists who were always attentive listeners to her strange and eventful stories. Despite her lack of education the most polished persons would sit and listen to her as she recounted, in the simplest manner, the incidents of her life, always seasoned with good sense. The historian said that while she was in Boston she made several trips to the South and it was these that resulted in her receiving the cognomen, "Moses." Actually she had received that name from the Negroes in Maryland several years earlier. "Men from Canada, who had made their escape years before, and whose families were still in the prison-house of slavery, would seek out Moses, and get her to go and bring their dear ones away. How strange! This woman—one of the most ordinary looking of her race; unlettered; no idea of geography, asleep half of the time. . . . No fugitive was ever captured who had Moses for a leader." [9]

Despite Boston's important role in Abolition, and Harriet's early appearance there, this was not yet her significant background. Mainly she was a "world-traveler," passing constantly from the world of slavery to that of freedom, and living for brief periods in St. Catharines, Canada, with the members of her family whom she had rescued. Harriet, a restless agitator, found her way about to other Canadian cities and towns, Chatham, Toronto, Vernon Center, wherever there was something doing, wherever a meeting was being held or some committee work needed, or a helping hand for some fugitive just in from the distant South. Canada West was virgin territory, and the fugitives had the pioneer task of clearing the land for cultivation. The women kept house and sometimes worked out. Even Harriet took a few months of work whenever the opportunity presented itself, although by now she was regarded virtually a professional on the railway to freedom.

It was by no means all socially smooth sailing in the Canadian West towns. Although the Negro was legally free here, and although generally an open mind prevailed, there was some prejudice, and many whites remained firmly dissociated from their colored neighbors. By 1855 the eyes of America were on Canada West, on the many cities and towns that housed the refugees from the United States. Many of these places became anti-slavery centers and to these places there came Abolitionists from the States. Editors and political leaders investigated the ways of the Negroes living in freedom and many books appeared on the subject. One was written by Benjamin Drew who, in 1855, traveled through a score of Canadian towns and interviewed hundreds of fugitives. In St. Catharines he was shown around by the Reverend Hiram Wilson, and one of the first persons he met was Harriet Tubman.   To him she summed up the meaning of slavery:

"I grew up like a neglected weed—ignorant of liberty, having no experience of it.   I was not happy or contented: every time I saw a white man I was afraid of being carried away.   I had two sisters carried away in a chain gang—one of them left two children.   We were always uneasy.   Now I've been free, I know what slavery is.   I have seen hundreds of escaped slaves but I never saw one who was willing to go back and be a slave. I have no opportunity to see my friends in my native land.   We would rather stay in our native land if we could be as free there as we are here.   I think slavery is the next thing to hell. If a person would send another into bondage he would, it appears to me, be bad enough to send him to hell if he could." [10]

All through the mid-'fifties Harriet continued as the "subverter," talking to individuals and groups, urging them to find freedom in Canada.   She stayed in the Maryland-Delaware district for various lengths of time, spreading the gospel of free Canada, educating the slaves about the Abolition movement in the North. When she had confidence in particular groups she gave them addresses of aides on the Underground and sped them northward, without herself conducting them.   Sometimes she escorted parties as far as Philadelphia or New York; then they were placed in the hands of others who forwarded them to the British dominion while she returned South to start new groups onward.   It was toward the close of April of 1856 when William Still thus recorded her arrival in the Quaker City with a party:

"The next arrival numbered four passengers, and came under the guidance of Harriet Tubman from Maryland.   They were adults, looking as though they could take care of themselves very easily, although they had the marks of slavery on them.   It was no easy matter for men and women who had been ground down all their lives, to appear as though they had been enjoying freedom. Indeed, the only wonder was that so many appeared to as good advantage as they did, after having been crushed down so long." [11]

Only a few weeks after Still made his latest entry in the Underground chronicles, he and his associate, J. M. McKim received a letter from Thomas Garrett. To his "esteemed friends" the Quaker wrote, revealing the heat of operations on the Road: "Those four I wrote thee about arrived safe up in the neighborhood of Longwood, and Harriet Tubman followed after in the stage yesterday. I shall expect five more from the same neighborhood next trip." [12]

*   *   *   *   *

If there are few insights into Harriet's personal side, there is at least one which throws a shaft of light into all of this lack. It is the poignant bit of how Harriet "kidnapped" a niece named Margaret Stewart, a child who remained throughout life the favorite kin of Harriet Tubman. There is only one explanation for the unbroken, life-long shower of affection which Harriet vented upon this girl. It grew out of Harriet's dislocated love life. She was warm enough to require and to have the most personal emotions, to have a need for a husband, and a need for her own children; and her affection for Margaret Stewart, in some way, supplied this lack. Harriet seized upon Margaret Stewart as the object of her personal emotions, lavished care and love upon her, and never relinquished this affection. The story is related by Mrs. A. J. Brickler of Wilberforce, Ohio. The event belongs to the mid-'fifties: it occurred after Harriet became acquainted with William H. Seward, but before she settled in Auburn. It belongs to the years 1855 or 1856. Mrs. Brickler recites the following history of her mother and the fascinating relationship of her mother to the liberator:

"My mother's life really began with Aunt Harriet kidnapping her from her home on Eastern Shore, Maryland, when she was a little girl eight or nine years old. I say mother's life began then because her memories of her Southern home were very vague. One thing she knew and that was that neither she, her brothers or her mother had ever been slaves. Her grandfather on her mother's side had bought his wife and children's time which made them free. Her mother's marriage to Harriet's brother, an ex-slave, seems not to have hindered the family's progress for mother said they had a pair of slick chestnut horses and a shiny carriage in which they rode to church. That was all she remembered of her home. Her next memory was of Aunt Harriet's visit to the home. She fell in love with the little girl who was my mother. Maybe it was because in mother she saw the child she herself might have been if slavery had been less cruel. Maybe it was because she knew the joys of motherhood would never be hers and she longed for some little creature who would love her for her own self's sake. Certainly whatever her emotion, it was stronger than her better judgment, for when her visit was ended, she, secretly, and without so much as a by-your-leave, took the little girl with her to her Northern home. I wonder what her thoughts could have been as she and her little partner stood side by side on the deck of the steamer looking far out over the water. They made the trip by water as that was what impressed mother so greatly that she forgot to weep over her separation from her twin brother, her mother and the shiny carriage she liked so much. Aunt Harriet must have regretted her act for she knew she had taken the child from a sheltered good home to a place where there was nobody to care for her. She must have known that the warmth of this new love was not great enough to calm her restless soul and turn her into a domestic. She knew she had violated her brother's home and sorrow and anger were there. I suppose she thought of her white friends in the North and decided to place her dearest possession in their hands. She gave the little girl, my mother, to Mrs. William H. Seward, the Governor's wife. This kindly lady brought up mother—not as a servant but as a guest within her home. She taught mother to speak properly, to read, write, sew, do housework and act as a lady. Whenever Aunt Harriet came back, mother was dressed and sent in the Seward carriage to visit her. Strange to say, mother looked very much like Aunt Harriet. . . ." [18]

END CHAPTER VII

CHAPTER VIII

THE ESCAPE OF JOSIAH BAILEY

Song, or the spiritual, as a means of communication, was a definite part of each of Harriet's campaigns. The spiritual with its hidden meaning, was employed usually when the situation was most dangerous. The idea of song was, in itself, disarming; thus, when the Negro sang he pampered his master's understanding of him as a "loyal, satisfied, slave." With a melody on his lips to cloak words which held an important and immediate significance, it was possible to dupe the slaveholder.

Once, when Harriet had been concealed in the woods with a party of Negroes who were hungry, she left them long enough to go to a "station" to find or buy food. She dared not return to them until night for fear of being watched and so revealing their hiding place. She had arranged with them to keep alert for her song when she came back, for by this she would warn them of safety or danger. As she neared her brood she sang the following stanzas to let them know of her arrival:

Hail, oh hail, ye happy spirits,
    Death no more shall make you fear,
Grief nor sorrow, pain nor anguish
    Shall no more distress you here.

Around you are ten thousand angels,
    Always ready to obey command.
They are always hovering around you,
    Till you reach the heavenly land.

Jesus, Jesus will go with you;
    He will lead you to his throne;
He who died has gone before you,
    Trod the winepress all alone.

He whose thunders shake creation;
    He who bids the planets roll;
He who rides upon the tempest
    And His sceptre sways the whole.

> Dark and thorny is the desert,
> Through the pilgrim makes his way,
> Yet beyond this vale of sorrow
> Lie the fields of endless day.

Harriet's fugitives understood that if this song was sung twice it was secure for them to emerge. As it happened it was unsafe for them to come out of hiding and she communicated the danger to them in one short stanza within which the ominous note can be detected:

> Moses, go down in Egypt,
> Tell old Pharoah, let me go;
> Hadn't been for Adam's fall,
> Shouldn't have to have died at all.[1]

That was sung in allegro tempo and the stanza is one that belongs to the nationally known, "Go Down, Moses."

The much-heralded spiritual, "Swing Low, Sweet Chariot," had a definite association with Harriet, but not necessarily an origin with her. Harriet was known by various names, one of which was "Old Chariot," perhaps as a rhyme to her own name.[2] The term also connoted the idea of escape by "chariot," that is, by any means which a company could employ to proceed northward. When the enslaved black sang, "I looked over Jordan and what did I see, Coming for to carry me home," it was over the Mason-Dixon line that he was looking; the band of angels was Harriet or another conductor coming for him; and "home" was a haven in the free states or Canada. Here is a stanza of one of Harriet's songs with such a reference:

> When that there old chariot comes,
> I'm going to leave you;
> I'm bound for the promised land,
> I'm going to leave you.[3]

This spiritual was underlain with a most material purpose. The words "meant something more than a journey to the Heavenly Canaan."

Harriet's use of song shows one of the origins of music in the American Negro. Music was an expression largely of his struggle, and not necessarily of his "light-heartedness." It was often an expression of his labor, his fight, his tragedy. Music was frequently a means, a leverage, a shrewd resort; it was a mask for the real Negro who was, beneath the melody, thinking, planning and advancing. Harriet, better than any other Negro is the best illustration of this. She has been cited as a case in point to illustrate that "religious" songs, so-called, had social meanings. "Once in America when men owned other men as chattels, Negro slaves chanted thinly-disguised songs of protest set to the meter of spirituals—"Go Down, Moses," the fighting song of Harriet Tubman who came like Moses to redeem her black kinsmen from the "Egypt-land of the South," "Steal Away," which invariably meant a summons to sneak off to the woods for a slave meeting; and the militant, "Follow the Drinking Gourd" which meant following the Great Dipper to the Ohio River and freedom." [4]

Alice Stone Blackwell, white suffrage leader, recalls Harriet's description of her use of songs. "If I remember correctly, Harriet Tubman told me that when she was convoying parties of fugitives, she used to guide them by the songs that she sang as she walked along the roads . . . it was when her parties of fugitives were in hiding, that she directed them by her songs, as to whether they might show themselves, or must continue to lie low . . . No one would notice what was sung by an old colored woman, as she trudged along the road." [5]

The use of spirituals on the "middle passage" is best illustrated in the record of one of Harriet's trips, a journey in which a Negro named Josiah Bailey took a part. The escape, with four slaves accompanying Harriet, occurred near the close of the year 1856 when her activity was of the most intrepid sort. By now the spirit of escape was rampant all through the Eastern Shore.

Josiah Bailey, who was called Joe, was regarded as a valuable slave, a large reward having been offered for his capture. He was a compelling physical specimen and a man of more than ordinary sensitivity. At the time there was widespread notice of this flight.

One of the advertisements, published in an Eastern Shore newspaper, described the three male members of the company:

HEAVY REWARD

TWO THOUSAND SIX HUNDRED DOLLARS REWARD

Ran away from the subscriber, on Saturday night, November 15th, 1856, Josiah and William Bailey and Peter Pennington. Joe is about 5 feet 10 inches in height, of a chestnut color, bald head, with a remarkable scar on one of his cheeks, not positive on which it is, but think it is on the left, under the eye, has intelligent countenance, active and well-made. He is about 28 years old. Bill is of a darker color, about 5 feet 8 inches in height, stammers a little when confused, well-made, and older than Joe, well dressed, but may have pulled kearsey on over their other clothes. Peter is smaller than either the others, about 25 years of age, dark chestnut color, 5 feet 7 or 8 inches high.

A reward of fifteen hundred dollars will be given to any person who will apprehend the said Joe Bailey, and lodge him safely in the jail at Easton, Talbot Co., Md., and $300 for Bill and $800 for Peter.

W. R. HUGHLETT,
JOHN C. HENRY,
T. WRIGHT.[6]

The fourth slave, not mentioned in the advertisement, was a woman, Eliza Nokey, of whom little is known, except that she was a member of the caravan.

Late in the Fall of 1856 Josiah had been administered a severe flogging by his master, William R. Hughlett, and this had decided him upon the course of escape. Immediately he made his way to the cabin of Harriet's parents, told them what had happened, avowed his determination to flee, and asked to be notified when next Harriet should put in an appearance. Meantime he interested his brother in going along with him. Josiah must have suffered much to think of escaping, for he was prepared to leave behind a wife and three children.[7]

Soon afterward Harriet arrived, and the party took to the Road. They were pursued. They were hidden in "potato holes" while their pursuers passed within a few feet of them; they were passed along by friends in various disguises; they scattered and separated, and were led by guides by devious routes to a new meeting place; they were taken in by Sam Green, an important conductor who was later jailed for his Abolition work, and at last they reached the outskirts of Wilmington.[8]

The Wilmington bridge, which the party must cross, was heavily guarded by police. Placards announcing the escaping party were posted everywhere. A twelve thousand dollar reward notice for the capture of Harriet was among the posters. But in spite of the heavy guard, Harriet was able, by means of scattering her group, to place them in various colored homes in the vicinity. For the purpose of crossing the bridge she communicated with her regular stand-by, Thomas Garrett. As soon as the Quaker learned of the plight of the slaves he evolved a plan to aid them. He engaged two wagons and filled them with bricklayers. He sent them across the bridge, and they went as if on a party, singing and shouting. The guards saw them pass, and of course expected them to re-cross the bridge later. After nightfall the wagons returned, but this time concealing the fugitives. The slaves were on the bottom of each of the wagons, and the bricklayers still sang and shouted and diverted attention as the fugitives entered the gates of Wilmington.

When the pioneers reached Philadelphia William Still made special notes on Josiah Bailey, and he concluded by observing of the party that their spirits never flagged and they had determined not to stop, short of Canada. Yet one of the company was destined to "flag," and it was none other than the much-admired Josiah Bailey. When he walked into the anti-slavery office of Oliver Johnson, in New York, that Abolitionist recognized him from descriptions that had already been sent ahead, and he greeted the hulking slave with the statement, "Well, I'm glad to see the man whose head is worth fifteen hundred dollars."

Immediately this plunged Josiah into the deepest gloom. The black man believed that if he, an unknown slave, could be recognized at a glance so far from home, the enemy must be too strong for resistance, and capture was certain. He settled into a despair that could not be shaken, and he refused to speak throughout the remainder of the journey.

Josiah had not counted upon the careful organization of the Road, and at last he, and the others, arrived at Niagara Falls, the crossroad between the United States and the British dominion.

The conductor and the fellow slaves tried to stimulate their melancholy companion to at least take a look at the famous Falls, but even to this he would not assent. Finally they were traveling, by "iron horse," across the Suspension Bridge, the span that cut off bondage from freedom, and the whole party broke into song. To the tune of "Oh, Susannah," they poured out several stanzas:

> I'm on my way to Canada,
>   That cold and dreary land;
> The sad effects of slavery,
>   I can no longer stand.

> I've served my master all my days,
>   Without a dime's reward;
> And now I'm forced to run away,
>   To flee the lash abroad.

Farewell, old master, don't think hard of me,
I'm on my way to Canada, where all the slaves are free.

> The hounds are baying on my track,
>   Old master comes behind,
> Resolved that he will bring me back,
>   Before I cross the line;

> I'm now embarked for yonder shore,
>   There a man's a man by law;
> The iron horse will bear me o'er,
>   To shake the lion's paw.

Oh, righteous Father, will thou not pity me,
And aid me on to Canada, where all the slaves are free.

> Oh, I heard Queen Victoria say,
>   That if we would forsake
> Our native land of slavery,
>   And come across the lake;

> That she was standing on the shore,
> With arms extended wide,
> To give us all a peaceful home
> Beyond the rolling tide.

> Farewell, old master, don't think hard of me,
> I'm on my way to Canada, where all the slaves are free.

Mid-way across the Suspension Bridge the United States ends and Canada begins; and Harriet knew from a slight descent on the Canadian side that they had "crossed the line."

She sprang to Josiah's side, and she shook him with all her might as she shouted, "Joe, you've shook the lion's paw! Joe, you're *free!*"

Her words broke through his emotional apathy and he looked up. He raised his hands, and with tears streaming he broke out in song:

> Glory to God and Jesus too,
> One more soul is safe!
> Oh, go and carry the news,
> One more soul got safe!

That is how "spirituals" were born; they came from the slave's very soul, from his experiences in desperation and his victories; they grew out of the Negro's hope and struggle for a better life *here.* If that stanza had not originated with Bailey, still, some slave in the same situation had first sung it.

Now Josiah could not be stopped. His voice reared above all others, over and over singing,

> Glory to God and Jesus too,
> One more soul got safe!

When they stepped out of the car Josiah continued his hosannah of joy. The attempts to quiet him failed; white people gathered about to listen to his paen of celebration, and behold his wild emotion. There was only one more trip for him, he said, and that was to heaven.

At that, Harriet uttered a comment that must have thrown the whole scene into a new tangent: "Well, you old fool you, you might have looked at the Falls first and gone to heaven after-wards!" [9]

Josiah had aroused himself with thanks to Jesus but he knew, and the other fugitives knew that it was very real forces that had freed them: Harriet Tubman, and the money, kindness and bravery of the station-masters, and their own will to liberation. Josiah sang a song full of hosannas to the Lord, but afterwards he did as all other newly-freed: he simply thanked Harriet Tubman, and asked her to convey his heartfelt appreciation to all of those on the "line" who had helped him out of bondage. When Josiah Bailey raised his paen to Jesus Christ it was Harriet Tubman that he meant, for as one observer of the Negro, the spiritual and the black man's strug-gle has aptly said, "King Jesus is not just the abstract Christ; he is whoever helps the oppressed and the disfranchised, or gives him a right to his life." [10]

END CHAPTER VIII

CHAPTER IX

THE LOCOMOTIVE OF HISTORY

The locomotive of history was speeding along on the Underground Railroad. Harriet Tubman, piloting her broods northward to a new life, watched John Brown in Kansas, and was amazed at how an old man fought for her people. "Bleeding Kansas," they called it correctly. It had bled since 1854 when pro-slavery men swarmed into the state to settle it for the South and slavery, while anti-slavery Northerners flocked into the territory to make it safe for a free labor-capitalist economy. It all dated back to 1820, to the time when there had been a Missouri Compromise, when the North and South had established a boundary line, the famous Mason and Dixon, north of which there was to be no slavery. But the slavocracy had grown powerful and aggressive, and in May of 1854 there took effect the Kansas-Nebraska bill, a measure which invalidated the Compromise and made it possible for Missouri pro-slavers to rush into Kansas and attempt to seize it for slavery. Up to now the fugitive question, in the center of which was Harriet, had been the sorest spot between the North and South, but this latest attack of the slave power brought the question of the settlement of Kansas to the fore. Then, for the next few years Kansas bled; Abolitionists swept into the state to oppose the inrush of the Missourians; Northern workingmen and farmers who had long been desirous of winning land grants in the West, rushed in alongside the Abolitionists, prepared to keep the Western territories free. Naturally a guerilla warfare opened up, with the anti-slavery forces on the defensive.

That was where John Brown led. He had long been involved in Underground operations, but this was an expanded type of guerilla warfare, and he was expert at it. Around him gathered stalwart young abolitionists and military men. Captain James Montgomery, a brilliant but wildfire type of Abolitionist rallied to the old man's side; James Redpath, journalist and reformer, and dozens of others joined Brown's forces: together, guns blazing, they fought for free-

84

soilers in Lawrence, Osawatomie, Pottowattomie, wherever pro-slavery men had rooted themselves on free territory, wherever the slave power's hoodlums had attacked an anti-slavery settlement. War in the West, that is what it was, and they called it "the winning of the West"; and the passage of the 'fifties more and more vindicated William H. Seward's prediction of an "irrepressible conflict."

Of course, Kansas was only an issue in the national picture: the question went deeper than that. Kansas, like the Underground Railroad, was only a development of a centuries' old question.

The founding fathers, formulating the Constitution, compromised over the question of slavery, and never even mentioned the word in that famous document. This paved the way for an incessant dispute that broke out around the early part of the Nineteenth Century. At the beginning of the nation, men believed that slavery was limited to the territory in which it then flourished, that it would not spread. But when, in the early 1800's there came a series of inventions that made it possible to produce cotton quickly and cheaply, resulting in an international demand for the goods, the slaveholders rallied around this commodity as their King. But the King, in order to be fed, needed ever newer and more fertile territories, because cotton growing used up the land quickly. These territories were in the West, and as the century advanced the South demanded these regions, resulting in a conflict with the Northern financial interests, with Abolitionists, workers and farmers. The slave power advanced with one aggression after another until at last it pushed into Kansas, hoping to open up the West for the cultivation of its cotton, tobacco and rice fields. Meantime the Southern rulers intensified their bonds with Britain, their largest importer, fought against a high tariff, prevented factories from coming South, and thus kept themselves tightly encased in their slave economy—and fought to expand it.

In the North the financial interests were equally desperate for expansion, but in their case desiring a West in which railroads could be built, modern cities created, factories opened. Northern capital was supported by labor in its drive westward. Northern laborers fought for the Homestead Act, a bill that would give them free land in the West. Small farmers in the North and West feared and hated the slave power, and wanted their region free of the blight of the plantation economy.

Alongside the struggle for the West, there developed a multitude of differences between the North and the South. The North, engaged in manufacturing, was deprived of the full-sized home market to which it believed itself entitled, due to the lack of buying power in the South, and the Northern industrialists dreamed of a free South in which the Negro and the poor white would buy their products. The North, if it could build a national domestic market, could break free of its dependence upon foreign markets always hard to obtain and harder to hold. Thus the South had bound itself to the present and the past, to a dying economy, and the North was in haste to rush ahead into the new Industrial Revolution that was sweeping the entire Western World.

All along the Mason-Dixon line, as both powers pressed against each other, there was a tremendous tension, and the bonds had burst in Kansas, and the fighting was on. It was Kansas now, and it would be Harper's Ferry later, and then. . . .

* * * * *

By now the plantations hooked onto each other in a vast chain, not even the State lines breaking their connection, except at the Mason-Dixon border, and they ran from coast to frontier and down along the Gulf of Mexico. Cotton and tobacco, sugar and corn and rice rooted the black millions to this soil. The slave trade had long since passed its climax; the greatest mass of Negroes had been here for generations and a melting pot process had begun to unify their social and economic characteristics. The American slave-mill was grinding to bits the African heritage, little of it remaining except some music and dancing, a few tribal words and an age-old color, but the latter was so important that by now it was turning the United States "upside down." The condition of slavery had made the Negro's relationship to this new earth fundamentally different than his attachment to the African terrain; here they were like oxen, yoked and burdened, and Africa, vast under the sun, free and primitive, was already little more than a tradition and a dim memory.

The white overlords, in creating plantations side by side, in forcing a strange language, a different religion, and alien customs upon the Negro, had themselves organized a new class, one with which it was engaged in a tremendous battle. By the time when the last tribal legions were smuggled into the land, the Negro character was so broadly evolved that these slave-shipments were assimilated and transformed as rapidly as they arrived. They were swallowed into the maw of the entrenched slave economy and ground immediately into the new, compressed conditions. They were overwhelmed with a different language, and an alien type of wearing apparel was forced upon them. Vital new currents of thinking were pressed upon them by their fellow slaves and by the rule of their white masters, and within a few months they were hardly distinguishable from those whose ancestors had been here a century and more.

Over the plantations there spread an increasingly native culture. There had developed a new and peculiar language—the famous Southern accent, with a transformed English which the King of England at that time might not have understood (and didn't care to understand later when the Civil War broke out, for the British rulers supported the slaveholders); it was a mellow, heavy tongue, r-less and soft, rich and ideal for pulpit, forum and song. The Negro's psychology had become religious; it was a hopeful type of thinking that had more to do with the freeing of the body than of the spirit.

The plantations, like cells in a human body, were knitted together into the bloodstream of a new, a soil-dwelling Negro nation—conceived in slavery, and dedicated to the proposition that some men, those with a certain color of skin, were created without freedom and unequal. But the black man, tilling the soil, extracted from his labor one observation: he beheld that that which has life within it needs freedom if it will survive.

*   *   *   *   *

Of the Abolitionists, Frederick Douglass did as much or more than any other, white or Negro, to the advancement of the Republican Party, and therefore, to the ending of chattel slavery. He was a Republican while Abraham Lincoln was still trying to find himself. When the Presidential campaign of 1856 was under way, Douglass came in for much criticism by the Abolitionists who were less far-seeing than himself. He endorsed John C. Fremont for President on the newly founded Republican Party ticket. This party had grown out of a long series of organizational transformations throughout the North and West. The Liberty Party had come and gone, and this had been followed by the Free-Soilers. Meanwhile the Whigs and Democrats, the chief parties, had been developing progressive, or anti-slavery wings which split away at the time the Kansas controversy broke, until at last there appeared in 1856 a fusion of parties that became the Republican Party. It was still weak, of course, but Douglass, who had helped build this alliance, knew that this was the party, that the years of Abolitionist organization had to be crystallized into this big, broad liberal onslaught. Once, in September of 1856, after he was bitterly attacked for his views, he took occasion to express his conception of political strategy, and in this statement can be seen the genius of the true political organizer, the one who knows how to fight on all fronts, to utilize all avenues of advance. "From our political philosophy, we are at liberty to consider the state of the public mind, and to look at immediate results, as well as remote consequences. We are at liberty to inquire how far our vote, at a given time, will forward what we conceive to be the highest interests of society; and having considered this, we are at liberty,—nay, it is our indispensable duty to cast our vote in that direction, which, upon a survey of the whole facts in the case, will largest promote that great end." [1]

It was the radicals of the National Abolition Society, guided by that strategy, who were doing the work which, historically, proved to be decisive. It was this group which, more than any other, welded the progressive sections of the severing parties into the movement that was becoming the Republican Party, the party that would vanquish slavery. Gerrit Smith was a leader of this movement, and a close associate of Douglass, as well as a heavy financial contributor to *Frederick Douglass' Paper.* The newspaper was a real organizing weapon; it was carefully read by most political leaders in the nation, and the policies of its writers were digested and often translated into the political life of the North. The leadership of the established parties knew that it was the criticism of Douglass—not Garrison— that was moulding the most far-reaching political consequences; they knew that the moral indignation of Garrison was instrumental mainly as an educational force.

Sometime in this period Douglass and William H. Seward developed a close relationship; and later, in 1860, the Negro liberator endorsed Seward for President. Although Seward's nomination did not mature, it does not minimize the importance of the relationship between the National Abolition Society and the wildfire growth of the Republicans.

James McCune Smith, a profound Negro critic and organizer, was associated with Douglass in the ranks of the National Abolitionists. Others, white, supported the Negro champion and acknowledged his critical and intellectual superiority. A. Pryne, an editorial associate of Douglass, who, in 1858, had a famous debate with a Southerner, W. G. ("Parson") Brownlow, publicly acknowledged the superior leadership of the black man. Other principal spirits of this society, S. S. Jocelyn, L. L. Matlock, A. G. Beman and William Goodell may not have achieved the public acclaim that went to Wendell Phillips, Garrison and other New England dis-unionists, but they were busy in behind-the-scenes work, knitting together the united front that became known as the Republican Party. Today, almost a century later, we can look back upon that period when the Abolitionists struggled for an effective policy and it is evident that it was the Douglass wing of Abolition that was most instrumental in bringing to an issue the question of slave labor versus free labor. Thus Republican wealth and power today can, in considerable measure, trace its origin back to the philosophical brilliance of a Negro born a slave.[2]

Harriet Tubman more and more saw the scene in the Douglass view, of utilizing all allies, of advancing step by step, by large and by small measures. Her developing friendship in this period with William H. Seward, whose home in Auburn, New York, housed her fugitive broods, is the best testament of this fact. The needs of a great principle called for a flexible strategy. It was this realization that enabled Harriet to work first on the Underground, later to side in with John Brown in an attempt and experiment at insurrection, to support Garrison and his school for their moral vigor and effect, to endorse and speak for women's suffrage (always primarily a white women's movement), and finally to rely a deep faith in liberal and radical parliamentarians like Seward, Sumner, Hale, Chase, and others, for these, she saw, had the power of government to enforce their views—and if they had full power, a dozen parliamentarians, fighting on the floor of the Senate, could do more than a hundred Abolitionist meetings or a thousand anti-slavery speeches. There was nothing sectarian or dogmatic about Harriet, save her love for liberty. True, the Underground Railroad remained her prime love, at least until 1858 when she acquired an equal devotion to the aims of John Brown, but she beheld a wheel with many spokes and she knew that the wheel could not turn unless all spokes turned with it: and she was at the hub, connected with all the spokes of the anti-slavery wheel of history.

END CHAPTER IX

CHAPTER X

JAIL THE "GODDESS OF LIBERTY!"

It was 1857 when Harriet decided to settle in Auburn, a small town in the central part of New York State. That had become a prominent station on the Underground Railroad, for here were many strong anti-slavery Abolitionists and Quakers. "Quick to recognize the friendly spirit of the place and encouraged by the kindness of Governor William H. Seward, his family and friends, Harriet decided by way of celebrating the Dred Scott decision in 1857 to bring her aged parents here for refuge. A little place on South Street was provided by Governor Seward." Thus has written one of the conductor's contemporaries, Mrs. Emma Paddock Telford, a white woman, who has described her impressions of Harriet's first settling in that town.[1] Thereafter, Auburn was Harriet's home, throughout life, except for her political excursions around the country. The reference to Harriet's flaunting of the Dred Scott decision was only in line with Harriet's reactions in the face all undue repressions. When the Supreme Court decided that a Negro had "no rights which a white man was bound to respect," it was a blow at all Negroes, and Harriet, naturally, was one of the first to reject this opinion. It is significant too that even William H. Seward supported Harriet in ignoring this ruling, for he sold to the conductor the property on which she lived the remainder of her life. Harriet was not even supposed to *be* in the North; she was a fugitive from Southern justice; she should be either in Canada or back in slavery; yet in the face of this, the prominent Seward had conducted a business transaction with her, albeit on generous terms. If the knowledge of this deal reached the South, it would have been scandalous, and Seward, aiming for the Presidency, might have been hard hit, and called an out-and-out Abolitionist, but it was kept quiet except in Abolition circles. Yet that transaction was a definite symptom of the close collaboration of the Abolitionists and the maturing Republican Party for it brought together the outstanding

91

woman Abolitionist in America with the outstanding contender for the 1860 Presidential race in the North.

Dred Scott time in America was not only one in which the threads of the nation were rapidly weaving into the fabric of Civil War, but it meant an inevitable maturing into public life for Harriet. It was a period in which the knowledge of her was becoming general and open: she was emerging from her secretive, underground existence. The year, 1857, was one in which her past work bore fruit. The Sam Green affair, growing out of a seed planted a few seasons earlier, developed and became a national cause; the Dover incident was an outgrowth of her years of operation in the Eastern Shore region; the rescue of her parents mid-year was hailed as her most daring campaign; and finally, in the fall, panic broke out among the slaveholders of the Eastern Shore, which was hats off to Harriet's influence. Taking the period chronologically, the matter of the violence at Dover was first. In this unfortunate affair, the man known as Humanitas, Thomas Garrett, had some bad hours worrying about Harriet, to whom he feared, in his soft, Quaker devotion, some terrible evil had befallen. . . .

*   *   *   *   *

It was March of 1857 when Harriet's name was seized upon by a slave named Thomas Otwell, and her identity and influence used in a scheme for the betrayal of an escaping party of eight Bucktown slaves, two of whom were women. Otwell, who had once made a trip north with Harriet, but had returned, used his knowledge of the Underground and his association with Harriet as a means of luring into his confidence this collection of unsuspecting Negroes, intending to win the reward offered for their capture. Far from planning to conduct the company to Canada, Otwell connived with authorities in Dover, Delaware, and so dexterously conceived the route of escape as to have it lead directly into a cell of the Dover Jail! Night operations and the innocence of the fugitives made efficacious this deception, in spite of its nervy and treacherous nature.

On the tenth of March, at night, Otwell piloted the band of blacks directly into a cell at Dover Jail. When a light was struck

and the slaves beheld where they were, they put up a valorous resistance. Despite the presence of an armed sheriff, the slaves broke
out of the cell and plunged down a flight of stairs directly into the
officer's private apartment. The leading spirit of the revolt, a husky
fellow named Henry Predo, smashed open a window, and immediately the two colored women leaped out. Someone, spotting hot
coals in the fireplace, spread a shovelful of fire around the room,
creating additional furore and alarming the sheriff's wife and his
two children. Predo smashed out the window entirely; the rest of
the party leaped through and dropped a distance of twelve feet.
Outside the walls the company scattered . . . and from thereon, for a
period of two weeks, the whole Underground system in Maryland,
Pennsylvania and Delaware was excited into an anxiety that was
new in its history.[2]

It was in the aftermath of this action, when the Underground
was shaken with fears, that the name of Harriet Tubman arose.
One of Thomas Garrett's correspondents informed him of what had
occurred and asked him to prepare to receive six of the party who
had found shelter with him and who were now ready to be sent on.
The Quaker notified his cousin, Samuel Rhoads, an Underground re-
ceiver in Philadelphia, to be on the lookout for the other two whose
whereabouts were unknown.

The first mention of Harriet appeared in a letter sent on March
23, about two weeks after the jail-break, by a colored conductor,
William Brinkley, of Camden, Delaware, to the Philadelphia office.
Brinkley, writing with an unsure quality in his spelling but a legible
correctness in his attitude toward the Underground, wrote in part:

> Dear Sir: I tak my pen in hand to write to you, to inform
> you what we have had to go throw for the last two weeks.
> Thir wir six men and two woman was betraid on the tenth of
> this month, thea had them in prison but thea got out, was
> conveyed by a black man, he told them he wood bring them to
> my hows, as he wos told, he had been there befor, he has come
> with Harr(i)ett, a woman that stops at my hous when she
> passes tow and throw yau . . ."[3]

That note indicates how spectrally the fear of the white patrol
hovered over the Underground. Thomas Garrett, who knew that

the betrayer had had some connection with Harriet, feared that she might have been revealed by the same informer. He had visions of Harriet at last captured and languishing in some Delaware or Maryland jail, and wrote to William Still at Philadelphia, inquiring of her whereabouts. Actually he had no reason to hold any fears: Harriet was nowhere in this vicinity at the time; she was either in St. Catharines or Auburn, and she knew nothing about the trouble at Dover, nor that her identity had been mis-used by a traitor. Garrett wrote:

Wilmington, 3rd mo. 27th, 1857

Esteemed Friend, William Still:—I have been very anxious for some time past, to hear what has become of Harriet Tubman. The last I heard of her, she was in the State of New York, on her way to Canada with some friends, last fall. Has thee seen or heard anything of her lately? It would be a sorrowful fact, if such a hero as she, should be lost from the Underground Rail Road. I have just received a letter from Ireland, making inquiry respecting her. If thee gets this in time, and knows anything respecting her, please drop me a line by mail tomorrow, and I will get it next morning if not sooner, and oblige thy friend.

I have heard nothing from the eighth man from Dover, but trust he is safe.

THOMAS GARRETT.[4]

William Still informed Garrett that Harriet was "all right," and this prompted the Quaker to pen a subsequent letter, expressing his satisfaction over that point, as good news, and he again spoke of the excitement occasioned by the Dover incident. "I was truly glad to learn that Harriet Tubman was still in good health and ready for action, but I think there will be more danger at present than heretofore, there is so much excitement below in consequence of the escape of those eight slaves." [5]

The matter died down. "The balance of these brave fugitives succeeded in getting off safely." [6] Such was the Underground, where traitors, though they did not abound, did, from time to time appear—and when they did, the whole movement girded itself, and then such comradeship as Garrett showed for Harriet was quickly manifest.

*   *   *   *   *

If the Dover affair was a result of the prestige that Harriet had acquired, there was, a few months later, another repercussion of her work, with more deep-seated consequences. This was the Sam Green case, a *cause celebre* of Abolition, in which the slavocracy pounced upon an aged Negro preacher and sentenced him to ten years in jail for having in his possession a copy of the Harriet Beecher Stowe book, *Uncle Tom's Cabin.* If there was ever an issue illustrative of the lengths to which the slave power resorted in its attempts to impose its will upon the colored population, it was this. Nor should it be surprising that at the root of the matter was Harriet.

The martyred Samuel Green, a slave-born Negro who had purchased his freedom, was a preacher in the Methodist Church.[7] But it was rather with this old man's son, also named Samuel Green, that the situation began.

Several years earlier, in July or August of 1854, when Harriet was cruising about on the Eastern Shore, planting the seed of escape in the minds of black men, she happened upon young Samuel Green, a blacksmith of twenty-five years, who was in the service of a Doctor James Muse of Indian Creek, in Chester County, Maryland. "He was quite too intelligent and liberty-loving, not to heed the valuable information which this sister of humanity imparted." [8] Recruited to the Underground, Samuel Green, junior, set out for Canada in August of 1854 and he speedily arrived there.

Ordinarily that should have ended the matter, except for Dr. Muse's wrath, but in this case the Chester County authorities directed their suspicions and hate upon the older Samuel Green. It irked them that the old man, a preacher, had been in any way a party to his son's escape, even to allowing it, and they decided to await the right opportunity to arrest him and make an example of him. When, in the summer of 1856, he went to Canada to visit his son, their suspicions of his Underground activities intensified and they increased their surveillance of him.

Early in the year 1857 "a party of gentlemen" raided Green's cabin. They found a map of Canada, several schedules of routes to the North, a letter from the son who was living in Canada, and above all they seized a copy of that scurrilous item, *Uncle Tom's Cabin*. A few weeks later, when the old preacher was arraigned on an indictment charging possession of the famous best-seller, the court held in abeyance its decision. The delay was for purposes of allowing the anger of the South to break loose against Sam Green and *Uncle Tom's Cabin*, to demand "proper" penalty, and to notify the North that Dixie liked neither Harriet Beecher Stowe nor her book, neither the Underground Railroad nor Canada, and neither Harriet Tubman nor the growing sense of Abolitionism in the North. The press, North and South, blared in the days that followed; and none doubted but that it would go hard with Sam Green.

A few days later the doom of Sam Green was pronounced, and the old man did go to jail, sentenced to ten years; and he stayed there, waiting and withering, until Abe Lincoln set him free with the Emancipation Act. The South had its share of victories in that historic struggle, and the reply to Harriet Beecher Stowe was one of them—at least for a few years.

Harriet Tubman's relationship to the Sam Green prosecution is an illustration of how the Abolitionists, planting acorns here and there, reaped the great oaks of revolt and slavery's end later. Moreover, Harriet brought the matter to a fitting conclusion. She accepted the slaveholders' challenge as laid down by the severe sentencing of old Green, and a few weeks later she irked them quite beyond their forbearance, for she then made one of the most dramatic journeys of her career. . . .

Harriet's abduction of her parents was an event in Underground annals. It was significant, not only because rarely did aged folks take to the Road, but because Harriet carried them off with an audaciousness and an aplomb that represented complete mastery of the Railroad and perfect scorn of the white patrol. Her performance was that, at once, of the accomplished artist and the daring revolutionary. Not only did this campaign attract the attention of all of Harriet's admirers, but it even drew the ire of a Philadelphia critic,

John Bell Robinson. His attack may be called the vindication of Harriet Tubman. He never intended it as such, but his words remain, to this day, the best compliment to the conductor's genius.

Franklin B. Sanborn declared that this, in 1857, was her "most venturesome journey, for she brought with her to the North her old parents, who were no longer able to walk such distances as she must go by night." [9]

Through one of her communicants in the Eastern Shore region, Harriet learned that her father was in trouble. The aged Ben had recently helped a slave to escape; in flight this slave had grown fearful and decided to return to his plantation. His identity is unknown, but whoever he was, he told his wife of Ben's help. Then the wife, desirous of ingratiating herself with her master, revealed how Ben had helped her husband. Immediately that old Ben was branded as an aide of the Underground, the authorities swooped down and arrested him.

To effect a rescue during an hour of emergency Harriet needed ample funds. Whatever might stand in the way, she decided, it should not be a lack of money. She would appeal to the anti-slavery office in New York, she told one of her friends, "and I'm not going to eat or drink till I get enough money to take me down after the old people."

Harriet did precisely that. She went to the Abolitionist headquarters and demanded twenty dollars. It was a larger sum than Abolitionists usually had on hand, and the sum was at first declined. They simply didn't have it. But Harriet refused to take no for an answer. She sat down and went to sleep, probably one of her intermittent sleeping seizures. She slept in the offices all morning and all afternoon, occasionally rousing herself to find people about and again to find herself alone. A few times she was urged to leave, "There's no money for you here," they said.

"No, sir. I'm not going till I get my twenty dollars."

Harriet's story became whispered about, and the Abolitionists went into action. They raised sixty dollars for her that afternoon and finally told her to take it and be on her way. And Harriet speeded southward to rescue her father and "remove his trial to a higher court"—Canada.[10]

The early part of the trip was the most hazardous. As Thomas Garrett described it: "She brought away her parents in a singular manner. They started with an old horse, fitted out in primitive style with a straw collar, a pair of old chaise wheels, with a board on the axle to sit on, another board swung with ropes, fastened to the axle, to rest their feet on.

"She got her parents . . . on this rude vehicle to the railroad, put them in the cars, turned Jehu herself, and drove to town in a style that no human being ever did before or since; but she was happy at having arrived safe. Next day, I furnished her with money to take them all to Canada. I afterwards sold their horse, and sent them the balance of the proceeds." [11]

Upon their arrival in Philadelphia the Vigilance Committee was impressed because not many of those thus far advanced in years ever succeeded in getting to Canada. William Still recorded their arrival, in part, as follows:

BENJAMIN ROSS, AND HIS WIFE HARRIET
Fled from Caroline County, Eastern Shore of Maryland
June, 1857

"This party stated that Dr. Anthony Thompson had claimed them as his property. Upon the whole, Benjamin pronounced him a rough man towards his slaves. But Ben did not stop here, he went on to speak of the religious character of his master, and also to describe him physically; he was a Methodist preacher, and had been 'pretending to preach for twenty years.' Then the fact that a portion of their children had been sold to Georgia by this master was referred to with much feeling by Ben and his wife; likewise the fact that he had stinted them for food and clothing, and led them a rough life generally, which left them no room to believe that he was anything else than a 'wolf in sheep's clothing.' These two travelers had nearly reached their three score years and ten under the yoke. Nevertheless they seemed delighted at the idea of going to a free country to enjoy freedom, if only for a short time. Moreover, some of their children had escaped in days past, and these they hoped to find." [12]

Harriet took them forward: New York, Albany, Syracuse, Rochester, St. Catharines . . . and liberation.

*   *   *   *   *

A sequel to this campaign occurred later when John Bell Robinson, a pro-slavery critic, devoted the conclusion of a book to an attack upon Harriet's abduction of her parents as "a diabolical act of wickedness and cruelty." His argument, largely a vilification of her Underground accomplishments, followed her appearance before a woman's suffrage convention, in 1860, when by then, Harriet had become nationally known.

"The most noted point in this act of horror," said Robinson, "was the bringing away from ease and comfortable homes two old slaves over seventy years of age. Now there are no old people of any color more caressed and better taken care of than the old worn-out slaves of the South, except the wealthy whites, who are few in number. A much larger proportion of the Southern slaves live to their old ages than do the colored people of the North, or free States. . . . Those old slaves had earned their living while young, and a home for themselves when past labor, and had sat down at ease around the plentiful board of their master, whose duty it was to support them through old age, and see them well taken care of in sickness, and when dead to give them a respectable burying. This ignorant woman must have been persuaded and bewildered by flattery by some fiendish source, or she certainly would not have been guilty of such a diabolical act of wickedness and cruelty to her parents, who had a fortune laid up for old age, and had come to the time when labor had ceased to be required at their hands, and were entitled to a peaceful home with him whom they had served so many years, and where the laws of the State compelled him to give them that support righteously due them the balance of their days, and where they had friends to comfort and console them in declining life."

This is the first time that we learn of the fortune which Ben and Ritty Ross had hidden away in the old sock. But the rescue of her parents was only part of Robinson's complaint, for he rapped the audience that listened to Harriet's description of her work:

"Can it be possible that so large an audience of white people can be found in so high a civilized community, professing so much love for the poor slaves, who could applaud such an act of wickedness and cruelty in a child to her parents, as this certainly was; and a thousand times worse than to sell young ones away! I admit it to be a great act of kindness to the master, or the estate that had them to support; and perhaps was a saving of some two hundred dollars a year to him or his estate. The notice (the newspaper account of Harriet's address) does not say where she took them to; but we suppose as far north as she could get them, and altogether likely into Canada, where they have nearly six months of severe winter out of the twelve. I cannot conceive of a more wicked act toward parents. Confinement in the penitentiary for life would be *'inadequate'* to her crime, for stealing her old parents away from a good home and friends, and a living already laid out sufficient for all their wants; and from a warm climate altogether congenial to their nature, to a very cold one, and where there is nothing to depend on but their labor. And in a climate where the thermometer is in the neighborhood of zero four months out of twelve, and no master's wood-pile to go to; and no rich white man or woman to call them 'Uncle Tom, and Aunt Lotta,' whose fortune was protected by the laws of the State in which they had labored for their support. Yet an audience of white people professing love of the slaves, could applaud a being in human shape, for so cruel an act."

There was, he argued, a reason for all of this. It lay in the witch-burning tradition of Boston's Puritan ancestors. "Therefore it was hardly to be wondered at in the summer of 1860, that their posterity should all assemble at Melodeon Hall, in the city of Boston, to worship the goddess of liberty in the shape of a poor deluded negro woman. And sing and shout with the loudest acclamations of glory and honor to her for the performance of as cruel an act as ever was performed by a child towards parents." [13]

END CHAPTER X

CHAPTER XI

"THE GREATEST HEROINE OF THE AGE"

Harriet was active on a variety of fronts after the year 1857, although the Underground remained a major occupation. She began addressing anti-slavery conventions in the late 'fifties, or at least, the record of her public appearances then begins. If anything took precedence over her work as a conductor, it was her developing association with John Brown, and their plans for raiding the Government arsenal at Harper's Ferry at a later date.

Harriet was never a full-time, paid Abolitionist. Even at this late date she was the main support of her parents, who were now too old to work, and she interspersed her Abolition activities with various temporary domestic jobs. Subsidy for her political life was irregular. Once, as shall be noted directly, she appealed to an anti-slavery body to aid her parents, because "the labor required for their support rendered her incapable of doing anything in the way of business (that is, politics)." [1]

With the widening of her scope of activities, her work on the Underground from 1857 into 1859 was converging into something of a climax, although she would not make her final rescue until late in 1860. "It now came to pass that . . . rewards were offered for the apprehension of the Negro woman who was denuding the fields of their laborers, and cabins of their human livestock . . ." [2] By the Autumn of 1857 Harriet, if not single-handedly, then primarily, aroused the Eastern Shore slaveholders to the point of organized action against the Underground. The Sam Green prosecution had not terrorized anyone. Not only had Harriet fled with her old folks a couple weeks after Sam went to jail, but the rate of slave exodus in the forthcoming months exceeded anything before in the history of Maryland.

At one time she collected and sent on a gang of thirty-nine fugitives in the care of others, as from some cause she was prevented from accompanying them. [3] That was in the month of October, 1857. They were Cambridge slaves: all left together, but for strategic reasons separated before reaching Philadelphia.[4] One contingent composed of twenty-eight men, women and children went heavily armed, with revolvers, pistols, sword-canes, butcher knives and other instruments of defense. It was common knowledge in every newspaper office in the North that the Bucktown-Cambridge region in Dorchester County, the Harriet Tubman country, was being plucked of slaves like a chicken of its feathers before roasting. Every Abolitionist editor knew of the high rate of flight in that region, and many found occasion to comment upon it in the ensuing months. When the party of twenty-eight arrived at the Quaker City, it made a profound impression on the station-hands. When William Still released his chronicle of slave narratives a few years later, the account of this caravan was accompanied by a vivid drawing of "Twenty-Eight Fugitives Escaping from the Eastern Shore of Maryland." [5] The brigade of thirty-nine was only part of the October outflux from the Cambridge region. Only a few days before they set out, a smaller company of fifteen had gone North, and had been duly registered by the Philadelphia historian. In fact, Still noted sixty arrivals from Harriet's region in that month alone.

If October, 1857, was an intensive month for Eastern Shore escapes, it was only somewhat more exceptional than others of the same year and of 1858. There was a constant procession of runaways, singly and in groups; the route from Harriet's region to the free states seemed accessible to any slave that desired to know it. It was no wonder then that the slaveholders, at about this time, began an organized drive against Negroes, free and slave, a movement that gained impetus in each county of the Eastern Shore, spread to the whole State of Maryland by 1858, and resulted in a State-wide convention by mid-Summer of 1859. It was this crusade, initiated by Dorchester County slaveholders in November of 1857, and culminating a year and a half later in a huge Baltimore convention against Abolitionism, the Underground, and calling for the re-enslavement of free Negroes, that was the greatest single tribute to the performance of Harriet Tubman, her fellow conductors, the station masters on the way north and the daring fugitives themselves. The panic that broke out at this time and lasted for so long was the major repercussion of Harriet's decade of activity.

The Cambridge slaveholders, meeting in that town on November 2, 1857, after the last decampment of blacks, resolved to enforce a number of ancient acts of the Maryland Assembly relating to servants and slaves.[6] They fished up one law dating back to 1715, providing that servants could not go farther than ten miles from their "master, mistress or dame, without a note in their hands . . . under the penalty of being taken for a runaway," and to suffer a runaway's punishment. The application of this was intended to give any white man the right to accost any Negro and question him. An 1806 act, intended to make re-capture of slaves attractive, provided for payment of six dollars to anyone seizing a runaway; and the resurrection of the most dangerous measures, those of 1825 and 1839, calling for the re-enslavement of free Negroes, and their sale and banishment from the State, would prevent them from aiding their enslaved brothers, it was thought.

Cambridge sounded a welcome tocsin to counties all over the Eastern Shore; and quickly, the slave powers called local meetings to revive the same set of acts and prepare for unified action. Ten months later, in August of 1858, the movement was rolling through the eastern half of Maryland, and the Dorchester County leaders undertook measures for the holding of a general Eastern Shore Convention.[7] It was the free Negro mainly against whom the assault was directed; it was he who encouraged the slave to resistance: therefore, re-enslave the free Negro! The Dorchester heads, long made frantic by their daughter, Harriet Tubman, dreamed of welding the whole South into a holy war against the free black, dreamed of being the spearhead in the whole question. "Let us not only have a Convention here on the Eastern Shore, but let it be held in view of the holding hereafter of a great Slaveholding Convention of the slave States. Similar laws with regard to free Negroes and Abolitionists and upon the subject of manumission, should be passed by all the States; and the initiatory to this result must be a great Southern Convention—not a Convention of mere words, but one of action —an action which coming events will force upon the South and upon us of Maryland. . . ."[8] A sinister crusade, but one into which the Maryland powers pushed, with all their vigor. The ancient acts were brought up to date, and free Negroes were re-enslaved. "Eighty-nine were sold in Maryland under the act of 1858 justifying such re-enslavement." [9]   Simultaneous with the intensification of the repression against both the slave and the free blacks, the slaveholders of both western and eastern Maryland drew plans for a State-wide Convention to be held in the Summer of 1859.

The Maryland panic had become the front-page news in both pro-slavery and Abolition journals ever since the close of the year 1857.   In the offices of Oliver Johnson's *National Anti-Slavery Standard* it was well understood why the Dorchester fathers had initiated the State-wide and the nation-wide movement.   Here Harriet had often stopped with her broods and received the assistance of the Abolition editors and their organization before going on to Canada. *The Standard* said, "The operation of the Underground Railroad on the Maryland border, within the last few years has been so extensive that in some neighborhoods nearly the whole slave population have made their escape, and the Convention is a result of the general panic on the part of the owners of this specie of property." [10]

*   *   *   *   *

When the State-wide Convention of slaveholders was held in Baltimore, in the Summer of 1859, they were defeated in their chief aim, that of effecting the removal of free Negroes from their State. There were in Maryland 80,000 free blacks, and by now they wrought enough political influence to thwart the aims of the 16,000 slaveholders of that State.   The slaveowners charged that these free Negroes were a threat to business enterprise, a competitive force with white labor, and they "subverted the slave population."   But there was a sharp struggle among the slaveholders; the black man had strong allies even among this group, and these friends were influential enough to compel a resolution that any such step against the free Negro was "impolitic, inexpedient and uncalled for, by any public exigency which would justify it." [11]

James W. C. Pennington, an ex-slave and a highly respected critic, commenting upon the defeat of this proposal, described it as a victory for the free Negroes and a "declaration in favor of free Negro labor." [12]   Thus there appeared, as early as 1859, a straw in the wind that would blow during the war period.   Even in the South, in the heart of the enemy's camp, there were powerful forces in favor of advancing the Negro from his slave status into that of free labor, or of defending the status of free labor after that was achieved. Speaking of the fugitive question, Pennington delivered an indirect compliment to the work of Harriet when he observed, as others had also declared, that Maryland, "more than any other State, had been drained by the exit of fugitive slaves"; he congratulated the fugitives for their work in the cause of freedom, but added that "their emancipated brethren at home have been doing even better." Thus the Negro fought on all fronts: as a slave, as a free Negro in the South, and as a fugitive in the North.

Some slaveholders' groups, wrathful over the defeat of their plan to expel the free Negroes from the State, stiffened their offensive against the slaves, and tightened their legislation to make more operative the capture of fugitives; and it was about now that Colonel Thomas Wentworth Higginson made the statement that if Harriet Tubman continued to go South on her slave-running expeditions, she would certainly be caught and burned alive.

Of the danger to Harriet, in this period, it was said: ". . . she was going down, watched for everywhere, after there had been a meeting of slaveholders in the court-house of one of the large cities of Maryland, and an added reward had been put upon her head, with various threats of the different cruel devices by which she would be tortured and put to death; friends gathered around her, imploring her not to go on directly in the face of danger and death . . . " [13] but she continued her work. Later the Abolitionist lecturer, Sallie Holley, wrote, "*Forty-thousand* dollars was not too great a reward for the Maryland slaveholders to offer for her." [14]

When the lynch spirit against her was at its highest she received from the Reverend Dr. Michael Willis of Toronto, the funds to make another trip to the Eastern Shore. Dr. Willis was the principal of Knox College, at Toronto, and he was President of the Anti-Slavery Society of Canada. In this position he could not but be closely associated with Harriet. Dr. Willis, a Scotchman by birth, had headed the Canadian anti-slavers all their organized history, since 1851. How often he and his followers aided Harriet cannot be ascertained, but in October of 1858, when the pressure against Harriet was heaviest, Dr. Willis stopped at *Frederick Doug-*

lass' Paper, in Rochester, and left a gift, probably funds, for the conductor. The *Paper* of October 29, 1858, carried a note on its editorial page, a communication addressed to Harriet, reading, "A valuable parcel left in our care by Rev. Dr. Willis, of Toronto, awaits the call of Harriet Tubman." [15]

Canadian aid was only part of the foreign support that her work merited at this time. As far away as Edinburgh, Scotland, there were persons vitally interested in her labors. Eliza Wigham, the head of the Anti-Slavery Society of that city, had a prolonged correspondence with Thomas Garrett, from about 1857 to 1860, and in the exchange of information the Quaker had described Harriet's operations. Thereafter Eliza Wigham and her Scottish associates sent funds for her, directing Garrett to place them with her.[16] She was receiving this aid at the time the Maryland slavemasters were on the march. She even had friends in Ireland, as Garrett's correspondence with William Still revealed.[17] Thus her labors were by now known on at least two continents, and in at least four countries. In spite of such a reputation she was still unknown to many sections of the American public, particularly in the West, and to large numbers of Negroes in some deep South areas. Her reputation was the typical one of the revolutionary who engages in subterranean operations, whose labors are often forced into the open by events. She was the scourge of the Eastern slaveholders, and her work was common gossip in Maryland, Delaware and Pennsylvania, where the heavy rewards were offered for her capture. Were her conspiratorial talents unknown to the Negro leadership in the West Indies, in Brazil, and in far off Liberia, Africa? Abolition and colored leadership was then in world-wide communication, and the "legend" of Harriet was certainly one of the communiques of the international grapevine.

*   *   *   *   *

Harriet traveled all through New England in the year 1859. She formed a fast friendship with Colonel Thomas Wentworth Higginson, then a Unitarian minister in Worcester. Higginson, once he became acquainted with Harriet, admired her above all other women then living, as his words frequently attested. Whenever he spoke of the anti-slavery figures he included mention of Harriet, directly or indirectly.

Only a few weeks after the execution of John Brown, Higginson, writing of his acquaintanceship with the old man, Harriet and others, said, "It had been my privilege to live in the best society all my life—namely that of Abolitionists and fugitive slaves. I had seen the most eminent persons of my age: several men on whose heads tens of thousands of dollars had been set; a black woman, who, after escaping from slavery herself, had gone back secretly eight times into the jaws of death to bring out persons she had never seen. . . ." [18] By the time that Higginson uttered that statement he was well-qualified to do so. In June of 1859, the fighting minister, as he was known, wrote a letter to his mother telling her that Harriet had been visiting him:

Worcester, June 17, 1859

Dearest Mother:

. . . We have had the greatest heroine of the age here, Harriet Tubman, a black woman, and a fugitive slave, who has been back *eight times* secretly and brought out in all sixty slaves with her, including all her own family, besides aiding many more in other ways to escape. Her tales of adventure are beyond anything in fiction and her ingenuity and generalship are extraordinary. I have known her for some time and mentioned her in speeches once or twice—the slaves call her Moses. She has had a reward of twelve thousand dollars offered for her in Maryland and will probably be burned alive whenever she is caught, which she probably will be, first or last, as she is going again. She has been in the habit of working in hotels all summer and laying up money for this crusade in the winter. She is jet black and cannot read or write, only *talk,* besides acting. . . . [19]

Colonel Higginson introduced Harriet only a few weeks later to an important anti-slavery audience at Framingham, Massachusetts, when the Fourth of July was celebrated. The Fourth was an event for the members and friends of the Massachusetts Anti-Slavery Society who were "to be counted by thousands." [20] The object was to remember the slave and "to renewedly consecrate themselves to his deliverance." It was an out-of-doors gathering, and according to *The Liberator,* the day was an exceedingly fine one. Colonel Thomas Higginson was elected President of the Society for the ensuing year. He regarded Harriet as an eloquent orator, and one of his statements reveals that he was familiar with the sight of her before anti-slavery groups. "On the anti-slavery platform where I was reared, I cannot remember one real poor speaker; as Emerson said, 'eloquence was dog-cheap there'. . . . I know that my own teachers were the slave women who came shyly before the audience . . . women who had been stripped and whipped and handled with insolent hands and sold to the highest bidder . . . or women who, having once escaped, had, like Harriet Tubman, gone back again and again into the land of bondage to bring away their kindred and friends. . . . We learned to speak because their presence made silence impossible." [21]

Harriet created such a sensation that James Yerrington, the phonographer (secretary), was a bit paralyzed, unfortunately, and he was compelled to report that words could not do justice to her; and he therefore did not undertake to repeat them! When Yerrington stopped reporting and turned to a moment of personal admiration, he expressed a mood that Harriet excited in most of those who came to know her:

.   .   .   .   .

The President then said that he wished to introduce to the audience a conductor on the Underground Railroad, who, having first transformed herself from a chattel into a human being, had since transformed sixty other chattels into other human beings, by her own personal efforts. It was rather hard to introduce her. She came here from a place in the slave states; she came by land, and had been here a reasonable time. (Laughter.) At the South she was called "Moses," after an ancient leader, who took men and women into the promised land. (Applause.)

"Moses," the deliverer, then stood up before the audience, who greeted her with enthusiastic cheers. She spoke briefly, telling the story of her sufferings as a slave, her escape, and her achievements on the Underground Railroad, in a style of quaint simplicity, which excited the most profound interest in her hearers. *The mere words could do no justice to the speaker, and therefore we do not undertake to give them; but we advise all our readers to take the earliest opportunity to see and hear her.*

Mr. Higginson stated that this brave woman had never asked for a cent from the abolitionists, but all her operations had been conducted at her own cost, with money earned by herself. Now, however, having brought her father and mother out of slavery, she found that the labor required for their support rendered her incapable of doing anything in the way of business, and she therefore desired to raise a few hundred dollars to enable her to buy a little place where her father and mother could support themselves, and enable her to resume the practice of her profession! (Laughter and applause.)

A collection was taken in her behalf, amounting to thirty-seven dollars, for which, at the conclusion of the meeting, in a few earnest and touching words, she spoke her thanks.[22]

Actually the Seward transaction had been cleared for some time, but she now sought funds to help pay for the property, and as she said, to be at the service of Abolition.

When Colonel Higginson introduced her as "Moses" this was a measure of safety to cloak her identity from the slavehunters as much as it was a crowning compliment to her leadership. The comment of Yerrington, that "it was rather hard to introduce her," further confirms the precaution taken to protect her. The slave power could have demanded of the Massachusetts government its right, under the Fugitive Slave Law, to have her returned to the South; and later, in fact, in anticipation of this development, Harriet's friends were stimulated to rush her off to Canada. Harriet had reached a stage in her career where she swung, like a pendulum, from the Underground into the open, and now the pendulum swung faster. That is why she was desirous of utilizing whatever uncertainties prevailed in official quarters about her identity and whereabouts; and that is why she hoped to remain out of the public eye, leaving this domain to the orators and writers. Had it not been for the dire need of assistance for her parents, in order that she might continue her political services, it is doubtful whether she would have risked appearing before such a major body as the Massachusetts Anti-Slavery Society. But Harriet's attempt to "labor in a private way," to be witnessed only by "the midnight sky and the silent stars," as Frederick Douglass put it,[23] was fast coming to an end, in spite of her desire for secrecy, in spite of her belief that she could be most useful so long as she performed behind the scenes. There were further efforts to maintain personal secrecy, but the bursting of the John Brown insurrection soon would definitely expose her in all of her past and present activity and make impossible further veiling from the publc gaze.

Similarly, she employed concealment in an address delivered a few weeks later at the New England Colored Citizens' Convention, which met in the Meionaon, in Boston. It was Monday morning, August 1st of 1859, when they met, and Harriet, still in New England, attended these sessions. Here she was introduced as Miss Harriet Garrison, "one of the most successful conductors on the Underground Railroad." Harriet told one of her typical stories, thus illustrating her anti-colonizationist attitude. As was usual in her expression of political views, she chose a figure of speech to illustrate the point. *The Liberator* account:

"Miss Harriet Garrison was introduced as one of the most successful conductors on the Underground Railroad. She denounced the colonization movement, and told a story of a man who sowed onions and garlic on his land to increase his dairy production, but he soon found the butter was strong, and would not sell, and so he concluded to sow clover instead. But he soon found the wind had blown the onions and garlic all over his field. Just so, she stated, the white people had got the Negroes here to do their drudgery, and now they were trying to root them out and ship them to Africa. 'But,' said she, 'they can't do it; we're rooted here, and they can't pull us up.' She was much applauded." [24]

This was Harriet Tubman. No other reference to a Harriet Garrison, colored, as "one of the most successful conductors on the Underground Railroad," has been found. Nor do any records of colored conventions indicate the presence a second time of a Harriet Garrison. Harriet Tubman had taken William Lloyd Garrison's last name and coupled it with her own first name for the temporary purpose of the Negro Convention. The figurative method of expression was peculiarly her own. Harriet Garrison was none other than Harriet Tubman, still living "underground," and now that her fugitive status was too dangerously revealed, she was making extra efforts to keep her identity secret.

* * * * *

If Harriet's career had ended at this point, if she had been burned at the stake somewhere in the South, as Colonel Higginson predicted she would be, if she had not lived to become possibly the outstanding woman of the Civil War itself, then her record in the 1850's alone (apart from other important events to be related directly), would have secured for her a lasting position among Americans as the ablest woman revolutionary, and a conspirator with but few peers among men. When it is realized that the Underground was the major means of struggle of the Negro people and their white allies in their drive toward the ultimate goal of emancipation, then we can better understand the generosity with which she gave herself to this work. For a half century the Underground system had been plunging its roots into the political fabric of the North and South. For the past ten years it had, like some huge social lever, separated the two sections, and rendered irreparable the breach. Millions of dollars worth of slaves, a total of 50,000, with an average value of one thousand dollars apiece, had flown to the North. Harriet had herself "stolen" about three hundred thousand dollars' worth of fellow blacks and stimulated other hundreds to flight. A few conductors spirited away larger number of slaves, as did Reverend Calvin Fairbank and Captain Fountain, but they were white, educated, and men. Harriet's achievement was in spite of her color, which was always suspect, in spite of her sex, and over against the handicap of her chronic illness. She was unable to read or write, she lacked knowledge of maps and geography, and she pursued her course in spite of being the support of her parents and others. Moreover, the uniform success of her campaigns was a record unrealized by any of the other conductors; and the excellence of her achievement lay in the fact that she was never martyred, never jailed, and never even for a day did she fall into the hands of her enemies, but outwitted them at every point.

It has been estimated that Harriet made nineteen excursions into the slave land, and most authorities have accepted this estimate. But if she had conducted only fifteen voyages, or even a dozen, her record of rescues, the moral influence upon the Abolitionists, the economic consequences in weakening the slaveholders, the increased stimulus to Negro morale in the South, and the culminating political result in intensifying the North-South contradictions, still add up to the career of an unparalleled conspirator and social fighter in any clime, in any nation, in any period of history. Her leadership of repeated blows at the Eastern slaveholders, with the hosts of the Underground network marshalled at her side, contending over thousands of square miles of embattled ground, created such a total effect in the ante-bellum period, laying siege, as it did, to the South's fundamental nature—the forceful containment of Negroes in slavery —that the prolonged guerilla operation can only be called the Battle of the Underground, and it must be compared to the victorious command of a major front in the Civil War itself.

END CHAPTER XI

END PART TWO

PART THREE

CAPTAIN JOHN BROWN AND "THE WOMAN"

CHAPTER XII

"THE MOST OF A MAN"

For several years John Brown had been battling in Kansas, until at last in the winter of 1857 he lost patience with the "peace" that prevailed in that territory and he veered his plans toward his long-dreamed-of conspiracy in the Virginia country. Kansas was not yet a free state, nor was it wholly in the hands of pro-slavers; the issue was simply not yet decided. But the struggle to make the region free had whetted Brown's appetite, confirmed his faith in the power of guerilla warfare, strengthened his hand with the wealthier Eastern anti-slavers; and a pack of vigorous young men had rallied to his side.

The genius of John Brown's raid at Harper's Ferry, West Virginia, lay in the fact that it combined in a single gesture most of the important political and economic features of that period, and it occurred at a time when it could have and did have the most possible effect on North-South relations. If it failed in its grand purpose, that of making good an insurrection which would liberate the slave and result in the establishment of a Provisional Government, which, in turn, would reconstruct the United States, then it succeeded in the political realm out of all proportion to the military debacle. The conspiracy utilized important political elements of that period, such as the need for black and white collaboration in the face of a common enemy, the resources of the Underground Railroad, insurrectionary theory (especially the experience of previous American revolts), and Christian zeal or the moral right of the Negro to freedom. In case the revolution failed—for a plan of revolution is exactly what it was—it was calculated to have a secondary, and an almost as desirable effect, the deflation of the slave's economic value.

With his revolutionary idea in mind, John Brown went east to New England in the Spring of 1858, to win the support of the men who had financed the free state campaign in Kansas. Among the more important persons whose aid was enlisted were those two wealthy anti-slavers, George Stearns and Samuel G. Howe of Boston; the Negro organizer, Lewis Hayden; the Reverend Thomas W. Higginson of Worcester, Massachusetts and Franklin B. Sanborn of Concord. These, probably the most daring male Abolitionists, excepting those who had already shouldered arms in Kansas or had run the gauntlet of the Underground Railroad, knew that at last the hoped-for movement to end slavery had a leader, and that the deed was in motion.

After making his contacts in New England, Brown turned into New York State. Gerrit Smith, whom he had seen in March of 1858 at Peterboro, was an important source for money and moral support; and it was through Smith that Brown now established his first connection with Harriet Tubman. Brown had long been curious to meet her. From hearsay he had pictured her as a vigorous and military personality. Since he planned to use the resources of the Underground Railroad, he believed Harriet could help out because of her knowledge of that system. The Underground was heavily entrenched in the Virginia, Maryland and Pennsylvania region, and if slaves rallied to his side they would have the assistance of the station masters, white and Negro. The Road would provide supplies; the Negroes, those who might become liberated in the Virginia region as a result of his revolt, could reach the station masters. Many who would not want to stay to fight in a warring South could be sent on to the North. The Underground Railroad would thus be a factor in numerous ways during the deliverance of the slaves. And who knew the Underground Railroad in the East better than Harriet Tubman?

When Brown visited Gerrit Smith's Peterboro home, the philanthropist gave him the funds to make a trip to St. Catharines, Canada,[1] and he also gave the Kansas warrior a check for twenty-five dollars, to be delivered to Harriet when Brown should meet her. That was the rich reformer's way of recommending Harriet.

Brown hastened on to Rochester to tell Frederick Douglass that he was making ready to enter the Virginia country, and to urge that now was the time to back up the plan. Whatever discussions occurred there, the most important result was Brown's decision to go to Canada and meet Harriet. She, he hoped, would be able to supply recruits for his liberation army from among her freed following in Canada. Douglass too had urged upon him an immediate interview with Harriet.

J. W. Loguen, the Negro minister and Abolitionist, of Syracuse, was in Rochester visiting Douglass at the time, and it was arranged that he should accompany Brown to St. Catharines and bring him together with Harriet. It was about April 4th or 5th of 1858 when Loguen and Brown went to the British dominion. Harriet was temporarily living there, although her more permanent home was already established in Auburn.[2]

One report has it that Harriet asked Brown to come to her home.[3] Whether or not that was true, Harriet was presently entrusted with the secret of the Virginia plan. By the time Loguen brought them together, Brown was prepared to meet an extraordinary creature. When he first set eyes on her he said, "The first I see is General Tubman, the second is General Tubman and the third is General Tubman." [4]

Brown wrote a letter a few days later to his son, John Brown, Jr., revealing that Harriet more than measured up to his expectations. He was virtually rapturous, and he was not a man given to the use of superlatives. He found it necessary to continue "masculinizing" Harriet in order to convey his estimate of her qualities for leadership. He wrote:

"I came here direct with J. W. Loguen the day after you

left Rochester. I am succeeding to all appearance, beyond my expectation. Harriet Tubman hooked on his whole team at once. He is the most of a man, naturally, that I ever met with. There is the most abundant material, and of the right quality, in this quarter, beyond all doubt. . . ." [5]

Whatever information of possible military resource Harriet had, she passed on to John Brown. She told him what she knew of the aid that would be forthcoming from the Underground Railroad in the East, gave him additional information about the terrain in which Brown expected to operate and promised to bring to his side her own personal following of fugitives in Canada West. Brown painted a picture of what might happen in the Virginia country once that hostilities opened up and explained that he had a special job for her at that time. He hoped she would be a chief guide to the North of the slaves he freed in the neighborhood of Harper's Ferry. [6]

In short, she was Brown's main reliance in Canada, his key to the fugitives and their various capacities for support.

"God's Angry Man," as Brown has been called, was still in St. Catharines on April 14th, and on that day, according to an entry in his diary, he paid Harriet Tubman in gold for Gerrit Smith's draft of twenty-five dollars. [7] By that time she was fully conversant with his plans, and he could now leave Canada and take up organizational problems elsewhere. He saw Harriet several times; he met many Negro allies through her, and he saw the advantage of calling a convention here to complete the organization of his army and his liberation plans. Before he left, he again called her General Tubman three times and informed her that she would hear from him through Douglass. [8]

While Brown was absent in Chicago for a few weeks, Harriet busied herself among the ex-slaves, seeking recruits to fight at the old man's side. The conspiracy went ahead rapidly, for Harriet and others in Canada were mobilizing a large number of blacks for an early meeting with Brown. Harriet was aided by Martin R. Delany, a prominent Negro critic and Abolitionist, in the selection of able men of color for service with Brown.

John Brown's intimates, those who had fought with him in Kansas and a few others that he had more recently taken into his confidence, clung together in small groups in Canada, in New England, in Central New York, in the far West, and they buzzed and rumored of the impending event. By now perhaps two score knew that a plan of revolution was fomenting. There was, especially in Canada West, since Brown made his visit to Harriet, a furtive, underground whispering. This atmosphere has been described by William Ellery Channing in a narrative poem, "John Brown," written many years after the Harper's Ferry explosion. Channing, describing a meeting in a house on the outskirts of Chatham, Canada, began his one hundred and forty-three-page drama with a scene of Harriet, Stevens, and John Brown in conversation. Stevens, a soldier with an extensive military background, was third in command of the Harper's Ferry expedition.

Harriet opens the conversation by asserting her profound interest in the conspiracy. Stevens replies, not doubting her hearty cooperation, and he avers his own staunch sentiments. Many or one, he says, be it even himself alone, he will take the road that goes to free her people. No more talk for him. . . .

> *For me I should not dare to live, and feel*
> *More like a slave than now!*

to which Harriet replies:

> *My people are unversed in strife and arms;*
> *Peace ever is the music of their hearts;*
> *And, long crushed down, even those who, with us now*
> *Sit under their own vine, dream but of rest.*
> *What think you of the meeting?*

That is a reference to the forthcoming Chatham Convention. Stevens says that the men must meet, must prepare to set up a Provisional Government; and he compares the event to Christ's last meeting with his disciples.

> HARRIET. *I have persuaded four to join your band.*
> STEVENS. *Four? One is an army in this cause!*

Harriet introduces the question of the risks of the campaign (one that, in reality, she never raised, according to any evidence.) Stevens cautions her to silence lest they be overheard and betrayed. Harriet calms him, and again predicts that the raid contemplated by the small band is doomed to failure. The soldier replies that, *"Someone must perish,"*—and he then speaks of the fortitude of old John Brown. At this point Brown enters, and addressing himself to Harriet, delivers himself of a conception of the Negro nation in freedom:

> *Harriet! We seldom can make sweet your days.*
> *The woman's heart is aching for its race.*
> *Their fate is hazardous, yet fear it not,—*
> *The sword of Gideon in our hands is set.*
> *Think of the men who till the wide-spread fields,*
> *Lands rolling o'er a continent,*
> *And every brother of the outspread race*
> *Waiting to clasp a brother to his breast.*
> HARRIET. *There is a pulse in that!* [9]

The poem continues, introducing John Cook, John Henry Kagi and others, unfolding the entire story of Harper's Ferry. As Channing has supposed, there were such conferences at houses in St. Catharines, Chatham and other places in Canada West. Harriet and others attended them and they discussed the hazards, the morale, the backing of the anti-slavers, and theorized about the possibilities of military success or failure. Channing advanced one line, in effect that Harriet had persuaded four to join Brown's band. The poet based his work on the various published accounts of the raid, and he may have known of this as a fact.[10] He was an intimate of Emerson, Thoreau, Sanborn and other Concord Abolitionists.

When the Chatham Convention opened in the second week of May, John Brown was chosen Commander in Chief, and John Henry Kagi, War Secretary. There was discussion on the Provisional Constitution and it was adopted. The "sword of Gideon" was indeed set by now, and had it not been for the development of a treasonable situation, Brown would have led his men to Virginia at about this time. Hugh Forbes, a military man and adventurer, who had fought with Garibaldi in Italy, had been for a short time in Brown's company. He revealed the plan to Senator Hugh Wilson. As a result, it was necessary to postpone the invasion of Virginia.

The movement that had grown to a considerable peak in May of 1858 simmered out in the succeeding months, and made necessary a postponement of the action until the year 1859. With the lapse of time, many of the followers vacillated, and the waning of interest at this point may have been fatal to the military success of the engagement when it finally did occur. Certainly Harriet was in a position to exert her fullest influence in the spring of 1858, when the plan was fresh to the fugitives, when they had neither time to develop doubts, nor time to enter into new engagements.[11]

END CHAPTER XII

Chapter XIII

HARRIET TUBMAN HEADS FOR HARPER'S FERRY

With operations indefinitely delayed Harriet decided to return to Auburn for the remainder of the fall. Here she had the responsibilities of a house to be paid for and her parents to be supported.

All through the autumn months she labored in the home town, but retained contact with her fellow conspirators.

By the time the snows fell she was restless with her domestic obligations, and she feared that these concerns might root her here permanently and prevent further Abolition labors. She decided to go to Boston, raise funds to pay for the property she bought from Seward, and plunge renewedly into the work.

That is what happened: she went to Boston, met John Brown who was then there, and managed to secure enough money to take care of the house, at least for a time. "Pains were taken to secure her the attention to which her great services to humanity entiled her," said Frank Sanborn, "and she left New England with a handsome sum of money towards the payment of her debt to Mr. Seward. Before she left, however, she had several interviews with Captain Brown, then in Boston. . . . He always spoke of her with the greatest respect, and declared that 'General Tubman,' as he styled her, was a better officer than most whom he had seen, and could command an army as successfully as she had led her small parties of fugitives." [1]

This is verified by Wendell Phillips, for the last time that he saw John Brown alive was the first day that he met Harriet—and that would be a memorable event in the life of any Abolitionist leader. Phillips said, "The last time I ever saw John Brown was under my own roof, as he brought Harriet Tubman to me, saying, 'Mr. Phillips, I bring you one of the best and bravest persons on this continent—*General* Tubman, as we call her.' "

Brown then went on to recount her labors and sacrifices in behalf of her people. After that, said Phillips, Harriet spent some time in Boston, earning the confidence and admiration of all those who were working for freedom.[2]

Hence, whatever the state of John Brown's affairs in the mid-winter period Harriet was acquainted with them.

With money in her possession to mitigate some of her debt to Seward, Harriet returned to Auburn. But she did not long remain there. She was anxious to return to New England in order to do "missionary" work for Brown: to win the support of prominent anti-slavers and to find recruits from among the host of young Abolitionists, white and Negro, who swarmed in Massachusetts.

From some indefinite date in the spring of 1859 through to the insurrection Harriet was in New England. During that time she was out of touch with the crucial Canada West quarter. She passed time with Smith at Peterboro, Higginson at Worcester, spoke publicly at Framingham, visited friends in Boston and Concord, and latterly stayed in New Bedford, Massachusetts, in ill health. It was a period when she could have lost touch with Brown's week to week movements.

Meantime her absence from Canada was taking its toll: the fugitives, those who had promised to bear arms at Harper's Ferry, were losing touch with the Brown conspiracy, and indeed, many of them may have believed it to have been abandoned.

It was early spring, when the conspirators' spirits were at low ebb, when the New England colleagues were writing long introspective letters to each other, bemoaning the slow estate of the plan, that Brown was working hardest and making ready to "take the field."

*   *   *   *   *

Harriet rarely if ever made a trip eastward without stopping to see Gerrit Smith, and it is from a letter written on June 1st by a young musician named Edwin Morton, an inmate of Smith's home, tutor of young Greene Smith, that we learn of her presence there sometime earlier. Probably it was a mere halt before she headed for her destination, New England. Young Morton, a Harvard classmate of Sanborn, who knew of the plot, wrote a letter to Sanborn which indicated with some finality, what the plan then was. ". . . I suppose you know where this matter is to be adjudicated. Harriet

Tubman suggested the 4th of July as a good time to 'raise the mill.' "

That letter is evidence that Harriet's proposal of July 4th as a striking day was seriously considered by Brown, that he may even have heard it directly from her. Brown was in Peterboro visiting with Smith in the month of April. He had also met Shields Green, a Negro protegé of Frederick Douglass, in Rochester, during the same month. It would be strange if, during that period in New York State, he had not seen Harriet, on whom he counted for so much. There had been a meeting at Peterboro, attended apparently by Harriet, Gerrit Smith, Morton, and possibly John Brown. Harriet had suggested July 4th as a desirable day for the beginning of the stratagem. The symbolism of the hour appealed to her, and she saw no argument against opening the hostilities in the hot weather when the authorities might be slowed up by the heat.

Meantime John Brown was in touch with Sanborn about the problem of getting soldier recruits. The old man wanted Sanborn or someone else to go to Canada with Harriet to get them. The Concord Abolitionist wrote to his friend Higginson at Worcester, on May 30, mentioning Harriet, and seeking the minister's speedy cooperation:

"He (Brown) is desirous of getting someone to go to Canada and collect recruits, with H. Tubman, or alone as the case may be & urged me to go but my school will not let me. Last year he engaged some persons and heard of others, but he does not want to lose time by going there himself now. I suggested you to him. Now is the time to help in the movement, if ever, for within the next two months the experiment will be made." [3]

There was no issue of Sanborn's plea to Higginson to make a recruiting expedition to Canada, with or without Harriet. Whatever Higginson's reason, he did not go.

By June 20, 1859 Brown "was already mustering his men and moving his arms toward Virginia, and it was about the Fourth of July, as Harriet Tubman had suggested, that Brown first showed himself in the counties of Washington and Jefferson, on opposite sides of the lordly Potomac.

"He needed now only recruits to serve with him and for these he relied on Tubman and the fugitives she had brought north with her." [4]

Only recruits. Only the most important thing of all, the men. And Harriet was the key to this.

It was too early for Brown to strike on the 4th of July. Not nearly enough preparation had been made. As late as July 3rd Brown made his first appearance in the vicinity of Harper's Ferry. After looking over the region he rented the Kennedy farm, near Harper's Ferry, as his headquarters; and at about that time, John H. Kagi, Brown's righthand man, was stationed at Chambersburg, Pennsylvania, as a liaison representative with the Northern backers. In spite of the year of delays, and even the slow movement and disappointments now, John Brown's general plan advanced. The treasonable Hugh Forbes was no longer a problem; and the morale of the financial backers was reawakening.

Early in August, John Brown, Jr., stationed in Ohio, undertook an important task in relation to the full development of the campaign. He was now the old man's chief representative in the North. He was designated to go east from Ohio on a "Northern tour," to round up recruits, gather additional funds, and test all the lines of contact. On August 11, young Brown, writing from Syracuse, informed Kagi at Chambersburg that he had seen Frederick Douglass and that the Negro leader would arrive there in a few days, that he would be accompanied by a Negro recruit for the campaign, Shields Green, and that if Harriet Tubman could be located, she would go along too. "Came on here (to Syracuse) this morning," he wrote. "Found L. (Loguen) gone to Boston, Massachusetts, and also said woman (Harriet)." In spite of extra expense he intended going on to Boston to find Loguen and "the woman." Frederick Douglass had urged this step upon him saying that Harriet's services might prove invaluable.

Arriving in Boston, John Brown, Jr., met everyone but "the woman." He had his first meeting with Dr. Samuel G. Howe and other staunch friends of his father. Consulting with them about what to do on the highly important question of going to Canada to get recruits, he was advised to have Loguen accompany him on his journey northward.[5]

Thus, months late, perhaps months too late, the matter of the Canadian fugitives was being taken care of; but from the time when the unavailability of Harriet as a Canadian recruiting agent was established, the whole question of fighters remained unresolved.

Harriet's location was unknown for several weeks or more, at the time Brown Jr. was looking for her. She was then in New Bedford, ill. Late in August Frank Sanborn, then in Springfield, Massachusetts, wrote to John Brown, reporting Harriet's whereabouts and illness. This letter, like the aforementioned John Brown Jr. letter to Kagi, was confiscated by the authorities at Kennedy Farm during the uprising, and eventually printed in the Senate Committee Report Investigating the Harper's Ferry Invasion. The schoolmaster's reference to Harriet read, "Harriet Tubman is probably in New Bedford, sick. She has staid here in N. E. a long time, and been a kind of missionary." [6]

Over-exertion in her Abolition labors, the years of toil on the Underground Railroad, and the intervals of hard domestic labor to maintain herself and her parents, had struck Harriet. Chronic illness was almost "natural" to her; she still suffered intensely from that bruise of slavery which left her with frequent visits of temporary unconsciousness. But now her illness was in a stage of general crisis; she was seriously weakened and abed.

In spite of her illness there was another attempt, this time by Lewis Hayden, to bring her into the operations. This was only a few weeks before the raid occurred. Lewis Hayden knew where Harriet was and he wrote to her, but he seemed to be unaware of her weakened physical condition, according to a letter that he sent to Kagi at Chambersburg. *The New York Herald,* which was violently opposed to Abolition, and subsequently wrote of the Brown campaign with a view to exposing its origins, remarked that "Harriet Tubman was not in good health and had been spending some time in a small New England town." [7] It then printed the Hayden letter, dated Boston, September 16, 1859:

My dear sir:—

I received your very kind letter, and would state that I have sent a note to Harriet requesting her to come to Boston, saying to her in the note that she must come right on, which I think she will do, and when she does come I think we will find some way to send her on. I have seen our friend at Concord (Frank Sanborn); he is a true man. I have not yet said anything to anybody except him. I do not think it is wise for me to do so. I shall, therefore, when Harriet comes, send for our Concord friend, who will attend to the matter. Have you all the hands you wish? Write soon.

Yours,

L. H.

That is an important letter, for it reveals how the Negro leaders, first Douglass, and later Hayden, looked to Harriet for leadership. It reveals that Chambersburg and Harper's Ferry were still requisitioning her, even though Sanborn had informed Brown two weeks earlier that she was in bad health. It was the plan of Hayden to send for Sanborn when Harriet arrived in Boston, and the schoolmaster's job was to provide funds to send her to the front.

That was John Brown's hope. Indeed, it was his last hope in the way of having a reliable Negro leader at his side when the gunfire would begin. A few weeks earlier when the Old Man met Frederick Douglass at Chambersburg, the Negro declared that he did not believe it sensible to bear arms himself at Harper's Ferry. The man of color foresaw the military failure with the same clarity as he understood most political situations in his own time. The Old Man badly wanted a colored leader at his side to rally the slaves: he wanted someone who could command, speak, and bear arms. From the time Douglass withdrew, the Old Man concentrated his efforts upon having Harriet with him. Thus, the hunt for "the woman" went on, and now, according to Hayden, there was a ray of hope that the little black conductor might be available. And she was . . . but too late.

*　　*　　*　　*　　*

John Brown would delay no longer. Fearing new obstacles, suspecting more treason, perceiving the lateness of the year, and realizing that he himself was growing old, he hastened his date with destiny, and on the night of October 16, 1859, history was made. The men struck, seized the important Federal arsenal, the bridges, the town of Harper's Ferry itself.

Franklin B. Sanborn says that Harriet was in New York City at that time,[8] which means that she was at last started on the way. The eminent Negro historian, W. E. B. Dubois, said, "Only sickness, brought on by her toil and exposure prevented Harriet from being present at Harper's Ferry." [9]

The loss of "the woman" to the cause, both in person and in the recruits she could have mustered had she been able to travel earlier, was a severe blow to the plan.

If Brown did not have with him Douglass or Tubman, he did have five other Negroes: slave-born Shields Green, who was captured in the engine house with the Old Man; Dangerfield Newby, first of the band to die in the struggle, for he was in the thick of it at the armory gate; John A. Copeland, who lived through the affray only to die on the gallows later; Lewis Leary, mortally wounded on October 17th and dying in agony; and Osborne Perry Anderson, who skirmished with the militia, fought to hold the arsenal, and managed to escape, being one of the five who did.

Of course, the story of the other sixteen white men who fought, died, hanged, or escaped, is to this day one of the most oft-told tales of American history. The episode snowballed into as large a political factor as anything which the Abolitionists had as yet achieved. If Brown and his men did not alone liberate the slave— and no single person or group did—then at least they struck a telling blow. The Old Man's military stroke miscarried, but an even greater political debacle was engineered by Governor Wise of Virginia when he hanged John Brown.

The impress of the affair never left Harriet Tubman's mind, never so long as she lived, and a generation later she wanted to name her own Home for the Aged and Indigent after John Brown. She never ceased to talk of the Old Man, and always referred to him as the true emancipator of her people. Harriet believed all of the days of her life, that it was not Lincoln who was the Negro's vindicator —not really Lincoln who hedged and vacillated in the war days—

but John Brown—there was the white man whom the Negro would forever remember!

*   *   *   *   *

As to Harriet's part in the Harper's Ferry invasion: while we must acknowledge the superior critical faculties of Douglass, and admit that he saw correctly the military failure of the plan, we cannot help but admire Harriet for her unmitigated fortitude, nor can we forget that one of Boston's leading Negro fighters, Lewis Hayden, and other Abolitionists, made a profound effort to send on, into blazing gunfire, the little black woman. More, to those who search for a principle or meaning in Harriet's relationship to Brown: she gave sanction and association to conspiracy and insurrection when she believed that these methods were necessary to the freedom of her people.

Brown found a personal inspiration in Harriet which few other living persons aroused in him. The highest expressions of admiration from him for another human being were spent upon her. She was "the woman" in whom he placed an implicit trust, the one person he admired above all other Abolitionists—"The General."

Great women's names have come out of that period, but they are not to be found mentioned in the pre-invasion days of Harper's Ferry. In the post-invasion period the five-foot high colored woman, with several front teeth missing, the wooly hair, and the sleepy eyes —she who was on her way to join the white-bearded deliverer, dropped from sight; and then the "great names" of the land were heard. When John Brown lay in jail, Lydia Maria Child offered to come to Charlestown Jail and be his nurse, and other articulate white women in the North flooded him with letters—and hoped for his replies. Lydia Child had been one of the most admired writers, but Brown already had a long association with Harriet and he happened not to have known Mrs. Child.

Harriet had functioned so deeply under cover that she was not revealed until months later. First the *New York Herald* indicated Harriet's complicity; then in 1860 she was mentioned again in the Report of the Senate Committee Investigating the Harper's Ferry Invasion. Within a year, it was common knowledge in the ranks of Abolition and among the New England and New York State woman suffragists that Harriet had been Brown's conspirator for a long time.   Only time has revealed how fully they collaborated.

Her presence alongside Brown is not only a score for Negro history, but it is a chapter in woman's annals, a role in "the woman's history of the world."   Harriet had pioneered for her sex as well as for the Negro nation.

END CHAPTER XIII

END PART THREE

PART FOUR

"I Know There's Going To Be War!"
Harriet Tubman to Frank B. Sanborn

CHAPTER XIV

THE BATTLE OF TROY

All through the Winter of 1859-60 the nation was agog over the John Brown affair; political parties girded for a great struggle in 1860; anti-slavery meetings increased, and Abolition demonstrations were unabated even in the face of the most furious official reaction. The Republican Party was busy denying that it had any connection with the John Brown affair; and in Auburn, Seward's and Harriet's town, the local newspaper, *The Auburn Union,* vigorously defended William H. Seward, the man who was expected to become President. *The Union* denied that Seward had any connection with Brown, that he had ever helped the man or the movement in any way. But the pro-slavery forces attacked him bitterly, for they wished to crush his Presidential aspirations, and the Brown matter furnished a fine pretext. It was becoming known that he was the personal friend of Harriet Tubman; that he had helped her abundantly in the past, even to making it possible for her to settle in Auburn. Birds of a feather flock together, the attackers reasoned; Seward had hobnobbed with Abolitionists, and he and his party were responsible.

They cited as proof of the matter that Northerners in high

places had aided Brown, that old Gerrit Smith had become mentally stricken by the excitement and had to be sent to a sanitarium: and Smith and Seward were connected in the pro-slavery mind.

The seizure of John Brown stimulated many a Northerner to an increased anti-slavery mood, and it so awakened Colonel Higginson that he extended his conspiratorial operations to the point where, directly after the raid, he was planning the rescue of two members of the party, Stevens and Hazlitt, who were awaiting trial. He tried to enlist the Kansan, Captain James Montgomery, in the plan, but this fell through; and Higginson even entertained, with others, the plan of capturing the Governor of Virginia and keeping him as a hostage for the safety of old Brown. But these ideas turned out to be flurries and gestures; the men were handicapped by lack of funds and by other circumstances.

In this period Harriet laid low. Business on the Underground Railroad went ahead, of course, for knowledge of the routes throughout the land could by now be acquired by any slave who was in earnest about finding his way North. But Harriet, who had been ill, still needed rest, and after the John Brown excitement she returned to Auburn and spent a few quiet months.

It was April of 1860 before she went into action again. Sometime in the spring Harriet was requested by Gerrit Smith, now recuperated, to go to Boston to attend a large anti-slavery meeting.[1] What happened immediately thereafter snapped Harriet out of her winter of quiet—and her first action of the year was one that only the memory of John Brown could have inspired. She staged her own personal Harper's Ferry at Troy, New York, in early spring of 1860. From this event it cannot be doubted what a force Harriet would have been at John Brown's side: and Brown, if he could have watched this action, would have said, "Lord, Harriet, why were you ill when I needed you most!"

* * * * *

Harriet Tubman, the escaped slave woman, was on the march again, once more trampling upon the hated Fugitive Slave Law. Black as plumbago, her small, fierce carriage eloquent with strength like a creature of the wildwood, she was leading the citizens of the town of Troy, New York, teaching them how to deliver a body blow to slavery. Cool brisk the day, noon sunny the hour, and the time, April 27, 1860.

Her presence in that town might have been called accidental, but her leadership of the anti-slavery action was not. En route to Boston to meet with the Abolitionists, in response to Smith's invitation, she stopped in Troy to visit a relative; a fugitive slave case had arisen during her presence and she organized the present demonstration. The fury of the Negro woman was the match struck to one of the fiercest outbreaks after John Brown's raid on Harper's Ferry and prior to the Civil War. The demand was that the fugitive mulatto, Charles Nalle, be seized from the hands of the Federal law and spirited away to freedom.

As the pack of cause-stricken anti-slavers swarmed into the street below the courtroom, and the pro-slavers crushed against them, political temperature and bodily heat mounted, and from the pavement the sun was blotted out. Harriet's brood was out there ready to live or die for Charles Nalle.

Eclipse of the business center became complete. The Trojans poured into the commercial area, many bearing arms that had been hanging on walls ever since the revolt from the British. Anxious eyes lifted to the second story of the drab, wooden building at State and First Streets where through the window, whose panes trembled from the tension below, the townspeople saw the figures in the slave case. Work stopped as all business closed in a spontaneous standstill. Keys turned in store doors. Running feet, clenched fists pointed toward the town center, now a marketplace, a man's life the article for sale, and the Northern law prepared to abide by its contract with the South.

At this minute General Tubman employed the effective ruse that she often used in her night-time operations on the Underground. Posted at the open door of the small courtroom, jackknifed into the crouch of a crippled and weak old lady, her intense ebon face covered by the strands of a shawl converted into a bonnet, and shielded by a nearly empty food basket which she maneuvered about her head, she whined to be admitted into the room. Being short she could posture decrepitude; but beneath this masked aspect of anility she was tensed as a tiger, and like a tiger, ready to spring.

She did a bit of acting that would have done justice to the then celebrated actress and anti-slaver, Fanny Kemble. Holding faintly to the broad guard's coat lapel as if to touch him by kindness, smiling gently and lifting her sable brows so that lines appeared in her forehead, she transformed her normally vigorous appearance into the mask of an octogenarian. Anguished of eye, wizened of body, she clung to two strong colored women who feigned supporting her. The guard was touched and he fell silent.

*   *   *   *   *

So brittle was the spring air in the Troy streets that fingertips and nosetips reddened and color came quickly to the cheeks. The pavement was dry and the jostlers, milling about, moving from one group to another to hear all sentiments, soon melted the air throughout the avenue, and waves of warmth arose from the massed body until the vague sense of it wafted into the open windows of the courtroom. But the cold passions of the pro-slavers were not so easily melted, for "Meanwhile angry discussion commenced. Some persons agitated a rescue, and others favored law and order." [2]

Troy was ready to fight for Charles Nalle as Syracuse fought for Jerry, Boston for Anthony Burns, as other cities fought for other great slave causes. Ten years of the Fugitive Slave Law had enraged anti-slavery sentiment in Troy, as throughout the North. For decades this town had been a station on the route of the Underground; for ten years it defied the national law and helped along escaped slaves, and today this heroic tradition was in danger of shattering if the law shipped Nalle back.

Planting themselves at strategic spots in the throng, Abolitionists, Negro and white, enspirited the crowd, and one Negro, William Henry, who had never orated publicly before, discovered that he had a natural eloquence to hold a crowd. [3]

If it was no longer Tom Paine's Age of Reason, it was still a period when the leader proclaimed the rights of man; but now, near the high point of the Abolition movement, after John Brown had struck his fatal gash into the slave system, new slogans, higher thoughts, deeper deeds spattered the air like a thousand volleys of buckshot. The unknown Bill Henry needed not to speak of "the irrepressible conflict" or "the Higher Law than the Constitution," for these realizations were deep in the American consciousness and by now every anti-slavery boy of ten years knew that these were truths. Bill Henry only said, "There is a fugitive in that office. Pretty soon you will see him come forth. He's going to be taken down South, and you'll have a chance to see him. He is to be taken to the depot, to go to Virginia in the first train." [4]

In this was contained all the meaning of the times; and Bill Henry might also have declared, as did the Abolitionist poet, Whittier:

"My voice, though not the loudest, has been heard. . . ."

Soon the murmurings for a forcible rescue became a clamor for immediate action. At the courtroom door, moaning like some helpless wind lost in a forest, Harriet listened to the roar in the street and viewed the scene in court. She waited for the right instant, measured every slightest motion, each developing factor, and waved the basket, shield-like, before her eyes.

She gazed incredulously at the witness from Virginia who was bringing the evidence against prisoner Charles Nalle. The Southern agent was the brother of the accused! A rare thing, but it happened sometimes; one could speculate that the agent was a free Negro or perhaps an especially favored slave of his master. The Virginian looked like the accused Negro; both were mulatto, but the testifying brother looked almost white.

The prisoner was about thirty, good-looking, intelligent of appearance, unnerved by his ordeal; and now he paced about before the tremoring window and looked down upon the whirlpool of friends and enemies. Perceiving that he had suddenly become a *cause celebre,* and encouraged by the manifestation of sympathy that thundered from the marketplace, he weighed his chances for escape. The stake was high; the cost might be death. The fugitive Daniel had been sent back to slavery from Buffalo; Hamlet had been captured in New York after a grim pursuit; but Shadrach had escaped to Canada, spirited there; and Ellen Craft, beautiful quadroon, had successfully fled to England with her husband William Craft. He looked down into the throng and realized that he had odds; that the time was later than he thought; it was 1860 and the Fugitive Law was old and hated now; here in Troy was enough anti-slavery sentiment to give him a two to one chance. Others had lost; he might win; and win or lose, it was better than slavery. A daring thought placed itself in his forehead. . . .

When, with a provincial majesty, the inevitable decision against Nalle was pronounced, as the guards began to squirm, and as Harriet's deep groan of protest suffused the room like a chant, Nalle leaped to action. He turned swiftly as a wheel, darted toward the window with a half dive, opened it with a fleet movement of his gray-white wrists, and stepped out on the ledge. As yells of welcome greeted him from the street, he twisted himself into position for a dangerous drop to the pavement.

"The crowd at this time numbered nearly a thousand persons," said the *Troy Whig*. "Many of them were black, and a good share were of the female sex. They blocked up State Street from First Street to the alley, and kept surging to and fro." Nor was it accidental that many of the anti-slavers were women; for women like the Negroes were on the high road too, grasping for suffrage, seeing in the anti-slavery struggle a stepping stone to their own freedom, and so, throwing themselves into such struggle, into the bloody street scenes, into the great fugitive cases.

The guards soon bayed the prisoner; hands encircled his neck, his sprawling limbs, his whole body, and they hauled him back into the offices of the Commissioner and held to him like crabs to food. Aching for breath in their hard grasp, Charles Nalle subsided; and he looked for help to the swaying Negro women who filled the doorway with their bodies and their bursts of lament at his recapture.

Harriet had straightened up during the fugitive's attempted flight, and she was prepared to barricade the door if the law attempted to come through and go down the stairs to recover him. Flight or forcible rescue was the correct policy, she knew. Flight was the main idea of the period. Negroes fled North from station to station; Abolitionists had flown before the Federal law; fugitives escaped pursuing masters, agents and bloodhounds. Everywhere men and women were running to freedom, to that ladder that led ever upward to human happiness. It was the whole meaning of the Underground Railroad, of the great cause itself. But escape was an art and a science, and it must succeed. Nalle had moved not quickly enough, she decided; so she resumed her patient crouch, moaning like a calm breeze that could not possibly whip up into anything stronger.

Time fiddled into the clenched hands of the anti-slavers. There was a vitally important half-hour's lull in the juridical proceedings, and during this period the whole town of Troy except the abject thronged into the center. While Attorney Martin Townsend for the prisoner hurried to a nearby office to appeal the judgment, the situation in the courtroom, presided over by Commissioner Beach, was stalemated; in here there was nothing but tension, two brothers glowering upon each other with a hate deep as death, an "old lady" waiting to rediscover her youth, an unnerved judge who peered outside at the expanding scene, the most historic in Troy, and the law grasping onto the convicted man's wrists with pressure that turned the mulatto's color white as newlaid paint.

As numbers spiral when they are multiplied so the crowd enlarged until the thousands merged and flowed, a great social and human tide. Suddenly there arose from the street a last desperate cry that cracked into the courtroom like a flame, *"We will buy his freedom. What is his master's price?"*

The Southern agent leaped to the rattling window, ready to strike a bargain. Money for flesh. Flesh for money. That was different. Flesh might not be higher than law, but money was.

"Twelve hundred dollars," shouted the Virginian.

Pools of citizens eddied with a new excitement as pouches flashed into the open and pledges loosed on the air. The well-to-do gave richly, and the poor heroically. Two hundred was mounted by three hundred more; a wave of notes and a jangle of silver lifted the sum to a thousand. Soon, like all tides that reach the shore, there was a mighty surf of final contribution.

"We have raised twelve hundred dollars!"

But the slaveowner's agent was avaricious, and he shouted back at the throng, *"Fifteen hundred dollars!"*

It was the typical Southern attitude, the same which later would provoke secession and rebellion; it was one more slap to rouse the North, and even now it reawakened all the quieted fervor of the anti-slavers. A stinging voice that was a clarion call of all the North shouted:

"*Two hundred dollars for his freedom but not one cent for his master!*"

The anti-slavers pressed forward, ready to give their lives if need be in the name of Freedom.

Simultaneously Martin Townsend returned with an order calling for the fugitive's immediate appearance before the judge of the Supreme Court. A husky deputy sheriff presented the paper; the Commissioner read it; and there was no alternative for the law but to undertake to deliver Charles Nalle to the higher court at once.

Harriet unraveled some of the kinks in her slight body. As several guards and deputies manacled the prisoner and headed him toward the door, ordering onlookers aside, she arose to her full height, which was not impressive, sent the basket reeling and bumping into a corner, magically dropped her aged appearance, and fleet-footed across the courtroom to the window. Her words, declaiming on the Troy air like some tonal bell in a hollow steeple, became the cue for the Abolitionists.

"*Here he comes! Take him!*"

She sped back to the door, with skirt flying and bonnet waving like a banner, glided down the stairway like a path of flame, and entered into the volcanic street, overtaking the guards with the demand that was nearest the heart of the North.

"*This man shall not go back to slavery! Take him, friends! Drag him to the river! Drown him! But don't let them take him back!*"

Adroitly Harriet gave directions to the battle. She wanted Nalle steered toward the river where by pre-arrangement a boat would whisk him across the cold water to temporary freedom in Albany County. As she shouted challenges and directions she locked her iron arms under the manacled bleeding wrist of Nalle, and began pulling him out of the lock-strong hands of his guards.

Oaken clubs and chisels struck against human heads and pistols blazed. Abolitionist, anti-slaver and sympathizer crushed with the pro-slavers and blood washed the Troy streets that afternoon.

"In the melee she was repeatedly beaten over the head with

policeman's clubs, but she never for a moment released her hold, but cheered Nalle and his friends with her voice, and struggled with the officers until they were literally worn out with their exertions, and Nalle was separated from them.

"True she had strong and earnest helpers in her struggle, some of whom had white faces as well as human hearts, and are now in Heaven. But she exposed herself to the fury of the sympathizers with slavery without fear, and suffered their blows without flinching." [5]

When after long attack, and after the fighting throng had swept down the town's blocks toward the river, and when the power of the police and the pro-slavers was smashed, Harriet, still clinging to Nalle, broke away, dashed to the river front, and protected by a brave band of hurt and bleeding whites and Negroes, placed the prisoner in a skiff manned by a sympathetic ferryman.

Harriet, who had fought the enemy in scores of battles, knew his tactics, his reserves, his cunning. She foresaw the possibility of the recapture of Nalle on the other shore and rallied the anti-slavers for a trip across the river. As the *Troy Whig* described it: "Then there was another rush for the steam ferry boat; which carried four hundred persons and left as many more—a few of the latter being doused in their efforts to get on the boat."

The prisoner, who was almost unconscious from his injuries, himself having fought furiously, was captured as soon as he reached the other shore, and there he was rushed to Police Justice Stewart's office. The law threw up barricades and prepared to fight anew.

With Harriet Tubman in the forefront, the conflict became sharpest and bloodiest at this point. "Not a moment was lost. Upstairs went a score or more of resolute men—the rest piling in promiscuously, shouting and execrating the officers." [6] Stones flew against the door, pistol shots came from the guards inside. There was a momentary retreat until someone shouted, "They can only kill a dozen of us—come on!" The citadel was stormed, amidst a hail of thrown stones and a returning theme of gunfire.[7]

"At last," said *The Whig*, "the door was pulled open by an immense Negro and in a moment he was felled by the hatchet in the hands of Deputy Sheriff Morrison; but the body of the fallen man blocked up the door so that it could not be shut. . . ."

Attorney Martin Townsend has said the last word. ". . . and when the men who led the assault upon the door of Judge Stewart's office were stricken down, Harriet and a number of other colored women rushed over their bodies, brought Nalle out, and putting him into the first wagon passing, started him for the West. . . ."

It was Harriet Tubman's victory as surely as Harper's Ferry was John Brown's, and more, it was a high point of the fugitive slave history that racked the nation's breast for ten years. If Brown's Virginia raid was a dress rehearsal for the Civil War, Harriet's action was a bugle call for the war to begin.

The law tracked after her for days, scenting her out as they might some thieving desperado. The wrath of the pro-slavers demanded her arrest, her trial, even her blood. But the Abolitionists had taken her deep into their underground bosom, and she lay hidden for days nursing her terrible wounds.

Later, by all the devious means of the Underground, she continued on her way—to Boston and her friends.

*   *   *   *   *

The memory of that struggle never faded from the life of Troy. A half century later, the townspeople placed a bronze tablet at the spot where the fight began, as an act of commemoration. As late as September 7, 1908, the memorial was erected on the National City Bank Building, at the northeast corner of First and State Streets, and it was inscribed as follows:

HERE WAS BEGUN

APRIL 27, 1860

THE RESCUE OF

CHARLES NALLE

AN ESCAPED SLAVE WHO HAD BEEN ARRESTED

UNDER THE FUGITIVE SLAVE ACT.[8]

And it is there to this day.

END CHAPTER XIV

CHAPTER XV

BOSTON TAKES HARRIET TO ITS HEART

Boston in 1860 was the long-haired son in the American family of cities, with a strong back for justice inherited in the revolt from Britain, large muscles for daring rescues of the Nalle type in Troy, a brain that bubbled ceaselessly with outpouring of pamphlets, newspapers and books, and social genitals that spawned Demosthenic young orators who flooded the streets, the plains and the plantations with their protest.

With its long, scrawly harbor, a harbor that was still hated by the British rulers, and its rambling expanse of small, wooden houses tilting puritanically on a criss-cross of alleys and lanes that led back onto each other or veered into maddening *cul de sacs,* Boston was like some whole city given over to a student's Latin quarter, as though the city fathers, foreseeing an intellectual culture for its sons, decided on a conscious experiment in esthetics, that of denying normal canons of form, as a first course in procedure. Early to set athwart the anti-slavery movement and even now the central stage of the battle, Boston, sheltered by three Olympian hills on its east, west and north, hurled its critical blasts up over these heights, whence the darts spread out to the whole nation, and even eastward across the ocean to inspire the hearts of Mazzini and Garibaldi liberating Italy, and O'Connell, Grattan and Curran fighting in Ireland against the sunset defying Tory Britain.

Drawing to their support economic theory, human rights, God and the Bible, the Abolitionists declared they were the carriers on of the founding tradition, still dedicated to the task begun by that adventuring worthy, John Smith, who in Plymouth and Boston worked "to the erecting of true religion among Infidells, to the ouerthrow of superstition and idolatrie, to the winning of many thousands of wandring sheepe, vnto Christs fold, who now, and till now, have strayed in the vnknowne paths of Paganisme, Idolatrie, and superstition." [1]

139

Today the "'wandring sheepe" were the Northern pro-slavers and the Southern slaveholders who must be won back "vnto Christs fold."

Flush-faced young women, zealous for the emancipation of their sex, took to the stump, and declaimed that woman's rights and Negro rights were one and the same. Elizabeth Cady Stanton's words would jar the rule of supine manhood. "Woman," she would say, "early learns the misfortune of being an heir to the crown of thorns, to martyrdom, to womanhood. For while the man is born to do whatever he can, for the woman and the Negro there is no such privilege." Inspirers like Lucy Stone, Lydia Maria Child, Abby Kelly Foster and Sallie Holley came to Boston, arose in convention, and demanded "an even platform with proud man himself." [2]

The times bred hosts of speakers and fighters, trained them and threw them into the public arena until the anti-slavery section of Boston was a hard-knuckled fist sticking up out of the Northeast, chastising his slower Northern brothers, and denouncing eternally his sister cities of the South. Boston Common was a sward for nightly collections of impassioned partisans, where heated argument ensued over the question whether the Constitution was a pro-slavery or an anti-slavery document. Often the patriotic blasts of either side were underscored in swift exchanges of fistic blows. The universities spawned a steady stream of birthlings for the great cause. Intellectuals of the nation trekked here to breathe the air of free thought, and to catch a sight of the revolutionaries on their home grounds. (Afterward they went to Concord where another, almost as remarkable set of talents flourished.) But it was proud, defiant, chin-smashing Boston that called himself vanguard, and dared the world to say he was wrong. Negro leaders walked the streets side by side with white men, already experiencing an equality that would belong to the colored mass in a few years—only to lose it again later.

At last, in the Spring of 1860 Boston, the Boston of Puritan John Smith, of the tea party, of Abolition, opened its lusty arms to a small black woman whose "voice has power to shake the nation that was so long deaf to her cries." [3]

*　　*　　*　　*　　*

In the month of May 1860, Harriet moved busily among the civic and reform notables of the region, tieing bonds of friendship which would be broken only by death. In Concord, effervescent with literary and political life, she resided at the houses of Emerson, Alcott, the Whitneys, the Brooks family and Mrs. Horace Mann, and other well-known persons.[4] In this pleasant and effective period Harriet favored the big-bodied, farm-born Frank Sanborn. They had been comrades of John Brown, which gave them an arterial link. Sanborn, like a guide in mountain country, rushed her from one Boston home of eminence to another, and then off to the literary peaks of Concord. In this latter town she visited at the home of Ralph Waldo Emerson, the renowned philosopher of transcendentalism. She stayed there, in the pine-surrounded, square, white house, which was a mecca for the nation's intelligentsia.

She could not be long alone, not long without a group, not long apart from people. It was as though she moved through life with outstretched hands, one palm touching the distinguished, the other ever touching the humble, the enslaved. At the house gatherings the Abolitionist notables studied her with rapt attention, for it was not merely the slave-thief to whom they listened. As much as the strained North rumored of her lightning achievements in running desperate Negroes off to freedom, of her relationship to the late John Brown, of Troy, so did all reaches of Abolition discuss her as an artist and personality. She dominated the anti-slavery parlors as Douglass, Phillips and Garrison dominated the lecture halls in which they spoke. Here was the woman and the Negro nation itself; here the guest, the cause, the figure, the symbol. In her ringing discourse, in her assured bearing of equality with all others, the anti-slavery leaders saw justified all for which they fought, saw the black people in freedom and in flourish.

She was not a boastful person, but she was an organic spinner of thrilling yarns; and that was because the days of her life were jammed with events impossible to the ken of any other's experience.

Harriet had long since discovered that there were white people with fine souls, and she had learned to give hers to these. As a child enslaved, she had always dreamed of kind, white women, and here, in Abolition, she had found them. To these now, and to the others, she opened her heart. She talked of her bondage and of her freedom, gave them of her rich experiences in elusion from the slave-owning enemy, and spoke of her friendship with the martyr Brown. She did not hesitate to perform the dances of Maryland and of the deeper South; singing too the folk songs of these little-known regions. It was not as an entertainer that she so exhibited; on the contrary, she knew that she was in the midst of artists and leaders, appreciators of other cultures, men and women who must be imparted with all of the black people's gifts; and it was proudly, as an example of her people, that she presented herself as a person of diverse skills.

She appeared these days, unlike one whose exploits were already legend over the country, hardly imposing enough to cast dread into the hearts of the pursuing slave catchers, and to irritate and tax the vigilant Northern authorities. Her clothes, according to photographs, were of Quaker-like simplicity, the two-piece dress she wore being somberly gray of color, the material of cotton, and the whole garb looking well-worn. Her crinkly shirt-waist fitted simply around a narrow torso, setting off the definite rise of her bosom, and disclosing an exceedingly small girth. A square dash of lace collar that rested chastely upon her throat brightened the apparel only slightly, and it served also to hide a few of the metallic buttons that formed a line from her neck to her skirt. This severe top-piece fitted tightly over a skirt that was amply ruffled at the top, spreading out over strong hips in a sharp curve, and then falling almost to the floor.

There were endless political discussions at the various anti-slavery homes. Harriet knew and declared where she stood. To her there was no such thing as merely a moral understanding of the evil of slavery. Understanding meant action, if it meant anything. Freedom itself was the recognition of the need for blows, more blows, and ever more telling blows against the enemy. Like Douglass, she favored the employment of all means of advance, parliamentary reform, moral suasion, critical education, slave-rescuing, petition, demonstration, insurrection, and finally large-scàle military struggle, should that be necessary. The latter, the likelihood of a war between the states, seems to have been her own real view of what would eventually transpire. She who had traveled back and forth between the two fires for so many years, was in a better position to know how really irrepressible was a large-scale conflict. Some time in this period she remarked to Sanborn, "They may say, 'Peace, Peace!' as much as they like; I know there's going to be war!" [5] In this knowledge she was well ahead of some men who even now were Presidential aspirants, and she was sounder in this respect than most Abolitionists with whom she traveled in Boston.

* * * * *

An incident, revealing and significant, occurred on the night when Harriet's gallant escort, Sanborn, guided her to his home. She entered a square, frame structure, wooden and simple like a farmhouse. ". . . she was shown into a room where Brackett's bust of John Brown was standing," Sanborn wrote later. "The sight of it, which was new to her, threw her into a sort of ecstasy of sorrow and admiration, and she went on in her own rhapsodical way to pronounce his apotheosis." [6]

Sanborn was much impressed that a soul untutored in art and reared in slavery reacted before sculpture, not with the restraint of a connoisseur, but with such sensitivity that, to her, the clay sprang into flesh. Harriet gazed, trance-like, into the stone eyes of the white-haired, white-bearded old man who had dubbed her General: and the veneration in her soul gushed forth into a virtual decretal that would be quoted all through Abolition, and repeated later even in England:

"It was not John Brown that died at Charlestown. *It was Christ;*—it was the Saviour of our people." [7]

* * * * *

East Wind. In historic Boston this has been for centuries a rubric for the spirit of the city. The salt-scented east wind brought the dissenting Puritans who breathed honest life into the new-born city and the infant country: the breeze vanished for awhile and then spiritually revived, washing in the angry Tories who failed to snuff out the growing life: and irregularly after that it circled about the town and blew up torrential storms for feminine suffrage and for religious toleration.

Now it returned again, ripping up a merry gale for Abolition. The illustrious New England caravan for Negro freedom was arriving, prepared to challenge the nation once more with its annual convention. But that was not all: ardent suffragists came on the same clattering trains and rickety stage-coaches for a woman's rights convocation called for the same time. Whether for good or ill, whether planned this way or not, the simultaneous assemblies made the salt spray spume: the editorial eyes of the conservative newspapers all through the United States were peeled on "bad boy Boston," anxious to thwack both "isms" and the rigid anti-slavery journals were girded to defend the irrepressible Boston tradition.

On May 27, 1860, the New England Anti-Slavery Society Conference opened. Row upon row of anti-slavers, breath-bated, listened to their leading spokesmen. Zealous churchmen, dauntless reformers, avowed suffragists, and calm philosophers one after the other denounced in pitched voice the institution of slavery, in ringing key eulogized John Brown, in grave tone mourned the churchman Abolitionist, Theodore Parker (who had just died), in steady, rolling eloquence foretold the freedom of the oppressed nation that agonized in the South. Harriet, avid for every gem-like utterance in this historic auditorium, listened to one fighter after another as they mounted the rostrum: Garrison, Burleigh, Purvis, Anthony, Remond, Child, Foster, Ruggles, May. Busy at his littered table, phonographer James Yerrington recorded the lofty speeches for that day and for posterity.

Swells of applause spread through the eager assemblage when the soft-featured, modestly-attired Wendell Phillips strode confidently toward the platform. His speech would be the highlight, for it was general knowledge that Phillips' voice, in recent denunciation of Seward, may have cost that illustrious statesman the Republican nomination to the Presidency; and this would be Phillips' first public utterance since that act. The scholarly Seward, in a pre-convention speech, committed the folly of justifying the hanging of John Brown as "necessary and just." For that opportunist compromise with a vengeful South, he had aroused the wrath of Abolition, culminating in Phillips' public excoriation of him. With the fatal stamp of radical disapproval upon him Seward was slapped by a majority of his own party—slapped and relegated to a secondary position in history. Now Phillips, with the poise of a swordsman, but wielding words which would be nationally sonorous, unsheathed a blade of steel that flashed as one of the major pronouncements prior to the Civil War.

What Phillips declared was historic, not alone in that it beheld Lincoln as the greater liberal, nor even for the greeting that it extended to the Northwest which, preponderantly, nominated Lincoln, but chiefly for its affirmation of the Negro's right to arise in his own defense. His lengthy oration reached a climax when he sounded a clarion call to the Negro South to strike out for its freedom. (And indeed, in the half year or so that remained of 1860, local revolts took place everywhere in the South.) Yerrington recorded that there was "tremendous applause" when Phillips said:

"I thank God therefore, that William H. Seward was rejected after making such a speech. (Seward's pre-convention rebuke of John Brown.) It is a good sign that far off in the Northwest there is a leaven of that spirit, that looks upon the Negro as a nation, with the right to take arms into its hands and summon its friends to its side, and that looks upon that gibbet of John Brown, not as the scaffold of a felon, but as the cross of a martyr." [8]

If Harriet was disappointed in Phillips' repudiation of Seward, she must have been earlier equally disappointed in Seward's rejection of Brown. At the moment she took consolation in the increasing political acumen of Phillips and the other Garrisonians. Apparently they were moving away from their inflexible dis-unionist position and beginning to see that the Republican Party, if granted Governmental control, might, at least, stop the advance of slavery. The wavering Garrisonians were already preparing for the time when they would go with the North and the Union.

Even before the anti-slavers closed their doors, the suffragists gathered in a "Drawing Room Convention" to present the artistic and esthetic view of the woman's rights question. [9] The contest for women's rights was old hereabouts. As ancestrally as 1668 the colonial Anne Hutchinson, a passionate religionist, had been banished from Boston for demanding the right of assemblage for women. In the seventeenth century, too, the fire-tongued Mary Dyer was publicly hanged for defending persecuted Quakers. Later Louisa Morton Green pioneered for woman's rights in industry; and in the revolutionary period Phyllis Wheatley, the brilliant young Negro poet who died in poverty, succeeded in representing the womanhood of her color in the field of culture. For centuries, even milleniums, women, dominated by men the world over, had grappled for economic independence and the rights of citizenship. Here, Down East, these dreams had become clearer, and now a veritable tidal wave capped the age-old struggle. The woman's crusade, with its spearhead in Boston, would mount and mount until one day, in the whole western world, womanhood would be legally free. In this onward march, alongside Susan B. Anthony, Elizabeth Cady Stanton, Lucretia Mott, and others, Harriet Tubman played her part and spoke, "in words which brought tears to the eyes and sorrow to the hearts of all who heard her for the unspeakable suffering of her brethren. She made the weak strong, the strong determined, and the determined invincible. After her words of untutored but fiery eloquence, her hearers stood like Martin Luther of old, body and soul and spirit devoted singly and untiringly to one end." [10]

Negro women figured prominently in this sphere for they, more than any other group, epitomized the period: they were both women and slaves. Harriet was only one in this pioneering core, and indeed, in the express circle of woman's rights, her friend, Sojourner Truth, played a more active part. Sojourner, tall and eloquent, religious and witty, was the first colored woman orator in the nation. But today was Harriet's, and the cooperative anti-slavers loaned her out long enough to make an appearance before the suffrage group to represent Negro womanhood.

In the wooden-walled Melodeon on a Friday that was the first day of June, the women gathered, Caroline Severance presiding over them, telling them that they would consider mainly woman's advancing position in the sphere of culture. The capable organizing talent, Caroline Dall, made the chief report, and statistical though it was, it reached the assemblage as a paen to the advance of their purpose. One thought they often used, like ammunition, and it issued from that animated clerical, Samuel J. May. There is nothing man has done that woman cannot do, he told them, and some things which they alone can do. The writer, Richard Hinton, had rushed hither from Kansas, long enough to announce that their cause advanced out his way with seven-league strides. Then came Harriet, introduced as Moses, and following her the weighty voice of Garrison. As if that was not enough celebrated company for a single platform, there appeared later, in the evening, Wendell Phillips, whose ardor and easy address was like a sunset crowning a blue-skyed day.

When Harriet mounted the rostrum, she fed water to the great thirst of the period. The slogan, "Tell Us of the Negro," rang through literature, the press, the church, the home and the salon, like a theme song of the cause. Of her speech this afternoon, *The Liberator* said:

> "A colored woman of the name of Moses, who herself a fugitive, has eight times returned to the slave states for the purpose of rescuing others from bondage, and who has met with extraordinary success in her efforts, was then introduced. She told the story of her adventures in a modest, but quaint and amusing style which won much applause." [11]

It was about this time that the Quaker City pro-slaver John Bell Robinson, writing his book, *Pictures of Slavery and Anti-Slavery,* studied the Melodeon Convention and beheld in Harriet the apotheosis of the whole question. He said that her work, and similar activities in the North, made matters intolerable, secession inevitable. She had not only committed treason against the United States Government, but against the State Governments. . . . "Now I ask all the candid men to look at this congregation of traitors a little, and see if the South had no reason not only to be insulted, but alarmed to the extreme, when they learned that enough such men and women could collect at Melodeon Hall in Boston in 1860, to densely fill it, and would laugh and shout over such wickedness, in a poor weak-minded negro woman, in trampling upon the rights of the South with impunity.   What could be more insulting after having lost over $50,000 worth of property by that deluded negress, than for a large congregation of whites and well educated people of Boston to endorse such an imposition on the Constitutional rights of the slave States.   Had we any right to expect anything but a rebellion against a government that refused to protect them against such outrages on their rights?" [12]

END CHAPTER XV

END PART FOUR

PART FIVE

THE WAR YEARS OF HARRIET TUBMAN

"She deserves to be placed first on the list of American heroines."
Samuel J. May, in
Some Recollections of the Anti-Slavery Conflict, p. 406.

CHAPTER XVI

1861

MUSKET IN HAND

Harriet divided the summer and fall of 1860 between New England and New York State. It was an intensely political period, for it was the year of the Presidential election. She was disappointed when, at Chicago, Abe Lincoln was nominated for the Presidency, and her friend Seward rejected. It was the season when the Northern Democrats, led by Stephen A. Douglas, split from the Southern Democrats, a move as fatal for the slave power as it was inevitable. The American Party came forward, nominating John Bell of Tennessee, trying to straddle the issue of slavery by ignoring it; but, succeeded only in further splitting the national vote, and making it easier for Lincoln to win. When, in the fall, Lincoln's nomination was secured, it was the cue for South Carolina to react immediately by seceding. That move was important in Harriet Tubman's life, for, during the next few years, this State was her battleground.

149

When events in the States drew toward their hostile conclusions, there were serious clashes in the North between Abolition and pro-slavery groups. This conflict was especially sharp in New England where the mere mention of John Brown excited violent partisanship. As an example, just before the war, Harriet was in an important demonstration in Boston. This was not long after Brown had been executed. Wendell Phillips, William Lloyd Garrison, as well as others, attempted to speak and the meeting was raided. She was one of several prominent women who escorted the speakers from the hall in order to prevent attempts to mob them.[1]

With the tightening up of political lines after the election, Harriet decided it was all the more necessary to bring out of bondage whomever she could, for slave-rescuing might become more difficult later. Her last visit to Maryland was made in December, 1860. In spite of the agitated condition of the country, and the greater watchfulness of the slaveholders, she brought away seven fugitives. One of them was an infant, which had to be drugged with paregoric to keep it from crying on the way and so revealing the hiding place of the party.[2]

Harriet had no difficulty in raising funds with which to make this journey, for her New England friends now supplied her with most of her war treasury. It was late in November when she tramped through the slave states with Stephen Ennets and his wife Maria, their six-year-old daughter Harriet, four-year-old Amanda, and a three months' infant. Though she started out with only these five, she collected two others, a man and a woman, while on her way. Thomas Garrett wrote a letter to William Still on the first of December, 1860, in which he described the dangers of Harriet's last excursion:

> *Respected Friend*:—William Still:—I write to let thee know that Harriet Tubman is again in these parts. She arrived last evening from one of her trips of mercy to God's poor, bringing two men with her as far as Newcastle. I agreed to pay a man last evening, to pilot them on their way to Chester County; the wife of one of the men, with two or three children, was left some thirty miles below, and I gave Harriet ten dollars, to hire a man with a carriage, to take them to Chester County.

She said a man had offered for that sum, to bring them on. I shall be very uneasy about them, till I hear they are safe. There is now much more risk on the road, till they arrive here, than there has been for several months past, as we find that some poor, worthless wretches are constantly on the look out on two roads, that they cannot well avoid more especially with carriage, yet, as it is Harriet who seems to have had a special angel to guard her on her journey of mercy, I have hope. Thy Friend,

THOMAS GARRETT.

N. B. We hope all will be in Chester County tomorrow.[3]

Historian William Still, who interviewed the party when it reached Philadelphia, wrote scantily for fear that his records might be seized. The capture of John Brown's papers and letters, he wrote, "with names and plans in full, admonished us that such papers and correspondence as had been preserved concerning the Underground Rail Road, might perchance be captured by a pro-slavery mob."[4]

*   *   *   *   *

There was a startling development for Harriet when she reached New York. When the party arrived there, the anti-slavers registered more concern for her than for her parcel of slaves. The Abolitionists would allow her to take no more risks. She must abandon the Underground Railroad. "It was the mad winter of compromises," said Frank Sanborn, "when State after State, and politician after politician went down on their knees to beg the South not to secede. Mr. Seward and many of the most patriotic and distinguished citizens of the country went over to the side of compromise. They were anxious to avert the horrors of civil war at any cost. . . . Those anxious months, when darkness settled over our political prospects, were viewed by all classes with deep forebodings, and by none more so than those who, like Harriet, had rendered themselves obnoxious to the supporters of slavery by running off so many of their race from its dominions. Fear for her personal safety caused Harriet's friends to hurry her off to Canada, sorely against her will."[5]

Here was irony! Harriet, who had run off hundreds to Canada, was now *conducted* there for her own security! She had been in too

151

many battles to escape the watchful eye of a Government ready to conciliate the slaveholders. Harriet could well be the "head on a charger" of any compromising Northerner who wished to ingratiate himself with the slave power. The Underground Railroad, John Brown, Troy, her speech-making: these had made her known and hated to every pro-slaver in the North, and to the Eastern slave-masters. Canada was now an even more urgent haven for her than for the slaves!

It was sound sense for Harriet's colleagues to ship her off to Canada. In December of 1860 the contest in the Senatorial Chambers was especially bitter: the representatives of the slave power were as uncompromising as the Republicans were concilia-tory. Senator John J. Crittenden of Kentucky, presenting an "olive branch" for the South, virtually asked the Republicans to unite upon a pro-slavery program and to guarantee an air-tight slave-nation. The "compromise" plan of Crittenden was a request for a whole and unadulterated slave power control. It was a virtual demand for the right to make of Mexico and Central America a slave region sub-servient to the South. It demanded the full suppression of every anti-slavery voice in the North. It was especially specific for the return of fugitive slaves and the prosecution of slave conductors. No wonder that Harriet's Abolition associates, fearing that the Re-publicans might give way to these demands, hurried her to free soil.

*   *   *   *   *

A spectral spirit hung over the North, over Abolition, over Harriet. "We live but today," said Frederick Douglass in a solemn moment late in April of 1861, "and the measureless shores of the future are wisely hid from us. And yet we read the face of that sky, and may discern the signs of the times. We know that clouds and darkness, and the sound of distant thunder means rain. So too may we observe the fleecy drapery of the moral sky, and draw conclusions as to what may come upon us. There is a general feeling amongst us, that the control of events has been taken out of our hands, that we have fallen into the mighty current of eternal principles—invis-ible forces, which are shaping and fashioning events as they wish, using us only as instruments to work out their own results in our National destiny." [6]

Douglass' general vision was correct. Events were making of Abe Lincoln—and of all Americans—but instruments of the period. When the President took office and the South decided upon rebellion, the division of North from South occurred as correctly as a child emerging from the womb. The South unfurled its banner, proclaimed slavery eternal and universal in America as its aim, and the North proceeded to the only course it could take—the subjugation of the South, the pounding of sense into its reprobate soul. Lincoln, like a parent, proved as kind as possible under the circumstances of a rebellious family of States taking a fatal course—but the war was on.

There occurred one dramatic event after another: first the President's call for volunteers, resulting in a mighty response, mainly by Abolitionists, then a Federal march through Maryland to defend Washington from attack or capture by the Secessionists.

*　　*　　*　　*　　*

Harriet remained in Canada until about the Spring of 1861. When the war broke out, she hastened to her New England friends, ostensibly to prepare for another expedition to Maryland, to bring away the last of her family.[7] But Harriet rescued no more slaves via the Underground Railroad. The next record of her whereabouts reveals that she was at the earliest scenes of warfare.

The Negro historian, William Wells Brown, declared that long before Butler's "contraband of war" doctrine was recognized by the Government, Harriet was hanging upon the outskirts of the Union Army, and doing good service for those of her people who sought protection in the Union lines.[8]

This means that Harriet followed General Butler's army as it marched through Maryland on the way to the defense of Washington during the months of April and May, 1861, when Maryland debated whether to secede and when the Federal troops met with violence at Baltimore. It was, after all, her home country; she knew how to get in and out of here speedily, and she had friends who could shelter her. It was an opportunity to stimulate slaves to escape to the Union Army or to take care of them as rapidly as they came into the Federal camps.

The "contraband of war" ruling to which William Wells

Brown referred occurred in May of 1861. Three fugitives, the property of a Southern colonel, escaped to the Union camp at Fortress Monroe, saying that they were about to be sent South and requesting protection. A Southern major approached the Federal quarters with a flag of truce and claimed the return of the people of color under the terms of the Fugitive Slave Act. But General Butler took the position that in view of the military outbreaks, the virtual but undeclared state of war, he considered the fugitives "contraband of war." Thus was coined a term which described the plight and state of the Negro until Lincoln proclaimed the black man free on January 1st, 1863. The war itself was not being fought for freedom, but Negro freedom was resulting from it, even at the outset. The black man, physically free, but not legally so, would bear the twixt-heaven-and-hell appellation of *contraband* until declared free.

There was sporadic fighting all through the summer and fall of 1861 in the Virginia region; the Union had entrenched in the vicinity of Washington; slaves were escaping regularly to the Federal forces and the *contraband* was already a major problem, forecasting the reconstruction problem of the future. Harriet, "hanging upon the outskirts of the Union army," was possibly the first American woman to visit or work on the battlefields of the Civil War.

*　　*　　*　　*　　*

Harriet was back in New England when the news came of the fall of Port Royal, South Carolina, to the Union forces. Instantly she conceived the idea of going there and working among her people on the islands and the mainland.[9]

That victory was the first heartening news of the year's fighting to the Union sympathizers. It meant that a blockade of the slave-holding coast was effective, that the Southern power would be broken of its reliance upon the support of the British aristocracy. Trade between the cotton South and the textile wealth of Britain was shut off; the beginning of the economic undermining of the Confederacy had begun.

With the capture of Port Royal Harbor, the Sea Islands in the vicinity, with their rich plantations, became Union property. As the Northern forces took over the islands and the harbor, the Secessionists retreated to the South Carolina mainland, leaving their plantations to the care of the Negroes. The blacks were exultant over the defeat of their masters. Many of them, because they would not accompany their masters to the mainland, were shot down. The town of Beaufort, located on the mainland, was taken on December 8, 1861, and the Confederates continued their retreat to the interior. The slaves quit the regional plantations and poured into Beaufort from all directions, seeking the protection of the Northerners, and, as they supposed, their freedom. From the time of the capture of Port Royal, it was evident to the whole North that the freeing of the slave would be a result of the contest. The war might be waged under the slogan of defending and retaining the Union, but the process of unseating the Southern masters automatically placed the Negroes in the hands of a new set of men—Northern soldiers, who did not know or care to administer slavery. The Federal military brought with it a new economy, the free-labor economy that prevailed up above the Mason-Dixon line. All of this was realized by the Abolitionists in the North. It was evident that Reconstruction could begin at once among the *contraband*. It was clear that the Negroes, pouring into Beaufort, were now—probably forever—separated from the slaveowners and that it was a Northern problem.

The Port Royal victory had occurred under the leadership of General T. W. Sherman (not to be confused with General William Tecumseh Sherman). For a month or more after the Sea Island country was marshalled under Northern forces, and while the slaves kept coming to the Beaufort and Hilton Head bases of the South Department, the military men saw that something must be done to protect the colored people.[10] General Sherman issued an "order" which spread like wildfire through the North, taking especial effect in Abolition centers. Sherman pointed to the helpless condition of the Negroes and to the enormous extent of land now occupied by the Federal troops. The Union was responsible to the Negroes; it must adequately provision them, instruct them how to govern themselves, and urge them to continue cultivation of the land. Sherman called help to the philanthropic North. He asked for instructors and aides, wanting them to come South right away. "Never was there a nobler or more fitting opportunity," said the General. Immediately thereafter, freedmen's aid societies formed throughout the

North, and men and women volunteered for service among the black people.

Diverse reports came to the North of the conditions of these ex-slave-but-not-yet-freedmen, and in Boston there was a buzz of Reconstruction talk, of sending teachers to the South. The Abolitionists, in particular, realized that whatever the hesitations of Lincoln and his Cabinet, the Port Royal Negroes must be ushered into Reconstruction. If Government was unprepared to handle them, then independent Abolition action was necessary.

It was this situation that Harriet Tubman beheld. And who would be more effective than she to act as liaison representative between the Northern soldiers and the Negroes?

Despite Harriet's immediate desire to go South and aid in the new work, it was some time before she actually went. In a matter such as this, Government authorization, transport passage, and other details were involved. A Federal policy toward the *contraband* must be established and monetary aid must be extended to the Reconstructionists.

The Abolitionists were agitated by Lincoln's refusal to set the Negroes free, or to acknowledge free those who had crossed over to Union lines. The hesitation had clogged up many important political and military processes. Soldiers were slow to join the Northern army because there was uncertainty as to the issue or the worth of the issue. The official declaration to fight to preserve the Union, everyone knew, was a half-truth. Slavery was at the root of it and slavery would have to go, but even yet there was the desire to compromise on the question. There was not yet a correct Northern morale for the struggle. Negroes wanted to join the fight but Lincoln and others did not want them as soldiers. Meantime the Confederacy was using the Negro in its labor battalions. More and more the black man loomed as the balance of power in the contest. Frederick Douglass was vehement in his attempts to drive Lincoln leftward toward freedom of his people. Abolition criticism no longer spared the compromiser, William H. Seward. Garrison and Phillips were now with the Union, and they too were calling for a free-the-Negro mandate.

Harriet, like the other Abolitionists, was critical of Lincoln. Sometime in this period she met Lydia Maria Child with whom she discussed Lincoln's vacillating policy. What Harriet said to the Abolition writer summed up, in her especial, figurative form, the radical view of Abe Lincoln. She selected the aphorism, "Never wound a snake but kill it," as the figure to describe the approach that she would employ toward the slave power, the approach that Lincoln must and finally did take. Lydia Child, writing to the poet John Greenleaf Whittier, from the New England town of Wayland, on January 21, 1862, reported Harriet's view.

"She talks politics sometimes," wrote Lydia Child, "and her uncouth utterance is wiser than the plans of politicians. She said the other day: 'They may send the flower of their young men down South, to die of the fever in the summer and the ague in the winter, (For 'tis cold down there; though 'tis down South). They may send them one year, two year, three year, till they tire of sending or till they use up the young men. All of no use. God is ahead of Mister Lincoln. God won't let Mister Lincoln beat the South till he does the right thing. Mister Lincoln, he is a great man, and I'm a poor Negro; but this Negro can tell Mister Lincoln how to save the money and the young men. He can do it by setting the Negroes free. Suppose there was an awfully big snake down there on the floor. He bites you. You send for the doctor to cut the bite; but the snake, he rolls up there, and while the doctor is doing it, he bites you again. The doctor cuts down that bite, but while he's doing it the snake springs up and bites you again, and so he keeps doing till you kill him. That's what Mister Lincoln ought to know.' " [11]

*   *   *   *   *

Boston Abolition was girding for the task of aiding the ex-slaves as fast as Union victories brought them out of slavery. *The Liberator* was filled with accounts of the problems of the Negroes in the Department of the South, and calls for help came from the officers of that Department. It had been known for some time that Harriet wanted to go South and at least one group raised some money for her, either for that purpose, or for other Abolition labors.

She had been in Boston early in February, and before she left a party was given in her honor. *The Liberator,* in an item written by "N" reported:

HARRIET TUBMAN

A meeting was held at the Twelfth Baptist Church, in Boston, a few days before Harriet Tubman left the city, where addresses were delivered by several gentlemen and also by the Beneficiary herself. A donation festival took place immediately after in the vestry, the pecuniary result of which was not large, as the ladies had but little time to prepare. It is, however, hoped that on some future occasion a testimonial will be tendered, more in keeping with their appreciation of her services in the cause of emancipation.[12]

Just below the item dealing with Harriet there appeared a notice of a meeting of persons interested in sending teachers to the *contraband* at Fortress Monroe and Port Royal. Mostly the leaders of this movement were anti-slavery clericals, including Harriet's friend, James Freeman Clarke. Below that news story there appeared still another referring to "Instruction for the Contraband," all of which is illustrative of the ferment for Reconstruction which was going on in New England—three years before the final Union victory!

Harriet went from Boston to Auburn long enough to notify the local Abolitionists to watch out for her old parents while she was away and not to let them want. It was a time for a last sight of her friends, Frederick Douglass, Gerrit Smith, J. W. Loguen, and others. At last, in May of 1862, Harriet was ready to go South.

There may have been other Reconstruction workers who went to Hilton Head on the same boat that carried Harriet, but it is doubtful whether any, except military men, arrived there before she did. She was sent at the suggestion of Governor Andrew of Massachusetts. The Governor believed that she would be a valuable operator within the enemy lines. She was forwarded by Colonel Frank Howe, the Massachusetts state agent in New York, on board the Government transport *Atlantic.* Her destination was Beaufort, and she was assigned to the headquarters of General Stevens.[13]

If Harriet or any other believed that the work of the Department of the South would be of a solely Reconstruction nature, it was a mistake. There was war, bitter and hard, to be fought in that region. The South Department had a significant role to play in military affairs. If Governor Andrew was able to arrange for Harriet's shipment there it was because the South had need for a liaison worker, someone to connect the military men with the Negroes. It needed an organizer of the secretive type, with experience in espionage and scouting such as she had had: nor did it object to a woman who knew how to fire a musket.

END CHAPTER XVI

CHAPTER XVII

NURSE, SCOUT AND SPY

When Harriet arrived at Beaufort, South Carolina, Major General David Hunter was in charge of the Department of the South. He had, on March 31, 1862, succeeded General T. W. Sherman. Hunter was one of the first to try the enlistment of Negro soldiers; he was attentive to the problems of reconstructing the blacks along the lines of the Northern social system. Harriet reported to Hunter, and from the outset, he regarded her as a valuable woman.[1] She was an ideal liaison representative. The Northern white soldiers were by no means able to understand the Negroes, and the latter, used only to slavery at the hands of the whites—all whites, had reason to suspect and mistrust them. Harriet, therefore, became a perfect intermediary between these groups, one whom the Negro followed and whom the whites understood. When she first plunged into the task of aiding the bewildered people of color seeking readjustment, there was little knowledge among them of the regard in which she had been held in the North. It was news to the Southern Negroes that she had been the famous Conductor and conspirator with John Brown, and that she had already been with the Union army in the North. The Carolina Negroes did know that she was from the North. Harriet has related that their language differed sharply from hers. "Why, their language down there in the far South is just as different from ours in Maryland, as you can think. They laughed when they heard me talk, and I could not understand them." [2]

Harriet had to win her spurs anew among these people. The Charles P. Wood history of Harriet's service, (the most authoritative account, a Government record written after the war), reveals the uncertainty with which she was at first received by her fellow blacks. "When she first went to Beaufort she was allowed to draw rations as an officer or soldier, but the freed people, becoming jealous of this privilege accorded her—she voluntarily relinquished this right and thereafter supplied her personal wants by selling pies and root beer—which she made during the evenings and nights—when not engaged in important service for the Government." [3] That is understandable. At a time when the military leaders were unable to supply the needs of the Negroes, when they were trying with might and main to reorganize the blacks, to make them self-supporting, any act like taking care of Harriet's personal needs would have seemed to the *contraband* a matter of favoritism.

From the start, her position with the Department was one of an irregular attachment, yet a service solicited by the officials. She was to serve the Government, but make her own way. During her service of more than three years, she received from the Government only two hundred dollars. This was received at or near Beaufort, but Harriet, with characteristic indifference to herself, immediately devoted that sum to the erection of a wash house. She spent a portion of her time there, teaching the freedwomen to do washing, so as they might learn to be self-supporting. During her absence with an important expedition in Florida that wash house was taken over by a regiment of troops fresh from the North. They had occupied it as a shelter for themselves but without giving her any compensation whatever.[4]

*   *   *   *   *

Harriet's earliest work was directly with her own people, primarily nursing the sick. There was widespread illness among them: largely the diseases sprang from malnutrition due to the social upheaval in this part of the country. The process of passing over into a free economy, of existing alongside military detachments and submitting to a semi-military discipline, together with securing from the environment their own food, made readjustment a great drain upon the Negro people. Privation led to illness, and the latter to the need for the creation of hospitals. Many slaves had been hiding out for months from their masters, fearing to venture into the Union lines or to encounter Confederate detachments that would seize them and hasten them back into the interior plantation service. The blacks lived in the open, in jungles and swamps, usually close to starvation. As there was a constant procession of stricken Negroes entering the Union encampment or being brought there by Union parties out on scouting trips, this more and more loomed as a state of affairs equal to the military problems faced by the leaders of the Union camp. Harriet merged herself with her people, heard their complaints, learned their needs, and made such representations to the military men and the white soldiers as would effect cooperation between the two groups and ameliorate the suffering of her kin. She taught the Negro women how to adjust themselves to the new conditions, to produce and create articles for their own consumption, to wash, sew, keep their own living quarters clean, and to make and sell various articles to the soldiers.

It was the medical need which, from the start, impressed Harriet as the most urgent. Sometime early in the development of the Port Royal freedmen's colony, a hospital for the Negroes was established. This was for a period Harriet's central location and work, in association with Medical Director Henry K. Durrant. "Among other duties which I have, is that of looking after the hospital here for contrabands," she wrote to Franklin B. Sanborn later. "Most of those coming from the mainland are very destitute, almost naked. I am trying to find places for those able to work, and provide for them as best I can, so as to lighten the burden of the Government, as much as possible, while at the same time they learn to respect themselves by earning their own living." [5]

News of the Union occupation had long since traveled all over the States of Florida, South Carolina and North Carolina. The Negroes, in a new type of Underground Railroad, tried to make their way to this location, and many black men and women lost their lives by Confederate bullets in trekking toward Port Royal and Hilton Head. The blacks, by the time they arrived, were often ready for the hospital. Harriet's nursing was not limited to her labors among the colored. She gave similar assistance to the whites, "to our soldiers in the hospital and our armies in the field." [6] There was constant need of such service, especially in the years 1863 and 1864, when the Union troops often engaged Southern forces, and during some especially severe campaigns, notably the siege of Fort Wagner and the battle of Olustee.

Harriet, describing her efforts as a nurse, said, "I'd go to the hospital early ever morning. I'd get a big chunk of ice and put it in a basin, and fill it with water; then I'd take a sponge and begin. First man I'd come to, I'd thrash away the flies, and they'd rise, like bees around a hive. Then I'd begin to bathe their wounds, and by the time I'd bathed off three or four, the fire and heat would have melted the ice and made the water warm, and it would be as red as clear blood. Then I'd go and get more ice, and by the time I got to the next one, the flies would be around the first ones black and thick as ever." [7]

It does not sound as if the hospitals of the army were of the most sanitary nature, nor that the means for caring for the soldiers was the best. In fact, Harriet's words indicate that the medical and sanitary conditions were about the world's worst; but whatever could be done, Harriet was willing to do. A pass that was issued to her in the fall of 1862 reveals the type of "antiseptic" on which chief reliance was placed. This note, dated at Beaufort, August 28, was written by Surgeon Durrant, and it was directed to a commissary representative, Captain Warfield:

> Will Captain Warfield please let "Moses" have a little Bourbon whiskey for medicinal purposes." [8]

There is no wonder that there was a high death rate in the Department of the South; that fevers, plagues and agues swept the Union encampment, taking toll among Negro and white at frequent intervals.

At one time Harriet was sent from Hilton Head to Fernandina, Florida, where the men were "dying off like sheep" from dysentery. Harriet had acquired quite a reputation for her skill in curing this disease. It has been reported that she prepared a medicine from roots which grew near the waters which gave the malady. She found thousands of sick soldiers and *contraband* at Fernandina and she immediately gave her time and attention to them. Later, according to the same account, she nursed hundreds who were seized with small pox and "malignant fevers." She had never had these diseases, but she survived these dangers as easily as she had other forms of death. [9]

Thus Harriet went from camp to camp in the Department of the South, wherever there was a call for her services, wherever someone of the indefatigable type and the right spirit was necessary, wherever she could be spared from one task to fly to another. "In this way she worked, day after day, till late at night; then she went home to her little cabin, and made about fifty pies, a great quantity of gingerbread, and two casks of root beer. These she would hire some contraband to sell for her through the camps, and thus she would provide her support for another day...." [10]

* * * * *

Many of the officers, General Hunter included, knew that Harriet's Northern work on the Underground Railroad fitted her for espionage on Confederate territory. There was no reason why Harriet could not go among the white Southerners, act as a "loyal" slave, denounce the Unionists, and gain their confidence. As a short, not impressive-looking woman, she could travel about in Rebel country with more ease than any white spy. She either volunteered or was coopted for such work.

Harriet was a natural guerrilla fighter. She, who had worked her way through the Maryland swamp country, was well-fitted to spy out enemy encampments, to trail along or even penetrate their picket lines, and gain a picture of the hostile defenses. As a Negro she could secure the confidence of other Negroes, and she could find out who, in this region, knew the country, the rivers, the hideouts, the likely spots for military operations. The Union encampment was constantly engaged in forays up and down the coast, taking or abandoning towns like Jacksonville and Pensacola, holding the various islands, taking fortresses such as Pulaski, assaulting Secessionville, and lengthening the Union picket line which extended for many miles around the Union occupation: it therefore needed an effective secret service to function over the whole area.

It was during or before the spring military operations of 1863 when Harriet organized a scouting service for the Department of the South. There is evidence that late in 1862 her work was still of a utility nature, with nursing as her chief occupation. By then, Harriet's good friend, Colonel Thomas W. Higginson, had arrived in the South, aiding General Saxton in the organization of Negro troops. Higginson was located at Camp Saxton, a few miles from Beaufort, when he received a visit from Harriet, she having heard that her Abolition associate had arrived. Higginson wrote to his wife on December 10, 1862:

"Who should drive out to see me today but Harriet Tubman who is living at Beaufort as a sort of nurse & general care taker; she sends her regards to you. All sorts of unexpected people turn up here." [11]

Their meeting was a symptom of the change in Federal policy at about that time toward the arming of Negroes. Higginson was the first of the Abolitionists to arrive at Hilton Head with orders to organize a Negro regiment. At that time the military situation nationally was unsuitable to the Federal Government. The Union soldiers had been repulsed at Fredericksburg and Vicksburg, and had sustained great losses at Stone River. About 65,000 troops were to be discharged during the following year, while the Confederate army was growing. When the arming of Negroes was determined upon as a military measure in October, 1862, Higginson was one of the first white officers to respond to the problem of recruiting from among them. General Saxton had written to Higginson, declaring his intention of forming a body of soldiers from among the *contraband* who had come into the Union lines, he asked Higginson to accept the leadership of them, and the preacher-writer immediately went South. He had only been in the Department two weeks when Harriet called upon him.

There was little warfare in the Department in the winter of 1862-1863. It was a period when Higginson's Negro troops were being trained. Colonel James Montgomery, an expert in guerrilla operations, who had figured in the Kansas conflict, had also arrived, and he was forming another company of Negro volunteers. Montgomery and Harriet, both associates of the late John Brown, became friendly. It was about the time of the arrival of Colonel Montgomery that Harriet's services as a scout and spy became a permanent need of the high command of the Department. She was now engaged in "obtaining the services of the most valued scouts and pilots in the Government employ in that Department." [12] Harriet selected a picked corps of black people familiar with the terrain. She soon had under her command nine scouts and river pilots: Isaac Hayward,

Walter Plowden, Gabriel Cahern, George Chisholm, Peter Burns, Mott Blake, Sandy Sellus, Charles Simmons and Samuel Hayward. These men had lived hereabouts all their lives and were now *contraband* and allies of the Union forces.[13] With this company of which Harriet was *Commander,* as she said, "under directions and orders of Edwin M. Stanton, Secretary of War, and of several Generals," [14] she surveyed the countryside. Harriet sent forth this band to learn the whereabouts and movements of the enemy, to discover the strength and weaknesses of his defense, and to report whatever else they might. This meant that Harriet had charge of the Intelligence Service of the Department, that espionage was under her direction, and that she was acting as a liaison between her colored aides and Generals Hunter, Saxton and Gilmore.

*   *   *   *   *

The Department of the South diffused its military operations over an area of hundreds of square miles, from the region of Charleston, South Carolina, as far south as Jacksonville and Palatka, Florida. The coast line of this area was extremely jagged, marked by countless islands, bays, inlets and rivers that ran deep into the interior. Towns, rice plantations, and large expanses of jungle and swamp composed the general sphere of operations. The Union's objective was to harass and keep occupied the Confederate forces guarding Charleston and Savannah, to advance where possible, to seize the major cities if practicable, to make secure the Union occupation, and to maintain the blockade. The Department did not then realize it, but they were holding at bay the entire Southeast, limiting the number of Confederate soldiers who could be sent from this region to the battlescenes of the North. They were making this region secure for the time when Sherman, marching in from Tennessee, would complete the job of conquering the Southeastern States.

The Department decided upon a tactic of numerous local movements, and of "capturing" or welcoming Negroes who could swell the Union ranks. It struck out from its bases at Beaufort and Hilton Head in all directions, and sent small parties up the rivers to break up rebel batteries and destroy rebel defenses. It established picket lines at points many miles distant from the harbor bases, surrounding the center of operations with lines of men who could protect the occupation from any attack by the rebels. In fact, in the fall of 1862, the Unionists expected a Rebel invasion, and extensive preparations to meet it were made at Beaufort. Although the Department never had the numbers to dare any large-scale command of the Southeastern States, the general staff decided that Charleston must be seized, and it settled down to the job of taking that place. The siege of Charleston lasted virtually from the time of the opening of warfare in 1861 until the closing days. Continual attack was inevitable because South Carolina was detested by the Union forces as the seat of secession and slave power.

It was in the scattered forays, the raids for Negro bondsmen, the harassing of the enemy in guerrilla occupations of local defenses, the seizure of the lesser towns, in keeping the enemy occupied, and in preparing the ground for the later conquests of the Southeast by General Sherman that the leadership of the Department, and the Negro and white soldiers under their command, performed a continuous and exhausting task. There were other hazards that drew heavily upon the men in these ranks. The tropic weather, maladies like yellow fever and dysentery, and the bad food took a continuous toll among the Unionists. All of this meant ceaseless labor for Harriet. She leaped from the post of nursing, to that of scouting, to that of cooking and washing, like a grasshopper in a lettuce bed. "When the Negro put on the 'blue' "Moses" was in her glory and travelled from camp to camp, being always treated in the most respectful manner. The black men would have died for this woman. . . ." [15]

Official records give to Colonel Montgomery the formal credit for engineering the guerrilla operations that occured all through the summer of 1863 in the Department of the South, but the leadership of Montgomery's most celebrated raid, the Combahee, has been attributed undisputably to Harriet. Montgomery's excursions up the various South Carolina and Florida rivers and overland into the plantation interiors were made possible largely through the scouting service of Harriet's corps, through the information of the inland areas that she and her squad unearthed.

One of the earliest evidences of the work of Harriet's espionage corps appears in a letter sent by General Saxton to Secretary of War E. M. Stanton, on March 6, 1863, discussing the possibilities for an assault on Jacksonville. "I have reliable information that there are large numbers of able bodied Negroes in that vicinity who are watching for an opportunity to join us." A few days later Colonel Montgomery made a successful expedition up the St. John's River and captured the town. Subsequently, in a similar raid, also based upon information gleaned by Harriet's spy squad, Montgomery made a successful expedition further up the St. John's to Palatka. These excursions convinced Montgomery and the Department officers of the possibility for a more extensive type of guerrilla warfare, and the preliminary raids culminated in the important engagement of the Combahee, organized and led by Harriet, on June 2, 1863. . . .

END CHAPTER XVII

CHAPTER XVIII

CAMPAIGN ON THE COMBAHEE

The following dispatch, quoted in part, appeared on the front page of *The Commonwealth,* a Boston newspaper, on Friday, July 10, 1863:

HARRIET TUBMAN

Col. Montgomery and his gallant band of 300 black soldiers, *under the guidance of a black woman,* dashed into the enemy's country, struck a bold and effective blow, destroying millions of dollars worth of commissary stores, cotton and lordly dwellings, and striking terror into the heart of rebeldom, brought off near 800 slaves and thousands of dollars worth of property, without losing a man or receiving a scratch. It was a glorious consummation.

After they were all fairly well disposed of in the Beaufort charge, they were addressed in strains of thrilling eloquence by their gallant deliverer, to which they responded in a song
"There is a white robe for thee,"
a song so appropriate and so heartfelt and cordial as to bring unbidden tears.

The Colonel was followed by a speech from the black woman, *who led the raid and under whose inspiration it was originated and conducted.* For sound sense and real native eloquence, her address would do honor to any man, and it created a great sensation. . . .

Since the rebellion she has devoted herself to her great work of delivering the bondman, with an energy and sagacity that cannot be exceeded. *Many and many times she has penetrated the enemy's lines and discovered their situation and condition, and escaped without injury,* but not without extreme hazard.[1]

The foregoing newspaper account, published a few weeks after Harriet led the engagement, is doubtless one of the most unique in American journalism. The communique had been sent to the paper by a correspondent of the *Wisconsin State Journal,* stationed in the Department of the South. It was followed by a few comments from the *Commonwealth editor,* then Franklin B. Sanborn, who promised his readers that the following issue would contain a description of Harriet's "remarkable" history. This was Boston's first knowledge of her activity since she had left the North early in 1862.

*   *   *   *   *

The Combahee River, in South Carolina, was the first one visited by the Spaniards in the year 1520. Vasque de Ayllon, having discovered it, gave it the name of the "River Jordan." [2] Although subsequently renamed the Combahee, the stream now became a River Jordan literally for more than seven hundred and fifty Negroes who, under the leadership of Harriet Tubman and the auxiliary command of Colonel James Montgomery, delivered this number of blacks into the free lines. The River Jordan has been in biblical history a reality, and in modern Negro allusion a symbol of the barrier between bondage and freedom, and it is an interesting coincidence, therefore, that the Combahee campaign should so parallel the ancient situation. It is significant as the only military engagement in American history wherein a woman, black or white, "led the raid and under whose inspiration it was originated and conducted."

The first information received by the Confederate forces which intimated that somewhere in the Department of the South a new or unique type of engagement was being planned, came to them in the form of information gleaned from *The New York Tribune.* Horace Greeley's paper carried information which Confederate agents dispatched to the South as a military circular, reading, "The N. Y. *Tribune* says that the Negro troops at Hilton Head, S. C. will soon start upon an expedition, under the command of Colonel Montgomery, differing in many respects from any heretofore projected.[3] This should have been sufficient to frighten the Southern forces in the South Carolina area into some vigilance, for they had already felt the wrath of Montgomery in his earlier attacks. He was a ruthless soldier, unhesitant about terrorizing the enemy, despoiling property, and not much concerned with the usual amenities of warfare. His recklessness became known to the Secession leaders of the region and they were anxious to destroy him personally. In fact, in the earlier

Palatka raid, according to a Confederate report, Montgomery was wounded.

The Combahee strategy was formulated by Harriet Tubman as an outcome of her penetrations of the enemy lines and her belief that the Combahee River countryside was ripe for a successful invasion. She was asked by General Hunter "if she would go with several gunboats up the Combahee River, the object of the expedition being to take up the torpedoes placed by the rebels in the river, to destroy railroads and bridges, and to cut off supplies from the rebel troops. She said she would go if Col. Montgomery was to be appointed commander of the expedition. . . . Accordingly, Col. Montgomery was appointed to the command, and Harriet, with several men under her, the principal of whom was J. Plowden . . . accompanied the expedition." [4] Actually in this raid it was Montgomery who was the auxiliary leader. The whole venture owed its success to the complete preliminary survey made by Harriet Tubman's espionage troops. In the *Official History of the War of the Rebellion*, the report of Captain John F. Lay, the Confederate investigating officer, discussing the movement afterwards, said, "The enemy seems to have been well posted as to the character and capacity of our troops and their small chance of encountering opposition, and to have been well guided by persons thoroughly acquainted with the river and country." [5] It was a commentary, however indirect, on Harriet's work and the labor of her subordinates.

*   *   *   *   *

About ten miles north of Port Royal Island, Harriet's station, was St. Helena Island, and between this island and the mainland of South Carolina was the water known as St. Helena Sound. The Combahee River, a narrow, jagged stream that ran about fifty miles into the interior of the State, began at the Sound: and on its banks were rice fields and marshes.

During the night of June 2, 1863, Harriet and Colonel Montgomery, with a party of about 150 Negro troops in three gunboats, started up the Combahee River. Pickets located at stations near the mouth of the stream spotted the oncoming boats and dispatched word to the Confederate commander, Major Emanuel, located deeper inland at Green Pond.

Confederate soldiers at posts along the river, Field's Point, Combahee Ferry and Chisholmville, were in motion by three or four o'clock in the morning, but as their forces were small they responded chiefly with a flurry of hurried retreats. While some went as couriers to the inland headquarters, others watched from hiding places along the shore the proceedings of the Abolitionists, as the invaders were called. A few sentries undertook movements toward neighborhood plantations to guard Negroes from fleeing to the Federal forces, and they attempted also to establish contact with each other and formulate some program of defense.

The Confederate Corporal Newton, chief of the Field's Point picket stated that about 3 A. M. he first saw two steamers about two miles in the river or sound below Field's Point; that the night was bright and he could see a long distance. When he saw the enemy land from eight to twelve men and heard them launch their boats, he sent a courier with the information to Lieutenant Hewitt, commander of outposts at Chisholmville, about ten miles distant. Soon afterward he sent off another courier. As the corporal had only five men left with him, and these poorly armed, he fell below to retire.[6]

The retreat on the part of Corporal Newton—he, in his haste, dispatching still a third courier to Major Emanuel—best expresses virtually all of the Confederate movement along the Combahee that night. The Union gunboats continued up the river, putting off small bands of soldiers at various points wherever there were a few pickets to be handled. The latter retreated and the Union forces, proceeding to nearby plantations to liberate the Negroes, set fire to Confederate property, and occasionally fired at Secession troops who did not retreat rapidly enough.

This action was more or less duplicated at each Confederate picket post every mile or so up the Combahee. The activity intensified about ten or twelve miles up the river at Combahee Ferry. The three Federal steamboats had made their way safely to this point, despite Rebel preparations against just such an incursion as this. Negroes in the service of the Secessionists had been reached by Harriet or her comrades, and as a result, the spy corps knew where the torpedoes had been placed by the Confederates. Later a Rebel report said of one of the boats, "She passed safely the point where the torpedoes were placed and finally reached the bridge at the ferry, which they immediately commenced cutting way, landed to all appearances a group at Mr. Middleton's and in a few minutes his buildings were in flames." [7]

Here too the previous Confederate panic was repeated. There occurred a retreat of the pickets, another call for help to the Confederate major who seems to have been tardy in opening defense operations (for it was now about 6:30 o'clock in the morning), and the Union raid took on larger and more decisive proportions.

Every plantation on both sides of the river was aroused; the Union soldiers, in small detachments, raced from one to another, creating a general devastation of the zone. In the Combahee Ferry region the Blake, Lowndes, Middleton and Heyward plantations were in ruins. The Negroes fled to the gunboats and the slavemasters skedaddled inland. The bridge at Combahee Ferry was burning too "but not badly." [8]

A company of Confederates under the command of a Lieutenant Breeden approached the vicinity, having been dispatched by Major Emanuel, but they were at a loss to consolidate, or to know where or how to strike. The only serious defense put up by the Confederates that night was the shooting of a young Negro girl. [9] This was at Nichols' landing, also in the Combahee Ferry region.

Major Emanuel himself went into action with a small force, making a few disjointed movements in the region of the stricken plantations . He attempted to prevent the escape of a band of Negroes to the gunboats but he failed. With a single piece of field artillery he decided to attack one of the gunboats in the river. He proceeded alongside the river in pursuit of a steamer now returning to St. Helena Sound. But he managed only to get himself ambushed between a Yankee crossfire, and at least one of his men, Fripp, was wounded and later died. The piece of artillery fired four shots and then Major Emanuel ordered a retreat. [10]

*   *   *   *   *

Harriet has related the story of that delivery over this modern River Jordan. [11] As the gunboats passed up the river, the Negroes left their work and took to the woods, for at first they were frightened. Then they came out to peer, "like startled deer," but scudding away like the wind at the sound of the steam-whistle. The word was passed along that these were "Lincoln's gunboats come to set them free." From that moment on, the overseers used their whips in vain, for they failed to drive the slaves back to the quarters. They turned and ran for the gun-boats; they came down every road, across every field, dressed just as they were when they left their work and their cabins. There were women with children clinging around their necks, hanging onto their dresses, or running behind, but all rushed at full speed for "Lincoln's gun-boats." Hundreds crowded the banks, with their hands extended toward their deliverers, and most of them were taken aboard the gun-boats to be carried to Beaufort.

This is about what happened all through the night and morning of June 2 when Harriet, Montgomery and the colored soldiers overran the Combahee. While the small detachments of Negro troops remained on shore, keeping the enemy occupied, the plantation Negroes were bundled aboard the boats.

"I never saw such a sight," said Harriet afterward. "We laughed and laughed and laughed. Here you'd see a woman with a pail on her head, rice a-smoking in it just as she'd taken it from the fire, young one hanging on behind, one hand around her forehead to hold on, the other hand digging into the rice pot, eating with all its might; a-hold of her dress two or three more; down her back a bag with a pig in it. One woman brought two pigs, a white and a black one; we took them all on board; named the white pig Beauregard (Southern general), and the black pig Jeff Davis (President of the Confederacy). Sometimes the women would come with twins hanging around the necks; it appears I never saw so many twins in my life; bags on their shoulders, baskets on their heads, and young ones tagging behind, all loaded; pigs squealing, chickens screaming, young ones squealing." [12]

When the boats were filled the slaves who could not be taken aboard clung to the ships. Colonel Montgomery applied a ruse to make the Negroes let go of the boats. He shouted from the upper deck of one boat, "Moses, you'll have to give them a song," and Harriet sang:

Of all the whole creation in the East or in the West,
The glorious Yankee nation is the greatest and the best.
Come along! Come along! don't be alarmed,
Uncle Sam is rich enough to give you all a farm.

At the end of each verse the Negroes, in their enthusiam, threw up their hands and shouted "Glory!" The boats took that opportunity to push off.[13]

*   *   *   *   *

The Confederate headquarters did not give credit to the Union command for having carefully prepared the region which it invaded —for knowing the terrain, for learning the Confederate weaknesses, even to having knowledge of where the torpedoes were placed. The Secession reports blamed the command of Major Emanuel, saying that the Major's forces had not been "properly drilled, disciplined or taught by him so as to be effective upon an emergency. His system of outposts is loose and men and officers badly instructed. On this occasion his pickets were neither watchful nor brave; they allowed the enemy to come up to them almost unawares, and then retreated without offering resistance or firing a gun, allowing a parcel of Negro wretches, calling themselves soldiers, with a few degraded whites, to march unmolested, with the incendiary torch, to rob, destroy and burn a large section of the country." [14]

So satisfied was General Hunter with the Combahee expedition that he wrote on the following day to Secretary of War Stanton that this expedition was but the initial experiment of a system of incursions which would penetrate up all the inlets, creeks and rivers of the department.[15] On the same day he also wrote to Governor Andrew of Massachusetts that he expected these operations to compel the Rebels either to lay down their arms and sue for restoration to the Union or to withdraw their slaves into the interior, thus leaving desolate the most fertile and productive of their countries along the Atlantic seaboard.[16] The General planned to continue these campaigns, so "injuring the enemy . . . and carrying away their slaves, thus rapidly filling up the South Carolina regiments of which there are now four."

*   *   *   *   *

Problems of Reconstruction immediately faced Harriet and the officers of the Department. The refugees had to be established at Beaufort, taught, fed, clothed and placed at work. There was established at Beaufort, at a place called Old Fort Plantation, a large refugee quarter which became known as "Montgomery Hill," after Colonel Montgomery, but it was not on a hill. "There was a row of a dozen or more buildings, which resembled huge wooden boxes. Each house was divided into four rooms or compartments, and in each room was located one family of from five to fifteen persons. In each room was a large fireplace, an opening for a window, with a broad board shutter, and a double row of berths built against the wall for beds. Benches, tables, dippers, and articles of wearing apparel somewhat filled out the interiors. It was rough and crude living, and compact and hasty, but the Negroes were free and they preferred this to the slightly larger cabins of the plantations they had quit." [17] Immediately large numbers of the Combahee Negro men joined the colored regiments and received training.

Harriet diversified her scouting operations with work in the *contraband* hospital and among her people now centered at "Montgomery Hill." Her popularity among the newly-freed was now precisely as great as it had been when she was a conductor in Maryland, and it was equalled only by "the great deference shown her by the Union officers, who never failed to tip their caps when meeting her." [18]

Even Harriet, usually a modest woman who did not speak of her experiences unless persuaded, had been impressed with the Combahee raid, and possibly with her own participation in it, for a few weeks later, in a letter that someone wrote to Franklin B. Sanborn, she described the operation. She asked for a bit of credit for the colored soldiers who had helped in the campaign. Harriet full well knew the nature of military reports: they would be covered with the names of colonels and captains, but not with the deeds of privates, and as for the black soldiers they would be referred to simply as "the colored regiments" with their contribution glossed over. The letter:

Beaufort, S. C., June 30, 1863
". . . Last fall, when the people became very much alarmed for fear of an invasion from the rebels, all my clothes were

packed and sent with others to Hilton Head, and lost; and I have never been able to get any trace of them since. I was sick at the time, and unable to look after them myself. I want, among the rest, a *bloomer* dress, made of some coarse, strong material to wear on *expeditions*. In our late expedition up the Combahee River, in coming on board the boat, I was carrying two pigs for a poor sick woman, who had a child to carry, and the order 'double quick' was given, and I started to run, stepped on my dress, it being rather long, and fell and tore it almost off, so that when I got on board the boat, there was hardly anything left of it but shreds. I made up my mind then I would never wear a long dress on another expedition of the kind, but would have a *bloomer* as soon as I could get it. So please make this known to the ladies, if you will, for I expect to have use for it very soon, probably before they can get it to me.

"You have without doubt, seen a full account of the expedition I refer to. Don't you think we colored people are entitled to some of the credit for that exploit, under the lead of the brave Colonel Montgomery? We weakened the rebels somewhat on the Combahee River, by taking and bringing away *seven hundred and fifty-six* head of their most valuable live stock, known up in your region as 'contrabands,' and this, too, without the loss of a single life on our part, though we had good reason to believe that a number of rebels bit the dust. Of those seven hundred and fifty-six contrabands, nearly or quite all the able-bodied men have joined the colored regiments here.

"I have now been absent two years almost, and have just got letters from my friends in Auburn, urging me to come home. My father and mother are old and in feeble health, and need my care and attention. I hope the good people there will not allow them to suffer, and I do not believe they will. But I do not see how I am to leave at present the very important work to be done here. . . ." [19]

Harriet asked to be remembered to various Boston friends, including the philanthropist-Abolitionists, Mr. and Mrs. George L. Stearns, and she concluded, "I shall be sure to come and see you if I live to go North."

Harriet's request for bloomers is most significant. It was a woman suffrage touch. Harriet, the suffragist, found herself in the situation of having a real right to "pants." She was a soldier; she could vindicate the suffrage mode of that time, the right to wear bloomers as a demonstration of equality with men. She wanted the women to know this.

A few days after Sanborn received this letter, his paper, *The Commonwealth,* printed the Combahee raid dispatch from the correspondent of the *Wisconsin State Journal,* and a week after that, on July 17, 1863, Sanborn printed a front-page biographical article on Harriet which remains, to this day, one of the most important sources of information about her. He opened his article with a very beautiful tribute:

"It was said long ago that the true romance of America was not in the fortunes of the Indian, where Cooper sought it, nor in the New England character, where Judd found it, nor in the social contrasts of Virginia planters, as Thackeray imagined, but in the story of the fugitive slaves. The observation is as true now as it was before war, with swift, gigantic hand, sketched the vast shadows, and dashed in the high lights in which romance loves to lurk and flash forth. But the stage is enlarged on which these dramas are played, the whole world now sit as spectators, and the desperation or magnaminity of a poor black woman has power to shake the nation that so long was deaf to her cries. We write of one of these heroines, of whom our slave annals are full—a woman whose career is as extraordinary as the most famous of her sex can show. . . ." [20]

END CHAPTER XVIII

CHAPTER XIX

THE REAPING OF THE HARVEST

All through the years 1863 and 1864 there were guerrilla forays and major engagements in the Department of the South and Harriet shared in the warfare. There was fighting against the Confederates on many of the Sea Islands; there was the siege of Fort Wagner, the bombardment of Charleston, the slaughter of Olustee, the fight on Morris Island and operations at a dozen other points in the zone of the Department. It was in the smaller engagements, the raids, that Harriet chiefly participated. "She made many a raid inside the enemy's lines, displaying remarkable courage, zeal and fidelity," said General Saxton of Harriet's guerrilla operations.[1]

Eventually she received those bloomers that she had sent for. "She was proud of the fact that she had worn 'pants' and carried a musket, canteen and haversack, accoutrement which she retained after the war and left as precious relics to her colored admirers." [2] She may have worn bloomers for awhile but throughout most of her service her dress was of a striped woolen material, a dark blue coat and headgear of the same material as the dress. She carried a service satchel filled with first aid necessities at all times, and she carried a rifle during raids.[3]

Harriet relied heavily on certificates in order to move about freely. She was such a plain-looking little woman that the average white man, officer or sentry, would barely notice her unless she placed irrefutable evidence before him. A few weeks after the Combahee raid, Colonel Montgomery wrote a note to Brigadier-General Gilmore, a commanding officer of the Department of the South: "I wish to commend to your attention Mrs. Harriet Tubman, a most remarkable woman and invaluable as a scout. I have been acquainted with her character and actions for several years. . . ." [4] She carried about a dozen such letters all of the time.

*　*　*　*　*

In July, 1863, there occurred one of the most celebrated battles of the Civil War, the assault on Fort Wagner, led by the white Colonel Robert Gould Shaw, who headed the famous Negro regiment, the Fifty-Fourth Massachusetts. Harriet was well acquainted with the Colonel, having dined with him on several occasions.[5] She went to Fort Wagner after the important charge was made, and she aided in burying the black soldiers and their white officers, and in nursing the injured.[6]

Fort Wagner guarded the city of Charleston and it was necessary for the Union forces to take the fort in order to seize the city. The black troops were selected to lead this famous charge, with Colonel Shaw at their head. The Union men met a fiery metal slaughter as they approached the fort. But Colonel Shaw and the Negroes believed that more than a fort was at stake here. The whole nation watched this attack to observe how the black soldiers would fare, as there had been much sentiment against their being employed as soldiers and doubt expressed as to their courage; and this was the first battle in which colored troops were used in large numbers.

Shaw gained the parapet of the fortress and stood on it, musket in hand, calling his regiment to follow him, the gunfire lighting him up as if in silhouette, as he fell inside the fortress riddled with bullets. The Negro soldiers pushed ahead in the face of a relentless fire. The regiment was almost decimated. It was a horrible loss of fine men, for the regiment contained some of the most active free Negro and ex-slave Abolitionists in the North. They proved that they could fight for their cause. Had they retreated when they should have in order to avoid being slaughtered, the cry might have gone up that they feared to fight. There was no alternative—but to die. From then on Negro soldiers were thrown into the fighting on all fronts, all over the nation, and their contribution was the balance of power in the ultimate Northern victory. At least Lincoln said so.

Harriet served Colonel Shaw his last meal before he led the battle.[7] Thereafter she spoke of him with a reverence second only to her regard for John Brown.

It was probably to the Fort Wagner battle that Harriet referred in her widely quoted passage chronicled by the historian, Albert Bushnell Hart, who knew and talked with her. Hart said, "Her extraordinary power of statement was illustrated in her description of a battle in the Civil War: 'And then we saw the lightning, and that was the guns; and then we heard the thunder, and that was the big guns; and then we heard the rain falling, and that was the drops of blood falling; and when we came to get in the crops, it was dead men that we reaped.[8]

The fierce grind of war wore on through the year 1863, Harriet functioning in the whole variety of labors that a war period creates.

At least once, the news of Harriet flashed to England. On the second of December, 1863, a public meeting was held in London to commemorate the fourth anniversary of John Brown's death. The Reverend Moncure Conway, an American Abolitionist, who had written a stirring anti-slavery book called *The Rejected Stone,* was the main speaker. He referred to Harriet and her work as the Negro's symbol, to illustrate how the colored population regarded the Harper's Ferry martyr. The minister was apparently influenced by the *Commonwealth* article on Harriet, published six months earlier. He quoted Harriet as saying, "We Negroes in the South never call him John Brown; we call him *our* Saviour. *He died for us."* Then Conway remarked, "How true it is that whenever a heroic life is lived, the Bethlehem star is rekindled for humanity." [9]

Some time during this period, Harriet became acquainted with the man who later became her second husband, Nelson Davis. Davis arrived early in the year 1864, having been recruited at Philadelphia under the name of Nelson Charles, with the 8th United States Colored Infantry Volunteers. Davis, a private in Company G, was a magnificent physical specimen,[10] and not more than thirty years old at the time of his service. He was due to see fighting at Olustee, Boykin's Mill, Honey Hill and other engagements.

*　　*　　*　　*　　*

In May of 1864 Harriet's thoughts turned homeward. She was worried about her parents, tired out and in need of rest; and she decided to go North. On the 3rd of May, Surgeon Durrant wrote a note of certification in which he spoke of knowing Harriet for nearly two years; he had frequent and ample opportunity to observe her general deportment, he said, particularly her kindness and attention to the sick and suffering of her own people.[11] General Saxton also signed the letter, concurring with Durrant's estimate.

Harriet needed such a voucher. Sometime earlier the Negro soldiers had their pay cut in half. That was on an order issued by the War Department. This act, by the Government, was the first of the endless chain of wage differentials applied to the American Negro from that time on. Government sanctioned what private enterprise had been doing, and the practice went on in business and industrial life thereafter. The Negro soldiers, knowing that their freedom was involved in the war, took this position: they refused to accept any pay and decided that they would fight anyway, and at last win all retroactive pay and their full rights. Ultimately the soldiers won their back pay. Harriet, from this time forward, realized the value of the written contract and thereafter she hoarded her certificates from the officers, intending to use them one day when she would ask the Government to make restitution for her services. She began her own fight for back pay soon thereafter, but she never did receive the sum that the Government owed her, which was $1800. One writer, referring to the money Harriet was entitled to for her part in the Combahee raid and for enlisting the liberated Negroes into the Union service, said, "It is one of the great injustices of the war that, although Harriet was promised the regular bounty, then offered for recruits, she never received a dollar for bringing about this wholesale enlistment." [12]

When Harriet came North to Auburn on leave of absence to see her parents she was taken sick. She had been through such illnesses many times before: it was nervous exhaustion, a loss of strength. Her sleeping seizures were especially troublesome and frequent.

The leading citizens of Auburn came to the Tubman home on the outskirts of the town and brought her food. She formed a friendship with Mrs. Sarah Hopkins Bradford, a Geneva, New York, woman, who afterward wrote a short biography of Harriet's life. Mrs. Bradford, sister of the Reverend Samuel Miles Hopkins, and herself a teacher, became fond of Harriet. During the war Mrs. Bradford had visited Harriet's aged parents, and many times she wrote letters for them to commanding officers at the South, making inquiries about Harriet.[13] Harriet described her experiences to Mrs. Bradford, and later, the Geneva woman wrote her *Scenes in the Life of Harriet Tubman.*

In a month or so Harriet was regenerated sufficiently to take a trip to Boston. *The Commonwealth* carried information on Friday, August 12, as follows:

HARRIET TUBMAN

This heroic woman whose career we described last summer, when she was engaged in the military service, in the Department of the South, has lately arrived in Boston, where her numerous friends will be glad to see her. She left Florida to come North in the latter part of June, and went from New York, where she landed, directly to the home of her aged parents in Auburn, whence she has come to this city. Her services to her people and to the army seem to have been inadequately recompensed by the military authorities, and such money as she has received, she has expended for others as her custom is. Any contribution of money or clothing sent to her at this office will be received by her, and the givers may be assured that she will use them with fidelity and discretion for the good of the colored race. Her address is "care of Dr. J. S. Rock, Boston."

Dr. Rock was a Negro Boston Abolitionist, who had helped in the recruiting of soldiers for the Fifty-Fourth Massachusetts Regiment.

Harriet met Sojourner Truth during this visit. Sojourner was in Boston at the time, on her way to visit President Lincoln.[14] She expected to see and did see Abe Lincoln in the autumn. Later Harriet told one of her interviewers, Rosa Belle Holt, that Sojourner Truth had expressed great admiration for the President at a time when she still rankled over the Lincoln Government's mistreatment of the soldiers in the South Department. Harriet said she did not then care to meet the Chief Executive.

"No," said Harriet, "I'm sorry now, but I didn't like Lincoln in those days. I used to go see Mrs. Lincoln but I never wanted to see him. You see we colored people didn't understand then that he was our friend. All we knew was that the first colored troops sent South from Massachusetts only got seven dollars a month, while the white got fifteen. We didn't like that. But now . . . I'm sorry I didn't go to see Mr. Lincoln.

"It was Sojourner Truth who told me that Mr. Lincoln was our friend. Then she went to see him, and thank him for all he had done for our people. Mr. Lincoln was kind to her, and she had a nice visit with him, but he told her he had done nothing himself; he was only a servant of the country. Yes, I'm sorry now I didn't see Mr. Lincoln and thank him." [15]

New England was a place where Harriet always found strength, where she could visit with solicitous friends and recuperate, and she stayed there for some time.

In the late fall she visited Gerrit Smith and the illustrious company which always surrounded him. From Smith and Mrs. A. Baird, who was visiting the Peterboro philanthropist, she secured additional letters to help her along in her travels.

*   *   *   *   *

It was early spring of 1865 before Harriet felt well enough to return to the Department of the South, but there is evidence that she did not go back, even though she wanted to be there for the final death blows to the Confederacy. At least two plans engaged her attention from the time when she made known her intention to resume work. One was military, and the other was in the medical service. Although she chose the latter, her connection with the military scheme was very significant, as a symptom of the influence which attached to her work and identity.

Abraham Lincoln decided upon a drastic course of action during February of 1865, the creation of a black army, to be officered by Negroes; and Harriet was immediately called upon to contribute in the effort.

For more than a year, since Lincoln had proclaimed the Emancipation Proclamation he had "hoped and prayed for" such an army, but he did not wish to initiate such a course unless it came as a policy suggested by others. The idea was at last put forward by the celebrated Negro, Martin Delany, a figure who ranked with Frederick Douglass and Harriet Tubman during the war period itself. Delany who had distinguished himself by a generation of activity as a physician, explorer, journalist and Abolitionist, had long been chafing at the Governmental reticence in the use of the slave population, which, he believed, could be aroused to war service in the cause of the Union. When, during the early part of 1865, a desperate Confederacy considered a course of arming the slaves and forcing them to fight the Federal troops, it became a matter of the utmost importance to the North to check and halt any such move. Had 200,000 slaves been forced to fight to maintain themselves in slavery, and had they confronted 200,000 Negroes fighting against slavery, only the most ironic and tragic situation would have developed.

Delany, conferring with the President, described a plan by which the blacks of the North would prevent the Confederacy from arming the slaves, by means of utilizing the Underground Railroad. Harriet Tubman and others familiar with the operations of that system would pass through the South, inform the slaves of their masters' plans, point out its meaning, call upon them to resist induction into the slaveholders' army, and finally prepare them to join the black army that would soon arrive. Delany would combine the Southern espionage work of the Underground Railroad, with the organization of an army, led by blacks. These troops, as soon as possible, would go into the heart of the South, and, as he told the President, "make conquests, with the banner of Emancipation unfurled, proclaiming fredom as they go, sustaining and protecting it by arming the emancipated, taking them as fresh troops, and leaving a few veterans among the new freedmen when occasion requires, keeping the banner unfurled until every slave is free, according to the letter of your proclamation." [16]

It was a bold plan, or, as Delany called it, "the crowning act of the noble President's life." Lincoln immediately gave his decision to proceed on the new path as rapidly as possible. Delany was given the commission of major, becoming the first Negro major in national history, and he was assigned to organize the black army and take the field in South Carolina.

Delany at once surrounded himself with a personnel of Negro leadership. Harriet was in Washington at that time, and Delany interviewed her. "Certain leading spirits of the 'Underground Railroad' were invoked," says the biographer of Delany, "Scouts *incognito* were already 'on to Richmond,' and the services of the famous Harriet Tubman, having been secured to serve in the South, had received her transportation for Charleston, S. C." [17]

A Government record of Harriet's order to the South,[18] reads as follows:

Pass Mrs. Harriet Tubman (colored) to Hilton Head and Charleston, S. C., with free transportation on a Gov't transport. By order of Sec. of War.

(Signed)   LOUIS H. PELONGE
Asst. Agt. Gener'l

To Bvt. Brig. Gen. Van Vliet, U.S.Q.M., N.Y.
Dated Washington, March 20, 1865.

But in spite of the magnitude of this project, Harriet decided upon another course. She was drawn into the nursing service of the hospitals of the Washington region. Actually it was the turning point in military affairs which determined her upon the hospital service. Sherman had marched through Georgia, reached the coast, and he was turning northward toward Richmond; Sheridan had made an important and successful raid north of the James River in Virginia; and Grant, with a large army of 125,000 men, was threatening the doomed Lee. When Sherman would advance on Richmond from the South, all would be over. Confederate morale was low; and the Unionists sensed an early victory.

As Charleston fell before Sherman and the war came closer to its end, and while Delany, in Charleston, went ahead with the recruitment of black-officered companies of Negro troops, Harriet found herself plunged into a new field of labor. . . .

"Returning (from Washington) with the intention of embarking at New York, she was intercepted in Philadelphia by some members of the Sanitary Commission who persuaded her to go instead to the James River Hospitals—where there was pressing need of such service as she could give in the Gov't Hospitals. And relinquishing her plan of returning to the Dept. of the South—without a thought as to the unfortunate pecuniary result of this irregular proceeding, she went to the Hospitals of the James River, and at Fortress Monroe or Hampton—where she remained until July 1865. In that month she went to Washington again to advise of some dreadful abuses existing in one or more of the Hospitals there. And so great was the confidence of some officers of the Gov't in her that

Surgeon General Barnes directed that she be appointed 'Nurse or Matron.' " [19]

Secretary of State Seward was instrumental in this appointment, for the Surgeon General sent a note to the Cabinet member informing him that the Medical Director of the Department of Virginia had been instructed to place Harriet as Nurse or Matron at the Contraband Hospital at Fortress Monroe. With a pass dated July 22, 1865, Harriet was permitted to proceed to the Virginia destination on a Government transport free of cost. [20]

Before Harriet left Washington she spoke to Seward of her claim against the Government. He felt that the first step was to secure confirmation from Major General Hunter, with whom she had served, and as Hunter was in Washington at the time, Seward directed a letter to him. It has been a much-quoted letter and in its entirety is as follows:

Washington, July 25, 1865

Major General Hunter—My Dear Sir:

Harriet Tubman, a colored woman, has been nursing our soldiers during nearly all the war. She believes she has claims for faithful services to the command in South Carolina, with which you are connected, and she thinks that you would be disposed to see her claim justly settled.

I have known her long as a noble, high spirit, as true as seldom dwells in the human form. I commend her therefore to your kind attention.

Faithfully your friend,

WILLIAM H. SEWARD

Major General Hunter [21]

Nothing profitable came of the attempt. Neither Seward nor Hunter was able to secure any satisfactory action.

Harriet did not remain long at Fortress Monroe, for the appointment of the officers did not materialize. Soon she returned to Washington. With this, Harriet's war work was at an end, and since the country's need had ceased, she prepared to return home to devote herself to her mother and father. [22]

Colonel Thomas W. Higginson, whose Abolition labors helped prepare the Northern victory, who organized the first colored troops, and who, save Frederick Douglass, may have been unexceeded by any other contemporary historian by participation in or understanding of the events of the period, has summed up the role of the Department of the South in which Harriet performed most of her services. He said that the operations on the South Atlantic Coast, which long seemed a merely subordinate and incidental part of the great contest, proved to be one of the final pivots on which it turned. The fate of the Confederacy was decided by Sherman's march to the sea. Port Royal was the objective point to which he marched, and he found the Department of the South, when he reached it, held almost exclusively by colored troops. "Next to the merit of those who made the march was that of those who held open the door. That service will always remain among the laurels of the black regiments." [23]

*   *   *   *   *

Harriet, *en route* home, carried a pass as a hospital nurse, and with this she was entitled to half fare on the train. She seems to have missed the connection that she should have taken and she got into the wrong train. When the conductor looked at her ticket he said, "Come, hustle out of here!" He called her an insulting name and declared that her people were not carried for half fare.

She explained that she was entitled to transportation as were the soldiers.

The conductor then took her forcibly by the arm, and declared, "I'll make you tired of trying to stay here."

Harriet resisted, but the conductor called three men to his assistance.

Nobody championed her, although the car was filled. Again she was insulted for her color as someone called for her to be put out. They nearly wrenched off her arm and at length, threw her, with all their might, into a baggage car. In intense suffering, she went on to New York.[24]

Thus early Harriet experienced the segregation of the street car and the railway line, that "democratic" feature of American life. Harriet was under medical attention for this injury for some time.

It was an irony that she who had soldiered in the deep South, escaping bullets and cannon fire, should meet up with her war wound upon her return to civilian life.

Harriet received this "reward" at about the time that the antislavers presented a gift of $30,000 to William Lloyd Garrison for his lifetime services to Abolition. Harriet's experience would indicate that if the Abolitionists believed their struggle was won and the job completed, they were, to say the least, a bit premature.

END CHAPTER XIX

END PART FIVE

PART SIX

THE NEGLECT AND DEATH OF HARRIET TUBMAN

"When the war was over she returned unobtrusively to her homely life in Auburn, where, after 80 years of service to her people and to the cause of justice, she is closing her life in poverty. It was not plaintively, but rather with a flash of scorn in her eyes, that she remarked to the writer last week:

"You wouldn't think that after I served the flag so faithfully I should come to want in its folds."

She looked musingly toward a nearby orchard, and she asked suddenly:

"Do you like apples?"

On being assured that I did, she said:

"Did you ever plant any apple trees?"

With shame I confessed I had not.

"No," said she, "but somebody else planted them. I liked apples when I was young, and I said, 'Some day I'll plant apples myself for other young folks to eat,' and I guess I did it."—Frank C. Drake, in *The New York Herald,* September 22, 1907.

CHAPTER XX

THE MATRIARCHATE

When Harriet returned to her home in Auburn she was tired to the point of illness, still badly hurt as a result of her railroad experience, and penniless. She was about fifty years of age, and neither she nor anyone else suspected that she would have another half century to live! She settled down in her house at the outskirts of the town, hoping to occupy herself only with a domestic life and the care of her parents: she believed that her period of fighting was over and that she had earned a few years of peace. Or did she? Did she believe that her people were free? Did she believe that struggle was at an end, that the Northern Government would now guarantee the right to life, liberty and happiness to her people? Perhaps she had doubts from the time of her experience with the brutal conductor, but in any case, she did not expect to engage in the intense work that had so far been necessary.

For some time her chief direction seems to have been that of securing from the Government the payment of its immediate $1800 debt for her war work. From the start there were heavy demands upon her energies, her health, her hope of some personal peace. There was great upheaval in the land; her people were striving for readjustment; Northerners had rushed into the South to invest their money: Southern whites were resisting the inrush of Northern capital which was buying up Southern property, and they were fighting to keep the Negro from advancing into social and economic equality. In Congress the Confederate Generals were now arguing across table with the Northern Generals they had met on the field of battle a few months earlier! Susan B. Anthony and Elizabeth Cady Stanton had resumed the fight for woman's rights, a battle that had been relatively dormant in the war years except for the work done by large numbers of women in the sanitary commission behind the lines.

Soon the aged, the maimed, and the impoverished of Harriet's color came to her door in need. She welcomed them, fed and housed the derelict, and nursed the sick. Harriet could not have been recuperating for longer than a few months, if at all, when the varied responsibilities of her house settled upon her shoulders. Her aged parents, Ben and Harriet Ross, were dependent solely upon her. The brood that settled about her was a drain. Now, for the first time since her days in slavery, she had the chance to work in a garden, to plant trees, to watch things grow, to bring produce into the house. She went among her rich Republican friends of the community, and they, still flushed with victory and the knowledge that their party had delivered the black man from his chattel bonds, gave generously of money, food and clothing to solace the weary ones under her shelter. Soon something like her effective energies were regenerated, and she began raising funds for the maintenance of schools for freedmen in the South. After awhile she was, of her own efforts, supporting two schools for Freedmen at the South.[1] By the year 1867 she had plunged into Reconstruction work and handling her personal responsibilities with the heartiness of her old self —but she was hard pressed, in need of money, and sometimes even wanting for food.

None knew better than Harriet that the real struggle began only after Lee surrendered to Grant. She had had enough heartaches in the South and enough disappointments at the early Government handling of her people, to know that there might be ushered in now a new period of compromise, a new set of betrayals and treasons, perhaps even a counter-revolution. There would be gains; yes, even a major gain: perhaps never would chattel slavery return, although millions of her countrymen in Africa would yet undergo severe trials under the handling of new European aggressors.

Harriet was happy that the suffragists and the Abolitionists combined as the Equal Rights Association. The conflict had welded all wings of Abolition, all reformers, into a single national body. Now the Equal Rights Association wielded the strength of a political party. It was a voice in the North: a hard, exacting, righteous, religious force. The South had played vampire to the Negro for two centuries; the North had stood by idly, watching the Negro blood flow until the past generation. Now the North had to be, *must* be stern if all this bloodshed meant anything at all. It was a new way of life from now on. If there didn't develop out of this a new way of life for the black man, then, come what may, thought Harriet, the whole thing (civil war) will happen again. But she believed that the great advance had come about. The rest was a long, slow process of education—*of the whites*. After all, it was not her people who was deluded with the thought of its superiority; that was a white madness. If the Northern adults began with their children, at the age of three or four, and taught them ordinary Christianity, ordinary morals and decency, the Negro man and woman would truly be free by 1880 or 1890.

So she believed—or hoped. Yet her experiences conflicted with her hopes. She brooded over the maltreatment by the conductor on her last trip home. It was not the physical pain, though she still had that, as a result. It was the awful humiliation after the way she had fought *for that very conductor*. It was his life she fought for as much as her own; it was to lift him out of the degradation of living in a tyranny-infested land that she risked bullets on the Underground and in the South Carolina campaigns.

More than once she wept—for the white man's shame.

* * * * *

Perhaps she shed tears too when she learned of the death of her husband, John Tubman.

Irony of ironies. She who had fought the slave power every day of her life and escaped all of its countless tentacles of fire and sword was still alive, but John Tubman, the "loyal" Negro, the free Negro who was "satisfied," the man who never wanted to accompany her to the North—he had been brutally murdered near Cambridge, Maryland!

It was a typical incident of Reconstruction. It was one of the long and endless chain of murders and lynchings that swelled up in "the tragic era" (tragic for the black man), and which have come to an end—not yet.

What happened? Did John Tubman speak up for once in his life? Did he defend himself? Was he at this late date learning how to fight for his rights? Did he realize by now what Harriet had talked about in those early days when she pleaded with him to come away to the North?

The Baltimore American, of October 7, 1867, carried an account of John Tubman's murder.

MARYLAND AFFAIRS
Outrage in Talbot County

———

A COLORED MAN MURDERED
(From the Easton Gazette)
A Colored Man Killed

On Monday afternoon, about 5 o'clock, on the road near Aireys, a colored man named John Tubman was killed by Mr.

Robert Vincent. From the evidence elicited at an investigation by Justice Winterbottom, acting Coroner, it appears that in the morning, about ten o'clock, Vincent and deceased had a quarrel about the ownership of some ashes; that Vincent threatened to kill him, and finally chased him away with an axe. In the afternoon, as Vincent was returning home in wagon, having been to Cambridge, he met Tubman on the road, and as he passed asked him if "he was the same man as he was in the morning." Tubman replied in the affirmative. Vincent drove on about forty yards, then took his gun and deliberately fired at Tubman, who fell and instantly expired. Vincent never stopped to see whether his shot had proved fatal, but continued on his way home. There were but two witnesses to examine—a colored woman named Rebecca Camper, who witnessed the difficulty in the morning, it having occurred at her house, and a son of the deceased, a lad of thirteen years, who was standing in the woods near the roadside, when his father was murdered. There was no other witness to the murder. Dr. Rogers, who made a *post mortem* examination of the body of the deceased, found a shot wound in the forehead which he said was of itself sufficient to produce death. There were also other wounds in the neck which he thought would have proved fatal. Most of the shot penetrated the breast and face. The jury of inquest returned as their verdict "that Robert Vincent feloniously, voluntarily and of malice aforethought, shot the said John Tubman in the head and throat and breast, of which mortal wounds the said John Tubman died; and so the said Robert Vincent then and there killed and murdered John Tubman against the peace and dignity of the State of Maryland."

The item concludes with this blithe comment, "The murderer has not yet been arrested, and we question whether he ever will be. When last seen he was in New Market, making his way to Bridgeville. That was on the morning after the murder. No effort, that we are aware of, has been made to overtake and bring him to justice."

But an effort was made to overtake the murderer. Correspondence of a Cambridge correspondent of *The Baltimore Sun*, appearing in that paper on December 17, 1867, carried a pro-slavery account of a trial.   There *had* been a trial, which indicated some rights for the Negroes over what they knew in former years, but there was small satisfaction.   The trial lasted from a Thursday through to Sunday morning, and the jury dallied over the facts for *ten minutes* to find a "not guilty" verdict.

The Baltimore American, reprinting a news item from the anti-slavery *Cambridge Intelligencer,* published in the very heart of the diehard Maryland country, wrote the following indictment of the trial:

ACQUITTAL OF A MURDER

The trial of Robert Vincent for the murder of the colored man John Tubman was brought to a close early on Sunday morning last, by the jury rendering a verdict of "not guilty." That Vincent murdered the deceased we presume no one doubts; but as no one but a colored boy saw him commit the deed, it was universally conceded that he would be acquitted, the moment it was ascertained that the jury was composed exclusively of Democrats.   The Republicans have taught the Democrats much since 1860.   They thrashed them into at least a seeming respect for the Union—They educated them up to a tolerance of public schools.   They forced them to recognize Negro testimony in their courts.   But they haven't got them to the point of convicting a fellow Democrat for killing a Negro. But even that will follow when the Negro is armed with the ballot."

The ballot for the Negro.   That was the big question then, as it is a major one today.   That was the crux of Reconstruction; that was the answer to whether white America would emancipate itself from its own bond to a bestial tradition.

$$* \quad * \quad * \quad * \quad *$$

And it was around just such issues as the killing of John Tubman that the North and the South, the Abolitionists and the unreconstructed rebels still fought.   The South meant to re-enslave the Negro—but this time within the framework of the "democratic process."

The North?   The North was splitting wide open.   Northern business, never much concerned with the life or death of the Negro, sprawled out over the continent, absorbing new territories into its economic embrace, investing capital, buying up land, making money. Northern Abolition, with Frederick Douglass the acknowledged leader, and Garrison and Phillips trailing behind, threw the full weight of its ranks into the struggle to win decisive amendments for freedom, for balloting privileges. Northern parliamentary representatives of the business interests pushed their own commercial expansionist legislation chiefly; the Confederate officer representatives in the Senate and House fought the Radical as well as the Conservative Northern spokesmen, and traded heavily on the indifference or outright hostility of some Northern men to the question of the Negro.

In the Equal Rights Association a fundamental split occurred over the question of the women's right to receive the ballot. Doubtless the women deserved the vote—then, and always—but there was panic among Abolitionists like Phillips, Garrison, and Douglass over whether the Negro was going to get any rights at all out of this long contest, whether he was free, or only half-free. Incidents all over the land, like the murder of John Tubman and the brutal beating of Harriet on her return from the war, made Phillips proclaim, "This is the Negro's hour!"

Douglass tried to convince Susan Anthony and Elizabeth Cady Stanton that when women (by which he meant white women) were beaten, lynched, and disfranchised in state after state, then their case would be as urgent as the Negro's. Until then all strength must be applied to winning the ballot for the black man. This was no time to dilute the energies, to diffuse strength.

The women leaders wanted the word *male* omitted from the Fourteenth Amendment, an omission, highly desirable, that would have given the right to vote to every adult man and woman, black or white, in the nation. Charles Sumner, offering the Fourteenth Amendment to the nation, tried hard to formulate the Amendment so as to omit this age-old domineering word. He is said to have written nineteen pages of paper, trying nineteen times so to frame the measure as to make it possible for women's rights to go through in the same Amendment. Susan and Elizabeth, and dozens of other suffragists had fought hard for the coming of this time; and they believed that the social upheaval was deep enough to be able to permit of woman's passage into political recognition. But the majority sentiment of the Abolitionists believed otherwise—saw a suffering Negro people that was already being deserted by Government representatives who were tired of the struggle, and desirous of accumulating interests for themselves. In the South the Ku Klux Klan was growing, and every Abolitionist knew what that would mean—counter-revolution. As late as March 4, 1868, when many Abolitionists believed that their cause was won and at an end, and that Abolition societies were no longer necessary, Sallie Holley wrote to one of her friends, again reminding of how Harriet had been thrust out of a car by a conductor. "Was there no need of anti-slavery teaching there?" ²

Susan Anthony and Elizabeth Stanton may have been correct in holding that this was a time for the woman question to be settled too; no historian can be certain; but they made a serious mistake in taking a threatening tone. In the columns of their suffrage organ, *The Revolution,* they delivered a blast against the Government's granting rights to Negro men while white women went politically unrecognized. Their words were trenchant, their thoughts unrestrained, their tone indignant—and the effect an insult to the Negro. The Abolitionists recoiled, called the argument a "deadly insult," called it a repudiation of what a whole great host of liberators had fought for—and then and there began the basis for the split that occurred in the Equal Rights Association. John Brown had died for the Negro, gladly, hanging thirty-five minutes before he was pronounced dead enough to be removed. Colonel Robert Gould Shaw virtually ran up on an enemy parapet and stood there taking shots through his body as a symbol to the Negro that there were white men who understood them—as men, as humans; Lincoln had been assassinated by the anti-Negro John Wilkes Booth; hundreds had languished in jails and thousands had died in battle (not as pro-Unionists, but as Abolitionists), yet Susan Anthony and Elizabeth Stanton, clear-eyed women who themselves had risked life and limb for the Negro, reneged. Nobody doubted, among the Abolitionists, that women, white and Negro, were entitled to vote; no one wanted that more than the Negro, Frederick Douglass, *the first man in*

United States history to call for the woman's right to the ballot.
But the women, with all of their zeal, failed to see the need for a
compromise, failed to admit that Negro suffrage was imperilled.
Douglass and others saw that they could not jeopardize Negro suffrage by attempting to put through woman's suffrage at the same
time, thus inviting the danger of the failure of *both.* One step
at a time. One lesser victory was better than a possible total political loss. That was the reasoning of Douglass, who had learned
much and taught much to others in the ante-bellum days and in the
war years. And the majority of the Abolitionsts, the overwhelming
majority, followed him.

Susan Anthony called for the breakup of the Equal Rights Association and the formation of a group that she called the National
Woman Suffrage Association. When the great Susan Anthony did
that she delivered a fiercer blow at her own rights and at the Negro's
rights than anything that the slaveholders themselves had accomplished since they had put through the Fugitive Slave Act. She
broke up the reform movement that had been fifty years building. It
had been the hope of Wendell Phillips that a woman suffrage
amendment would become law at the succeeding Constitutional Convention, but the impatience of Miss Anthony and some of her adher-
ents meant that, not only did it not come about later when that Convention was called, but it did not come about in her own lifetime,
and indeed, not for a half century and more later.

When the Equal Rights Association broke up, the reform movement of the great period of Douglass, Garrison, John Brown, and
Harriet Tubman came to an end—and progressive ideals limped
along thereafter, weakened beyond any recovery in that century.

There were deep enmities thereafter among the Abolitionists
and the suffragists, and the Southern Democrats took advantage of
the rift. They immediately invited Miss Anthony to their cause, and
she, amazingly, went along with them. Susan with the ex-slavehold-
ers! But it was true; and for a long time thereafter, throughout the
North, she was unable to recapture prestige for her movement.
There were two suffrage movements in the field from then on, and
the disunity among them was just what the legislators wanted. They
could now ignore the question of woman's rights. If this had had

only adverse effects on woman's suffrage, it would have little place in the understanding of Harriet, her life, and her people, and her relationship to her times. But from the time when the Equal Rights split occurred, the forces fighting for the Negro were weakened; and with Abolition cracked in two, the voices of the old leaders lost weight with the Northern legislators, and it was the black man who suffered.

Harriet saw all of this in the Reconstruction years, and was part of it all, even as her husband's death was part of it. There is no way of knowing where Harriet stood on the question of the split in the Equal Rights Association. A few prominent Negroes stayed with Susan Anthony, including Robert Purvis, an influential voice. Frances Watkins Harper, a prominent Negro writer, sided with Douglass, declaring in convention that she would be satisfied, for the time being, if Negro men alone were given the ballot.

Wherever Harriet stood in this critical dispute, though unascertainable, one thing is certain: she remained throughout life the firm admirer of Susan Anthony. Miss Anthony, in spite of a serious error, did regain prestige after awhile, and Harriet, whatever she thought of Susan's moves, did not doubt the *essential,* the honest, the great Susan Anthony. In the days to come they would meet and prove all this.

*　　*　　*　　*　　*

There was a deeper evidence in Harriet's life of how Reconstruction leaders were treating the black nation than her post-war experience on the railroad homeward bound. Harriet came to know a deep-seated, galling neglect on the part of the Government. She found, on all sides, that prejudice and discrimination continued; that it was a slow horror to eradicate. When it is realized that Harriet had now entered upon a *thirty-five year struggle* to win the recognition of Congress, to secure a few hundred dollars reward for performing in the Department of the South, *so that she could continue to help others,* then, and then alone is it possible to perceive the magnitude of the official indifference to the Negro's plight. When one of the most noteworthy women of the land could be spurned, over and over again, by one Congressional Session after another; when a figure of the stature of the Secretary of State in Lincoln's

Cabinet was unable to convince a *pension committee* of the black woman's rights; then we look inside of Reconstruction. Was it Seward who had so fallen? Or was it rather Harriet who had not yet arisen—to freedom? It was doubtless the latter.

Consider the difficulties that beset Sarah Bradford in this period when she undertook to write a biographical account of Harriet's life. To dare to attempt that in 1868 took courage. It was even then an Abolition act. Mrs. Bradford, preparing for the assault that was certain to come, said, "There are those who will sneer, there are those who have already done so, at this quixotic attempt to make a heroine of a black woman, and a slave; but it may possibly be that there are some natures, though concealed under fairer skins, who have not the capacity to comprehend such general and self-sacrificing devotion to the cause of others as that here delineated, and therefore they resort to scorn and ridicule, in order to throw discredit upon the whole story." ³

Scorn and ridicule. That was what the Negro faced, in spite of January 1, 1863, in spite of Brown and Lincoln, in spite of three amendments granting rights to a new life. And scorn and ridicule greeted Harriet Tubman's claims for a pension—in the Congress and the Senate!

* * * * *

In the fall of the year 1867 she went to visit Gerrit Smith at Peterboro. Sallie Holley was the guest of the philanthropist at that time, and she wrote on November 4, in a letter to a friend, that Harriet Tubman had just visited there and that she wanted Mr. Smith to help her win her claim against the Government.⁴ Smith wrote a letter for Harriet requesting that the Government give its attention to her claim.⁵

Sallie Holley decided to do something more about the matter. She wrote to Editor Aaron M. Powell of *The National Anti-Slavery Standard*, which was published in New York, and on Saturday, November 30, that paper published her letter. "Among American women," Miss Holley asked, "who has shown a courage and self-devotion to the welfare of others, equal to Harriet Tubman?" She spoke of the liberator's work on the Underground, compared her spirit to that of John Brown, and concluded with the story of her beating at the hands of the conductor. ". . . and as she told me of the pain she had and still suffered, she said she did not know what she should have done for herself, and the old father and mother she takes care of, if Mr. Wendell Phillips had not sent her $60, that kept them warm through the winter. . . ." [6]

In spite of the aid of Phillips, Smith, the Sewards, and others, Harriet, her parents, and the others who clung about her were not always warm in the post-war winters. Once, in the winter of 1867-1868, this happened:

"The old man (Harriet's father) was laid up with rheumatism, and Harriet could not leave home for a long time to procure supplies of corn, if she could have made her way into the city. At length stern necessity compelled her to plunge through the drifts to the city, and she appeared at the house of one of her firm and fast friends, and was directed to the room of one of the young ladies. She began to walk up and down, as she always does when in trouble. At length she said, 'Miss Annie?'

" 'What, Harriet?'

"A long pause; then again, 'Miss Annie?'

" 'Well what is it, Harriet?'

"This was repeated four times when the young lady, looking up, saw her eyes filled with tears. She then insisted on knowing what she wanted. And with a great effort she said, 'Miss Annie, could you lend me a quarter till Monday? I never asked it before.' Kind friends immediately supplied all wants of the family, but on Monday Harriet appeared with the quarter she had borrowed." [7]

That precarious mode of living went on until the spring of 1868 when Secretary of State William H. Seward and other Auburnians seriously took up the plan of securing a pension for her. Mrs. Mary Derby, an Auburn admirer of Harriet, wrote to General Saxton, in Atlanta, Georgia, soliciting his assistance. He wrote the following reply:

Atlanta, Ga., March 21st, 1868

My dear Madam:

I have just received your letter informing me that Hon. William H. Seward, Secretary of State, would present a petition to Congress for a pension for Harriet Tubman, for services rendered in the Union Army during the late war. I can bear witness to the value of her services in South Carolina and Florida. She made many a raid inside the enemy's lines displaying remarkable courage, zeal and fidelity.

She was employed by Gen'l Hunter and I think by Generals Stevens and Sherman—and is as deserving of a pension from the Government for her service as any other of its faithful servants.

(Signed) Very truly yours,
RUFUS SAXTON
Bvt. Brig. General.

to Mrs. Mary Derby
Auburn, N. Y.[8]

Another influential Auburnian rallied to Harriet's side. That was Charles P. Wood, a banker who had been active in relief work during the war, helping to provide for families in distress due to having lost kin in the conflict. He undertook to write an account of Harriet's war record, with a view to presenting this as evidence to Congress. He sat down with Harriet, listened to her story, examined the certificates which she had collected during the recent years, and wrote a 15-page account of her services. Most of his report was to establish the authenticity of her labors as a scout, nurse and spy in the Department of the South and in the Washington vicinity. He concluded his account by saying that Harriet was entitled to several thousands of dollars pay. The only difficulty seemed to be that she held no commission, and had not in the regular way and at the proper times and places, applied for her compensation.[9]

It was in May or June of 1868, when it was evident that Harriet was not yet to be recognized by the Government, that Sarah Bradford began the important job of writing Harriet's story. This effort proved more profitable. Mrs. Bradford was no practised writer; she never wrote anything else other than Harriet's story, but no matter. She did an authentic work, even if it was all too brief." [10] The biographer decided on a literary policy, chiefly, of allowing others to tell Harriet's story and of permitting them to appraise her. She

wrote directly to those who had been Harriet's most intimate associates in Abolition and war labors—to Wendell Phillips, Gerrit
Smith, Frederick Douglass, Franklin B. Sanborn, Thomas Garrett, and
others. She had the assistance of her brother, the Reverend Samuel
Miles Hopkins, a scholar and admirer of Harriet. The organizing
force in back of the book was an Auburnian named William G.
Wise. He went about raising a subscription list to make possible
the publication of the story. Gerrit Smith and Wendell Phillips contributed twenty-five dollars apiece; and others of New York, San
Francisco and Auburn donated to the fund. The foreword to the
book contained letters from various Abolition notables, including a
rather famous one from Frederick Douglass:

Rochester, August 29, 1868

Dear Harriet:—

I am glad to know that the story of your eventful life has
been written by a kind lady, and that the same is soon to be published. You ask for what you do not need when you call upon
me for a word of commendation. I need such words from you
far more than you can need them from me, especially where
your superior labors and devotion to the cause of the lately enslaved of our land are known as I know them. The difference
between us is very marked. Most that I have done and suffered in
the service of our cause has been in public, and I have received
much encouragement at every step of the way. You on the
other hand have labored in a private way. I have wrought in
the day—you in the night. I have had the applause of the
crowd and the satisfaction that comes of being approved by
the multitude, while the most that you have done has been witnessed by a few trembling, scarred and foot-sore bondmen and
women, whom you have led out of the house of bondage, and
whose heartfelt *"God bless you"* has been your only reward. The
midnight sky and the silent stars have been the witnesses of
your devotion to freedom and of your heroism. Excepting John
Brown—of sacred memory—I know of no one who has will-
ingly encountered more perils and hardships to serve our enslaved people than you have. Much that you have done would
seem improbable to those who do not know you as I know you.
It is to me a great privilege to bear testimony to your character

and your works, and to say to those to whom you may come, that I regard you in every way truthful and trustworthy.

Your friend,

FREDERICK DOUGLASS [11]

Even while friends were trying to raise the means to publish the book for her, she was going about with the greatest zeal and interest to raise a subscription for a Freedmen's Fair. She called on the Hon. William H. Seward for a subscription to this project, and he said, "Harriet, you have worked for others long enough. It is time you should think of yourself. If you ask for a donation for *yourself* I will give it to you; but I will not help you to rob yourself for others!" [12]

The book was a Christmas present to Abolition. In *The Commonwealth,* on Saturday, January 9, 1869, there appeared the following announcement of *Scenes in the Life of Harriet Tubman*:

". . . Mrs. Sarah H. Bradford, of Geneva, N. Y., has made quite an interesting memoir of this devoted woman, which has been published in neat book-form, and the proceeds of the sales of which go to her support, she being now very old and quite infirm. The price is $1 only, and copies can be procured at the rooms of the Woman's Club and the Freedmen's Aid Society, or they will be forwarded post-paid, upon receipt of price, by addressing 'Box No. 782,' Boston Postoffice."

Funds came in and tided Harriet over a bad period. Money went to the freedmen in the South, and the matriarchate took in the worn and the helpless of her people, and there was food for all.

END CHAPTER XX

Chapter XXI

THE TURNING YEARS

It was the flush spring of 1869 when there was cash in the Tubman till, and the fame of her spread in book form as once it had traveled by word of mouth for her deeds of the moment. A lush spring, with food and plenty. The book had brought in about $1200, enough for Harriet to pay off her debt to Seward and have a surplus. "There's cider in the cellar, and the black folks, they'll have some; must be now the kingdom coming, and the year of Jubilum," Harriet sang from time to time.[1]

It was in this spring that she remarried. It has been said that her husband, Nelson Davis, spite of being a large man was not a healthy man, that he suffered with tuberculosis, and she married him to take care of him.[2] Be that as it may, he had weathered the battle of Olustee and other engagements; he had the respect of his fellow men, and he knew that Harriet Tubman was a rare and an unusual woman.

When the Reverend Henry Fowler blessed them on the evening of March 18, 1869, at the Central Church in the center of Auburn, he did so in the presence of "the first families of the city," that is, the wealth. There were present the Sewards, Osbornes, Woods, Chedells, the Dr. Willards, Seymours and Steels. The next day a local newspaper carried an extensive account of the affair:

". . . Before a large and very select audience Harriet Tubman . . . took unto herself a husband and made one William Nelson (Nelson Davis) a happy man. Both born slaves, as they grew in years and knowledge recognized the glory of freedom, still later in the eventful struggle they fled from bondage, until finally, by the blessing of Divine Providence, they stood there, last evening, *free,* and were joined as man and wife. The audience was large, consisting of the friends of the parties and a large number of the first families of the city. Ladies and gentlemen who were interested in Harriet, and who for years had advised and assisted her, came to see her married. After the ceremony Rev. Mr. Fowler made some very touching and happy allusions to their past trials, and the apparently plain sailing the parties now had, when the ceremony ended amid the congratulations of the assembly, and the happy couple were duly embarked on the journey of life. We tender our congratulations to the bride and groom, and may they never see a less happy moment than when Shimer, that prince of good fellows, spurred on by a prominent Democratic politician of the Third Ward, rushed frantically forward, and in an excited manner congratulated them on the happy event." [3]

But the well wishes of the correspondent were to be anti-climaxed in another of those ironies that pursued Harriet all of her days and nights. The very man who rushed forward to congratulate Harriet, Anthony Shimer, would be involved with her a few years later in another, and one of the most tragic incidents of her life.

*　　*　　*　　*　　*

Whatever surplus of funds had been left for Harriet from the sale of her biography, after she liquidated her debt to Seward, she was soon bankrupt. Harriet did not know how to administer money; she knew no reason for saving it in a world where her people starved and wanted; and she could not have had her bit of wealth, the most she had ever had, for more than a few months. She sent much of it to her freedmen's schools in the South, but mainly the brood that now hung upon her skirts consumed the little treasury. Occasional Negroes still came North, arriving at her door; old Abolition friends of color came to her for loans. Latterly, when funds any larger than driblets came to her, friends, Negro and white, insisted on handling them for Harriet's heart was so large, and her feelings were so easily wrought upon, that it was never wise to give her more than enough for immediate needs. [4]

It was so easy to work on Harriet's feelings, she had such an unfailing faith in the essential goodness of human nature, that once she was seriously abused as a result. She allowed herself in 1873 to be victimized in a swindle that became a national whisper. If Congress had given her the pension she deserved when Seward first asked for it, Harriet would not have been driven by such fierce economic need as to make her the prey of confidence men. In this instance Harriet barely escaped with her life. Her great contemporary, Frederick Douglass, in a scandal involving the Freedmen's Bank, had also been mulcted for his great trust in his fellow men.

Harriet allowed herself to be "taken in" only because she saw in a money-making scheme that had been unfolded to her the chance to do something else, something big, for her people. Here was the opportunity to found a great home and hospital for the sick and suffering of her people, for this was the dream of her closing years. Here was the chance to pour life back into the bloodstream of drained ex-slaves. So signficant was "The Gold Swindle and the Greenback Robbery" in the ordinarily dull news life of the community of Auburn, that the account of the affair merited five full columns in *The Auburn Daily Bulletin,* and it was such a journalistic event that *twelve* headlines announced the full story to a town that was rife with rumors of what had happened. More, the news had gone over the continent. The account opened as follows:

> Harriet Tubman, the celebrated colored philanthropist, whose connection with the "gold" transaction and loss of Shimer's $2,000 in greenbacks which has, for the past week, created so much interest in this city and abroad, returned to her home, near the Fleming toll gate, on Saturday afternoon, having so far recovered from the effects of her adventure as to admit of leaving the shelter of Mr. Slocum Howland's roof at Sherwood's.

> From interviews . . . we are enabled to furnish a more connected and reliable account of the great gold swindle and robbery than has heretofore been obtainable.

> Our reconstructed history commences at the beginning, and has first to do with

The Rogues at Seneca Falls [5]

The "rogues at Seneca Falls" were two black men from the South named Stevenson and Harris who claimed to have a hoard of about $5,000 worth of gold which Harris had found during the war. This he dared not to exchange for the more convenient greenbacks in the South because the government would seize the gold.[6]

None in Seneca Falls would deal with Harris, or his right-hand man Stevenson, for it was known there that there had been a gold swindle a couple of years earlier in St. Catharines, Canada, and so the two went on to Auburn in the hope of finding "easy marks." In Auburn they were able to interest Harriet's brother, John Stewart. He went to Harriet and apparently he presented the situation in a highly favorable light, for she was prevailed upon to bring it to the attention of her so numerous white friends. Harriet was esteemed so highly in the community that she was able to find persons willing to participate in the "deal," although some dissuaded her from any connection with the strange men.

The plan rang a memory bell in Harriet's mind. She had seen a trunk full of gold and silver buried in Beaufort, S. C., during the war, and had that in her mind when this affair came up.[7]

Anthony Shimer, the man who was first to rush forward and congratulate Harriet at the time of her marriage, was now first to rush forward with $2,000 to exchange for the gold. Doubtless Harriet and Shimer and others involved arranged for some division of the "proceeds." The details complete, a party consisting of Shimer, Charles O'Brien, then cashier of the City Bank, Harriet Tubman and her husband, her brother John Stewart, and the man Stevenson started out to make the exchange in the seclusion of a forest in the South end of the county. The swindler arranged for Harriet, with the $2,000 in her possession, to become separated from the rest of the party. In a wild place in the woods, in the dead of night, Harriet was attacked and the money on her person forcibly taken from her. "When she recovered her consciousness she found she was bound and gagged. She says she succeeded in getting over the fences by resting her chin on the top rail, to steady herself while she climbed up, and then dropped to the ground."[8]

Shimer lost his money; the matter became something of a scandal; and Harriet added to her long life of adventure another set of scars in the service of the black nation. For if there is anything in the whole episode that is certain and irrefutable, it is Harriet's dream of the sudden realization of her hospital, the "John Brown Home" as she hoped to call it.

Perhaps that was why the leading citizens of Auburn resumed

busying themselves on a pension for Harriet. In 1874 Congressman MacDougall again presented the colored philanthropist's claim to the halls of legislation.[9] A few weeks later, on June 22, 1874, Representative Gerry W. Hazelton, of Wisconsin, also reported a bill for the same purpose.[10] But nothing came of the efforts. The liberator must go on using her wits how best to provide for herself and her small army of dependents.

*   *   *   *   *

The Secretary of State to Lincoln was spared the blow of seeing his friend injured in this last strange affair, so unlike those fights that Harriet had waged all her life and one of the few incidents since slavery in which she emerged the loser. Had William H. Seward, who died in 1872, lived long enough for Harriet to seek his counsel whether or not to enter into the "gold deal," he would have surely advised against it, and she would have turned aside the matter. Seward was gone, and with him her most devoted friend since John Brown.

"The great man lay in his coffin. Friends, children and admirers were gathered there. Everything that love and wealth could do had been done; around him were floral emblems of every possible shape and design, that human ingenuity, could suggest or money could purchase. Just before the coffin was to be closed, a woman black as night stole quietly in, and laying a wreath of field flowers *on his feet*, as quietly glided out again. This was the simple tribute of our sable friend and her last token of love and gratitude to her kind protector." [11]

The lean, hard days continued through the seventies, eighties and nineties, with Harriet toiling to provide for the helpless and aged who clustered around her. No poor helpless creature was ever turned from her door, although very often she had no idea where the next meal was to come from. The lame, the halt and the blind, the bruised and crippled little children, and one crazy woman dwelt in her humble home.[12] Once when the whole house hungered, Harriet went to the public market in Auburn and wandered about among the booths where food was on sale until the meat and vegetable tradesmen surmised her penniless plight, filled her baskets with food, and told her to pay them whenever she might. Another time Harriet borrowed seven dollars from an Auburn doctor, telling her she would repay it in a few days. Then she turned to her good friend, Mrs. Bradford, and borrowed from her to repay the doctor. Even if she had to borrow from Peter to pay Paul she must feed her charges and she did. There was a constant turnover of guests in her home, some staying only a few months, others remaining a lifetime, but she was never with less than a half dozen dependents, in addition to her parents. Throughout she dreamed of establishing a Home for the Aged and Indigent, and worked toward that purpose.

Harriet, in her latter years, became a kind of peddler, going from house to house, selling the produce that she and her dependents raised on their several acres, by this means earning a few dollars to supply their varied wants. Wherever she called the townspeople urged her to sit and talk of her anti-slavery work. One of those who persuaded her to speak occasionally has said, "Harriet when I knew her in her matriarchal phase was a magnificent looking woman, true African, with a broad nose, very black, and of medium height. I used to often sit and listen to her stories when I could get her to tell them. We always gave her something to eat. She preferred butter in her tea to anything else. That was a luxury...." [13]

*   *   *   *   *

As the years turned Harriet occupied herself with three or four major interests, other than those of the struggle to live from day to day and provide for others. She supported the woman suffrage movement, going to nearby meetings whenever she heard of them, took an active part in the growth of the African Methodist Episcopal Church in Central and Western New York, fought for her pension, and eventually established the Home for the Aged and Indigent.

Her parents passed away in the seventies, each of them said to be nearly centenarians when they died.

The older she grew the stronger became the hold of the church upon her thinking. Her reputation as a religionist spread widely, and religious journals often spoke of her work. The Salvation Army, through its journal, *The Evangelist,* sent her funds for the support of her "disciples." She never ceased to sing those roaring songs with the religious words and the revolutionary meaning, like "The John Brown Song," and "Go Down, Moses." She sang in church and, as it was called, "gave testimony." The colored population of Auburn, which revolved around Harriet, came to church as much to see Harriet mount the rostrum and to hear her, as from religious motive.[14]

Harriet's religion was primarily an expression of her love for life and for people. There was no superstitution within her, no fear of anything. Once, it has been related, she was visiting some white friends in the evening a mile or so from her own home. When she left them she took a shortcut across a cemetery, Fort Hill, where she was later buried. Her friends, fearful that she might be taken with a sleeping seizure while on her way, cautioned her about taking that route. Perhaps they had eerie and unnatural feelings about graveyards too, a mood that Harriet did not share.

"Why are you going that way?" she was asked.

"I'm going across the cemetery."

"Why?" they asked, revealing their fears for her safety.

"They're all quiet there," she said, "all peaceful." [15]

Harriet never did recover from her chronic "sleeping" illness. After the Civil War she underwent a head operation at the Massachusetts General Hospital in Boston, where an attempt was made to "raise the pressure." But she was not much helped, perhaps not helped at all. She continued throughout life to be seized three or four times a day with this strange affliction. Once she was found leaning against a fence, in broad daylight, sound asleep.[16]

Because of Harriet, Auburn became a shrine toward the close of the nineteenth century. Negroes and former Abolitionists, making pilgrimages to the North to the scene of the early anti-slavery events, made a visit to Harriet a major stop. From there they would go to the burial place of John Brown in the Adirondacks. Booker T. Washington, once the outstanding Negro voice in the nation, came to see Harriet from time to time. He regarded no trip to Auburn complete that did not include a visit with her.[17] Such visitors usually brought gifts to Harriet, but these tokens were quickly seized by Harriet's friends, and as Harriet did not place great value or sentiment upon such possessions she did not mind. If they were visitors who knew her well and were acquainted with her circumstances, they brought only food.

Throughout these years Harriet maintained her parental relationship to the growing Margaret Stewart, the girl whom she had "kidnapped" from Maryland and brought to the home of William H. Seward. The record of this strange mother-daughter association has been referred to as a peaceful and unfailing friendship. Subsequently Margaret Stewart married a man named Henry Lucas.

*   *   *   *   *

From the time Harriet returned from the war, friends referred to her age and to her ill health, yet she outlived many of those who feared that she had not long to remain. The majority of Abolitionists died during Harriet's declining years. Colonel James Montgomery passed away in 1871, leaving Harriet to live forty-four years longer than that soldier. She attended the funeral of Wendell Phillips and spoke there.[18] The great orator died in Boston in February of 1884. Frederick Douglass was there too, and he said, "I came not here alone only to see the remains of my dear old friend; I wanted to see this throng, and to see the hold that this man had upon the community. It is a wonderful tribute." And a few years later Harriet went to Frederick Douglass' funeral. His death was a great blow to her.[19] Garrison had gone many years earlier; Whittier passed away late in the century; the women, Abby Foster, Lucretia Mott, Lydia Child, and the others died, and still Harriet lived on. She got up occasional streaks of energy in which she dashed to New England to see her friends before they departed. The Alcotts and the Beechers, the Howes and Adamses, welcomed her and she passed weekends with them. By the time the nineties were well along the last of New England culture was in the hands of Franklin B. Sanborn and Colonel Thomas W. Higginson, two of the small group that lived on into the twentieth century. Edna Dow Cheney, a prominent suffragist and writer, always Harriet's devoted admirer, drew closer to her in the closing days.

The earliest mention of Harriet in a suffrage relationship with Susan B. Anthony and Elizabeth Cady Stanton has been described as an incident occurring in a Rochester church sometime during the eighties of the nineteenth century.

"The church was warm and Harriet was tired, and soon after she entered deep sleep fell upon her.

"Susan B. Anthony and Mrs. Stanton were on the platform, and after speeches had been made and business accomplished, one of these ladies said: 'Friends, we have in the audience that wonderful woman, Harriet Tubman, from whom we should like to hear, if she will kindly come to the platform.'

"People looked around at Harriet, but Harriet was fast asleep.

". . . it was some time before Harriet could be made to understand where she was, or what was wanted of her. At length she was led out into the aisle and was assisted by one of these kind ladies to the platform.

"Harriet looked around, wondering why so many white ladies were gathered there. I think it was Miss Anthony who led her forward, saying:

" 'Ladies, I am glad to present to you Harriet Tubman, the conductor of the Underground Railroad.'

" 'Yes, ladies,' said Harriet, 'I was the conductor of the Underground Railroad for eight years, and I can say what most conductors can't say—I never ran my train off the track and I never lost a passenger.' The audience laughed and applauded, and Harriet was emboldened to go on and relate portions of her interesting history, which were most kindly received by the assembled ladies." [20]

It was this statement, that she had never run her train off the track or lost a passenger, that was inscribed on the bronze tablet erected in Harriet's memory a year after her death by the people of Auburn. It may have been this statement that more or less labeled Harriet's chief contribution as her work with the Underground, and resulted in the neglect of her war record, her association with John Brown, and other Abolition and reform labors. It was as an Underground Railroad operator and Union fighter that Harriet spoke, but it was as a suffragist that she came to the Rochester meeting. [21]

At another time Harriet was visited by some women from out of town who invited her to attend a sewing circle in their city. Harriet went there, finding twenty or thirty persons gathered. They asked her many questions, and she told stories, sang songs and even attempted a few dances. She went away loaded with many tokens of the kind interest of these women. On the way home Harriet said to Mrs. Bradford, "What nice, kind-looking ladies they were. I looked in all their faces, and I saw nothing venomous in any of them." [22] Mrs. Bradford referred to this as a "peculiar expression" on Harriet's part. It was not at all peculiar. Harriet knew that prejudice against her people and herself was by no means eliminated, and that millions of parents encouraged color bigotry in their children. That Harriet could say she had seen no ill glance in an entire group of twenty-five or thirty women, speaks highly for the liberality of that particular company.

In April of 1897 the suffragists of Boston gave a benefit party for Harriet at the *Woman's Journal* parlors. An account in that newspaper says that ". . . Mr. F. J. Garrison planned the reception, Mrs. Edna Dow Cheney presided, and the survivors of the old Abolitionists in this vicinity, with the children of those who have passed on, gathered to do Harriet honor. . . . Mrs. Frances E. Harper also was present." [23] Harriet's visit to Boston was also noted in the *Woman's Journal* of April 17, 1897, under the "Concerning Women" column: "She has no pension, although her services during the war were worth hundreds of men to the government. . . ."

If the Government was slow to recognize her, the British Queen Victoria full well realized Harriet's significance. A copy of the Sarah H. Bradford biography had been sent to the Queen and it had been read to her. The Queen sent a Diamond Jubilee medal to Harriet and invited her to come to England. Harriet said of this incident, "It was when the Queen had been on the throne 60 years, she sent me the medal. It was a silver medal, about the size of a dollar. It showed the Queen and her family." The letter she received with the medal "was worn to a shadow, so many people read it." [24]

Susan Anthony and Harriet met again, for the last time, at a house gathering late in the year 1902, possibly a Christmas party, in the home of Eliza Wright Osborne in Auburn. The Osborne home was at that time the liberal center of Auburn where suffrage leaders gathered, where notables in the reform world visited when they called in the town. The home was an intellectual salon, a gathering place of the last of the Abolitionists, the oldest of the suffrage leaders, and the younger reformers. A noted suffrage leader, Anna Howard Shaw, wrote of that place, ". . . and the best talk I have heard anywhere was that to which I used to listen in the home of Mrs. Eliza Wright Osborne, in Auburn, New York, where Mrs. Stanton, Susan B. Anthony, Emily Howland, Elizabeth Smith Miller, Ida Husted Harper, Miss Mills and I were gathered there for our occasional week-end visits." [25] All of these were acquainted with Harriet, the Osbornes in particular, and Harriet was present at one of the gatherings Mrs. Shaw speaks of. Miss Anthony was surprised that Harriet was still living. The suffragist wrote at that time:

"This most wonderful woman—*Harriet Tubman*—is still alive. I saw her but the other day at the beautiful home of Eliza Wright Osborne, the daughter of Martha C. Wright, in company with Elizabeth Smith Miller, the only daughter of Gerrit Smith, Miss Emily Howland, Rev. Anna H. Shaw and Mrs. Ella Wright Garrison, the daughter of Martha C. Wright and the wife of William Lloyd Garrison, Jr. All of us were visiting at the Osbornes, a real love feast of the few that are left and here came *Harriet Tubman!*"

SUSAN B. ANTHONY
17 Madison Street
Rochester, N. Y.

Jan. 1, 1903 [26]

Harriet's reputation as a Negro leader continued to be utilized by the suffragists up to her dying day. As late as 1911 Harriet was interviewed by Elizabeth Smith Miller, who was the Geneva leader of suffrage.

"I remember seeing you years ago at a suffrage convention in Rochester," said Miss Miller.

"Yes," the old woman affirmed. "I belonged to Miss Susan B. Anthony's association."

"I should like to enroll you as a life member of our Geneva Club. Our motto is Lincoln's declaration: 'I go for all sharing the privileges of the Government who assist in bearing its burdens, by no means excluding women.' You certainly have assisted in bearing the burdens. Do you really believe that women should vote?"

Harriet paused a moment as if surprised at this question, then quietly said, "I suffered enough to believe it." [27]

END CHAPTER XXI

CHAPTER XXII

"SWING LOW, SWEET CHARIOT"

It was not until the death of Harriet's husband on October 14, 1888 that she received any Government aid. Nelson Davis was 44 when he died.

About a year and a half later a pension act was passed, granting relief to widows of Civil War veterans. That was on June 27, 1890, and a few weeks later Harriet applied for such a pension. She was awarded the sum of eight dollars a month, and she went along with this pittance for several years, although naturally it was inadequate to her needs.

Finally, in the late nineties, there was a concerted movement to end this matter that had dragged in and out of the Congressional Record ever since the Civil War. Harriet was by now a much written about woman. Newspapers and magazines found in her "good copy." A sketch about her could find a place in almost any newspaper or magazine. The story of the Underground Railroad was good drama, the mention of John Brown still aroused controversy. Since all of Harriet's biographers spoke very favorably of her, and as each denounced the Government treatment of her, the matter became something of a scandal. In July of 1896 Rosa Belle Holt, writing in *The Chatauquan,* said: "It seems strange that one who has done so much for her country and been in the thick of the battles, with shots falling all about her, should never have had recognition from the Government in a substantial way, but such is the fact." [1]

Harriet was advised to make out an affidavit as to the truth of the Charles P. Wood history of her war service, since he was now deceased. This Harriet did on the first of January 1898. The affidavit and other documentary material was placed in the hands of Congressman Sereno Payne, representing Harriet's district, and on February 5 he recommended the case to Congressman George W. Ray, of Norwich, New York, Chairman of the Committee on Invalid Pensions. [2] Meantime the citizens of Auburn drew up another petition urging the Congressman to "take up this affair" [3] and press the matter through Congress.

Early in 1899 the bill came before Congress. According to the debate printed in the Congressional Record [4] the bill was presented as a claim to enter Harriet on the pension rolls as a nurse, but the Congressman from South Carolina, W. Jasper Talbert of Parkesville, questioned the proposal. Congressman Ray, speaking for the bill, was speedily argued out of the claim as nurse at the first Southern questioning.

Mr. Talbert. I would like to have the report in that case read.

Mr. Ray of New York. If the gentleman will permit me, I will make a brief statement which may cover the point.

Mr. Talbert. That will be satisfactory.

Mr. Ray of New York. . . . This pensioner is now drawing the sum of $8 a month and we propose to increase it to $25 a month. She was the widow of Nelson Davis, who served in Company G, Eighth United States Infantry, from Sept. 1863, to November, 1865, and was honorably discharged. She also served long and faithfully as an army nurse. She acted as a nurse in the hospitals, as a cook in the hospitals, and as courier messenger and spy during the whole period of the war. There is a letter accompanying the report from Hon. William H. Seward, which refers to her services, and there are also letters from other officers of high rank in the service, attesting her faithfulness and efficiency.

She is now old and very poor, and an object of charity, unless the pension is increased.

Mr. Talbert. She is getting pensioned as a widow then, and also as a nurse?

Mr. Ray of New York. No, only as a widow. She is about 75 years of age, I may add, as I remember the testimony.

Mr. Jett (of Illinois). What does the bill provide for her?

Mr. Ray of New York. An increase of from $8 to $25 per month.

The bill was considered, and was laid aside to be reported to the House with a favorable recommendation.

In spite of the aim of the South Carolina Congressman to deny Harriet the credit of receiving her award as a nurse and intelligence representative, the *Congressional Record,* of course, had to print the information on Harriet's war service, making it an indelible part of the American record. In the printed Senate report, which published the officers' certificates of Harriet's war record, including Seward's exalted estimate of her, it was the contention of Congressman Shoup, from the Committee on Pensions, that Harriet ought to win her reward on the basis of her military services. "The papers in this case show that a claim for this woman was once presented to the House of Representatives and referred to the Committee on War Claims. Manifestly, that would be the better way to reimburse her for her alleged services to the Government, but her advanced years and necessitous condition lead your committee to give the matter consideration." [5]

When the pension was finally awarded to her, as the widow of Nelson Davis, five dollars was whittled off of the twenty-five dollar request, and she was granted twenty dollars a month for the duration of her life.

*   *   *   *   *

For years Harriet had looked from the porch of her residence over a 25-acre expanse of adjoining terrain, dreaming of what a fine community farm it would make. She was desirous of presenting this to the Negro church of Auburn, for that institution to operate collectively. At last, in June of 1896, by sheer audacity, she did come into possession of this property. The lot was to be sold at auction, and on the day of the sale Harriet appeared at the scene with very little money, but a determination to have the land, cost what it might.[6]

Harriet has described the circumstances of her purchase: "They were all white folks but me, there, and there I was like a blackberry in a pail of milk, but I hid down in a corner, and no one knew who was bidding. The man began down pretty low, and I kept going up by fifties. At last I got up to fourteen hundred and fifty, and then others stopped bidding, and the man said, 'All done. Who is the buyer?'

" 'Harriet Tubman,' I shouted."

They turned to her in astonishment, wondering where she would obtain the money to make the purchase, but Harriet went down to a bank and secured the money by mortgaging the land. But it was not easy to operate an enterprise like this, and because of lack of funds the permanent incorporation of what Harriet wished to call the "John Brown Home," was not achieved until 1903 when she deeded the 25 acres and her home to the African Methodist Episcopal Zion Church. In 1908 the center was formally opened, and the first inmates settled there.

That had been the chief aim of her latter years, and now it was realized. From that time on until Harriet's death, and long beyond her passing, ten or twelve persons were constantly sheltered there. The white people of Auburn were astonished at this place, for it had no specific character: it housed the sick and the well, the young and the old, sightless and seeing, whoever was in need. A young colored woman named Frances Smith became matron, doing the cooking and much of the other hard work, and watching out for Harriet.[7]

Once she broke off active participation in behalf of the home. "When I gave the Home over to Zion Church, what do you suppose they did? Why, they made a rule that nobody should come in without a hundred dollars. Now I wanted to make a rule that nobody could come in unless they had no money. What's the good of a Home if a person who wants to get in has to have money?"[8] Harriet was eminently philanthropic, as usual, but she may have been a bit impractical by now. The colored community of Auburn deemed itself unable to support a completely free institution. On another score, though, Harriet was correct. She came to grips with the colored leaders about the composition of the executive board of her home. She was in favor of a board combining membership of both white and Negro communities, but her colored advisers overruled her, and kept the directorship of the home exclusively in Negro hands. All of Harriet's Abolition and Civil War work had taught her the value of inter-racial cooperation.

How correct she was in her fight for white membership on the executive board is illustrated by the fact that a few years after her death the home which she founded had to be abandoned, while another Harriet Tubman Home, established in Boston in 1904, but operated with white and Negro cooperation, is still in existence (in 1942). The Boston home was founded by Julia O. Henderson of that city. She called together four others and they, seeing the need of a home for colored women in Boston rented a house for two years. With Harriet's permission, the home was named after her. Harriet was present at the dedication. The Boston home was one of the first community centers to be named after Harriet, but subsequently other Harriet Tubman Homes spread all over the land, especially after her death.

She kept moving through the streets of Auburn to the homes of her friends, to Syracuse, to Boston, to Rochester. She liked to travel. When she made a trip to Boston she didn't concern herself about time-tables. She simply went to the Auburn depot and waited for eastbound trains. She took the first that came along, and away she went. She was a legend in Auburn by now. A new generation was running the city, and the young bloods stood in awe of her and of the stories that had been related about her war days. The old and young pointed at her and said, "There goes Harriet Tubman."

She shriveled up as she became older. Her clothes looked more like drapes, and she always wore a couple of cloths around her head in bandana fashion.[10] Mrs. Emily Hopkins Drake has written: "We always loved to hear her sing, and I remember vividly how she would rock to and fro, pounding her hands on her knees in time to the rhythm." Mrs. Drake took some photographs of Harriet. "I remember well the day we took those snaps, how Harriet went to a mirror, and tied on her cape, pulling out the ribbons that held it, and the white ruffle about her throat with as much care and pride as a young girl. Her dress was a neat percale as I remember it, dull in color. I should say, a grey and white stripe, though I am not positive about that. The hat was a battered old black straw with ribbon trimming."[11]

In 1911 she was interviewed by James B. Clarke, who wrote a pamphlet about her and helped raise funds for her home. On the day of his visit she had without assistance gone down stairs to breakfast, and he saw her eat a dinner that would "tax the stomach of a gourmand." She resented the suggestion that someone should feed her. She only wanted the nurse to cut the chicken and place the tray on her lap.[12]

She was zestful to the end, as illustrated in a prank she played on her great grand-niece, Alice Lucas. The child, who was eight or nine years old at the time, was at play in the yard, when suddenly she was frightened as something seemed to be crawling along the grass behind her. It was Harriet, slinking over the ground, dragging herself Indian fashion, in imitation of the way she had worked on the Underground and in the Department of the South.[13]

In 1911 Harriet was under care at the Auburn City Hospital, and upon her discharge she entered the home which she had founded to spend her remaining days. *The New York World* of Sunday, June 25, 1911, reported this in a story headline, "Moses of Her Race Ending Her Life in Home She Founded."

"She was the friend of great men, but now, almost a centenarian, she awaits the last call. Now, with the weight of almost a hundred years on her shoulders, she seeks rest during the few remaining days. . . ."

On her last trip to church she stood before the colored people of Auburn and said: "I am nearing the end of my journey; I can hear them bells a-ringing, I can hear the angels singing, I can see the hosts a-marching, I hear someone say: There is one crown left and that is for Old Aunt Harriet and she shall not lose her reward." [14]

On the 18th of November, 1912, she made out a will, leaving her property to three persons, but in typical equalitarian fashion, "to share and share alike." The testament read, "I will and devise my real estate consisting of seven acres of land with brick house in the town of Fleming, Cayuga County, N. Y., to Mary Gaston, my niece, and Katy Stewart, grand-niece, and Frances R. Smith, share and share alike and I direct my executor hereinafter named to sell, and divide the proceeds from the said sale, said real estate and carry out the terms of this will." [15]

When Harriet lay abed, too feeble to get about, but still with a mighty heart beating and keeping her alive with an insistence almost that this woman must not die, she was visited by Mary B. Talbert. Mrs. Talbert, head of the New York State Federation of Colored

Women's Clubs, was highly esteemed by white as well as colored women. She knew, as did most Negroes, that when Harriet left, the greatest star in the Negro horizon—veritably the north star— would pass. It was a few weeks before Harriet's death when she told Mrs. Talbert "of the sweet spirit in that home, and of the happiness she felt was there." As Mrs. Talbert arose to go Harriet grasped her hand firmly and delivered her final message to the woman suffrage cause, telling the women to "stand together." [16]

*   *   *   *   *

Perhaps the most astonishing thing of all in the life of Harriet Tubman was the *strength* with which she died. She was the leader unto the last breath. "Conscious up to within a few hours of her passing, she joined with those who came to pray for her and the final scene in the long drama of her life was quite as thrilling as the many that had gone before." [17]

It was pneumonia, and there was no north star that could help her now. She called to her bedside a few of her friends. She was sorry she couldn't help Eliza E. Peterson who had come all the way from Texarkana, Texas, to see her. Mrs. Peterson was national superintendent for temperance work among colored people, and she had arrived here seeking the aid of Harriet and others in her work. The best that Harriet could do was to extend greetings to colored temperance advocates—greetings and farewell. There were two ministers present. She brandished her feeble hands, uttered some faint words to draw them about her and they joined in a final service *which Harriet directed.*[18]

That evening, March 10, 1913, the soft chant, "Swing Low, Sweet Chariot," drifted out of the front door of the Tubman home.

*   *   *   *   *

Harriet's last rites were *military*, the local Charles A. Stewart Post of the Grand Army of the Republic presenting the honors.

When Harriet passed the city of Auburn felt a great void. A year later it was decided that there should be an enduring memorial to this woman. The whites and the Negroes organized a day of demonstration for Friday, June 12, 1914. Booker T. Washington, Mary B. Talbert, and white leaders of the community of Auburn, met at the Auditorium and unveiled a bronze tablet to the memory of Harriet, which was afterward placed on the front entrance of the Cayuga County Courthouse (where it is to this day). On the day before the demonstration the Mayor of Auburn, Charles W. Brister, issued the following proclamation:

LET ALL DISPLAY FLAGS ON THE MORROW!
Is the Official Wish of Mayor Brister, That the Memory of Faithful Old Slave Harriet Tubman May Be Honored

The citizens of Auburn have very properly seen fit to erect a public monument to the memory of Harriet Tubman, as a tribute for her faithful services to the Nation, during the Civil War, and to her own people in the cause of freedom. As a further mark of respect and as a token of appreciation for her loyal and patriotic service to our country and flag, as Auburn's Chief Executive Officer I direct that on tomorrow, June 12, the date of the unveiling of the memorial, the flags be displayed on the municipal buildings, and suggest as there are many of our loyal citizens who may wish to honor the memory of this faithful old slave who was willing to die for her race, if need be, that they also at the same time cooperate and display the national emblem from their homes and places of business.

If the stars and stripes could float from every home in Auburn we believe that it would inspire patriotism and demonstrate that we are not forgetful of those who suffered for the cause of freedom and were willing to die that we might have one country and one flag.

CHARLES W. BRISTER,
Mayor

Auburn, N. Y., June 11, 1914 [19]

And on the day designated flags furled, and a white city celebrated the memory of a black woman, an unheard of tribute in American history. It never happened before, nor has it happened since. That night Booker T. Washington addressed the citizens of Auburn in the huge Auditorium. He described how she had "brought the two races nearer together, made it possible for the white race to place a higher estimate upon the black race." [20] Mayor Brister said that not because the subject of this memorial was a woman, nor because she was black, was this tribute tendered, but rather to commemorate the inherent greatness of her character.[21]

On the following day an editorial in *The Auburn Citizen* said:

"The meeting at the Auditorium last night may be said to rank among the most unique in the history of this state, if not the nation. Every thoughtful person in the audience carried away the thought—what a remarkable woman Harriet Tubman must have been to deserve this tribute, an enduring monument from the white race to one of the lowliest and most humble of the blacks! Where has anything like it been recorded! . . .

"How many of the white race exist today who will ever merit equal recognition with Harriet Tubman?"

DOCUMENTATION

PART I — CHAPTER I

[1] Reverend James Mason, *The Modern Amazon*, pamphlet, passim.
[2] Letters of Harkless Bowley, Tubman Collection, Schomburg Collection, 135th Street Branch Public Library, New York.
[3] Benjamin Drew, *The Refugees, or Narratives of the Fugitive Slaves*, p. 30. Fortunately a living relative has something to say upon this matter. This is Harkless Bowley, a grand-nephew of Harriet, who is now 88 years old (in 1941). In point of his years he may be regarded as the dean of the living relatives of Harriet. He lived with Harriet when he was a boy, and his own mother was one of those who fled North with the "Conductor of the Underground Railroad," as Harriet was often known. For the information supplied by Bowley, see his letters referred to in the preceding footnote. In the Sanborn article, *The Commonwealth* (Boston), July 17, 1863, there is further mention of Harriet's kin, and there is also some dealing with them in William Still's *The Underground Railroad*.
[4] Frank C. Drake article in *The New York Herald*, September 22, 1907, passim.
[5] Sarah H. Bradford, *Scenes in the Life of Harriet Tubman*, p. 10.
[6] *Ibid.*
[7] Harriet Tubman article, the Boston *Commonwealth*, July 17, 1863, passim.
[8] Statement of Mrs. William Tatlock, in Tubman Collection, Harlem Library.
[9] Sarah H. Bradford, *Harriet, the Moses of Her People*, in supplementary chapter added to the 1886 edition.
[10] *Letters of Harkless Bowley*, Tubman Collection.
[11] *Ibid.*
[12] *Scenes in the Life of Harriet Tubman*, p. 10.

CHAPTER II

[1] The Boston *Commonwealth*, July 17, 1863, passim.
[2] *Scenes in the Life of Harriet Tubman*, p. 13.
[3] The Boston *Commonwealth*, July 17, 1863, passim. Also described to the author in correspondence with historian Wilbur H. Siebert, who talked with Harriet. Letter, in Tubman Collection, is dated September 4, 1940.
[4] *The New York Herald*, September 22, 1907, passim.
[5] *Scenes in the Life of Harriet Tubman*, pp. 14-15.
[6] Statement to author by Mrs. Carroll Johnson, 64 Garrow Street, Auburn, N. Y. Mrs. Johnson is a great grand-niece of Harriet Tubman.
[7] *Scenes in the Life of Harriet Tubman*, p. 15.
[8] Herbert Aptheker, *Negro Slave Revolts in the United States*, p. 15.
[9] William Still, *Underground Railroad*, pp. 395-6.
[10] The Boston *Commonwealth*, July 17, 1863, passim.
[11] *Ibid.*
[12] Drake article, *The New York Herald*, September 22, 1907, passim.
[13] *Scenes in the Life of Harriet Tubman*, p. 10.

CHAPTER III

[1] Elizabeth Lawson, *History of the American Negro People*, p. 15.
[2] *Scenes in the Life of Harriet Tubman*, p. 16.
[3] Elias Jones, *Revised History of Dorchester County*, account of Tubman estate, passim.
[4] *Ibid.*
[5] *Scenes in the Life of Harriet Tubman*, p. 15.
[6] *Ibid.*
[7] *Ibid.*

[8] The Boston *Commonwealth*, July 17, 1863, passim.
[9] Letter to author from Clerk of Circuit Court of Dorchester County, Maryland, in Tubman Collection.
[10] *Scenes in the Life of Harriet Tubman*, p. 107.
[11] *The New York Herald*, Sept. 22, 1907, passim.
[12] *Ibid.*
[13] *Scenes in the Life of Harriet Tubman*, p. 24.
[14] The Boston *Commonwealth*, July 17, 1863.
[15] *Scenes in the Life of Harriet Tubman*, pp. 16-21.
[16] Statement of Mrs. William Tatlock, in Tubman Collection.
[17] *Scenes in the Life of Harriet Tubman*, p. 19.

It was stated at the outset that Harriet's master was Edward Brodas. That is the name and spelling given by Harkless Bowley, the living grand nephew of Harriet. Records substantiate the fact that slaveholders named Brodess lived at the same location where Harriet was reared, that the "Brodess brothers" owned property at that point. There are other records, noted in the chapters devoted to the Underground Railroad, which refer to several of Harriet's brothers being in the service of a mistress named Eliza Ann Brodins. That is the name and spelling as recorded, perhaps hastily, by historian William Still in his "The Underground Rail Road." This "Brodins" may also be one of the Brodas clan but there is no certainty on this point. We have used the Brodas spelling throughout when referring to her master.

One report, in a fictional account dealing with Harriet Tubman, states that upon her escape from slavery, she killed her master. That appears in Leonard Ehrlich's, *God's Angry Man*. Mr. Ehrlich admits that he took a fictional license, on this point, saying that if there were no other accounts of any such incident, then his treatment of this matter must be ignored. See the Leonard Ehrlich letter in the Harriet Tubman Collection, Schomburg Library, Harlem, New York.

PART II — CHAPTER IV

[1] *Scenes in the Life of Harriet Tubman*, pp. 19-20.
[2] *The New York Herald*, September 22, 1907, passim.
[3] The Boston *Commonwealth*, July 17, 1863, passim.
[4] Letters of Harkless Bowley, Tubman Collection.
[5] "A Moses in War-Time Maryland," *The Baltimore Sun*, April 21, 1928, p. 13.
[6] Wilbur H. Siebert, *The Underground Railroad*, p. 358.
[7] The Boston *Commonwealth*, July 17, 1863, passim.

Fred Landon, librarian of the University of Western Ontario, London, Canada, in a letter to the author, on August 15, 1939, sends a report from a Toronto newspaper referring to Harriet's arrival there with members of her family. Mr. Landon says: ". . . I came upon the enclosed extract from *The Globe* (Toronto). It was not dated but was plainly printed shortly after her death. I knew the Rev. R. A. Ball, when he was a minister in London (Canada), and I am sure that his statements can be relied on." The report sent by Mr. Landon is an editorial that appeared soon after the death of Harriet Tubman. In it the following was stated: "The Rev. R. A. Ball of B.M.E. Church of this city, who was a lad in St. Catharines while the underground railroad was in operation, remembers Harriet Tubman's arrival there on her first escape from slavery with two of her brothers. On her first rescue journey she led to freedom another brother, William, and his wife and child. On the next she brought her aged father and mother. By that time the desire to help in the destruction of slavery had become the passion of her life. Henry Ball of St. Catharines, a brother of Rev. R. A. Ball . . . tells how Harriet Tubman, after getting a party safely over the border— usually at Niagara Falls—would say to them: 'Shout, shout, you are free.' Some of the refugees in their ecstasy would clap their hands, kneel in prayer, kiss the ground that meant freedom to them, and say, 'This is British soil.'" There are several contradictions in the foregoing with other reports of the order in which Harriet rescued members of her family.

[8] The Boston *Commonwealth*, July 17, 1863, passim.
[9] *Ibid.*
[10] Frederick Douglass: *Life and Times of Frederick Douglass*, pp. 329-30.

[11] The Boston *Commonwealth*, July 17, 1863, passim.

[12] *Ibid.*

CHAPTER V

[1] *Scenes in the Life of Harriet Tubman*, p. 57.

[2] William Still: *The Underground Railroad*, p. 395.

[3] Sarah Bradford relates this story of a brother named John Ross, but William Still's record of this escaping party indicates that it was Henry Ross who was "the father of two small children, whom he had to leave behind." No John Ross is mentioned in this account. The likely explanation is that the Henry Ross named by Still took the name of John later, in freedom, and when Harriet told the story to Mrs. Bradford, she related it of one who was now named John. William Still, however, made his notes in the heat of the escape itself, fourteen years before Mrs. Bradford wrote her story; his notation definitely refers to Henry Ross as leaving a wife, Harriet Ann, and two children.

[4] *Scenes in the Life of Harriet Tubman*, p. 59.

[5] William Still, *The Underground Rail Road*, p. 298.

[6] *Scenes in the Life of Harriet Tubman*, p. 62.

[7] In a letter by William Brinkley to the Vigilance Committee of Philadelphia, dated March 23, 1857, in William Still's *The Underground Rail Road*, p. 74.

[8] William Still, *The Underground Rail Road*, p. 296.

(Still has reported six men in this company, Sarah Bradford five. Garrett either erred or sent on an extra man for some reason or other.)

[9] *Ibid.*, p. 297.

CHAPTER VI

[1] *Scenes in the Life of Harriet Tubman*, p. 22.

[2] William Wells Brown, *The Rising Son: or The Antecedents and Advancement of the Colored Race*, pp. 536-539.

[3] Wilbur H. Siebert, *The Underground Railroad*, p. 118. Siebert's interview with Harriet Tubman on April 8, 1897, in Boston.

[4] *Ibid.*

[5] Doctor R. C. Smedley, *History of the Underground Railroad in Chester County*, pp. 249-50.

[6] Reverend James E. Mason, *Tribute to Harriet Tubman: The Modern Amazon*, a pamphlet reprinting an address given by the Reverend Mason during the month of June, 1914, and first published at that time in the *Advertiser-Journal*, Auburn, New York.

[7] The Boston *Commonwealth*, July 17, 1863, passim.

[8] Elizabeth Cady Stanton, *Eighty Years and More, Reminiscences of Elizabeth Cady Stanton*, p. 51.

[9] Frederick Douglass, *Life and Times of Frederick Douglass*, pp. 329-330.

[10] Willis B. Knowles, in the *Rochester Democrat and Chronicle*, November 8, 1936, in a series of articles on the Underground Railroad in Western New York.

[11] John White Chadwick, *A Life for Liberty, Anti-Slavery and Other Letters of Sallie Holley*, p. 80.

[12] Reverend James Freeman Clarke, *Anti-Slavery Days*, pp. 81-82.

[13] Drake article, the New York *Herald*, Sept. 22, 1907, passim.

[14] Philip Green Wright and Elizabeth Wright, *Elizur Wright, the Father of Life Insurance*, p. 203.

[15] Letters of Harkless Bowley.

[16] *Scenes in the Life of Harriet Tubman*, p. 25.

[17] William Still, *The Underground Rail Road*, p. 297.

[18] Letter to author by Helen Storrow, Cornish Point, Buzzards Bay, R. F. D. 2, Mass., August 29, 1939.

[19] See Tatlock statement.

[20] Marion Gleason MacDougall, *Fugitive Slaves*, pp. 62-3.

[21] See Tatlock statement.

[22] *Ibid.*

[23] *Washington, City and Capital, American Guide Series,* 1937, p. 70.
[24] Letter to the author, May 31, 1939.
[25] *Scenes in the Life of Harriet Tubman,* p. 21.
[26] Letter to author from the Negro writer, George Schuyler, Sept. 1, 1939, Shomburg Collection.

CHAPTER VII

[1] Samuel J. May, *Some Recollections of the Anti-Slavery Conflict,* p. 283.
[2] James B. Clarke, *An Hour with Harriet Tubman,* passim.
[3] *Scenes in the Life of Harriet Tubman,* p. 50.
[4] Higginson collection of letters, Widener College, Harvard University.
[5] Colonel Thomas Wentworth Higginson, *Cheerful Yesterdays,* p. 8.
[6] Frank C. Drake article, *The New York Herald,* Sept. 22, 1907, passim. Drake reported this incident as occurring in Virginia, but that was unlikely as Harriet had no masters in that State. Other accounts say that the incident occurred in her home town, which would be Bucktown, and the master involved was Doctor Thompson.
[7] *Scenes in the Life of Harriet Tubman,* p. 63.
[8] According to Carter G. Woodson, in his *The Negro in Our History,* p. 269, William Wells Brown had done more than any other writer to popularize Negro history during the Abolition and Civil War periods. There is therefore a very authoritative source for the date of Harriet's arrival in Boston even though some of the Abolitionists do not seem to have met her until the late 'fifties.
[9] William Wells Brown, *The Rising Son; or the Antecedents and Advancement of the Colored Race,* pp. 536-9.
[10] Benjamin Drew, *The Refugee; or Narratives of Fugitive Slaves,* p. 31.
[11] William Still, *The Underground Rail Road,* p. 386.
[12] *Ibid.,* p. 387.
[13] Letter to the author from Mrs. Alexander D. Brickler, Jr., Wilberforce, Ohio, August 14, 1939. Mrs. Florence Carter, a close friend of Harriet Tubman in the closing period of Harriet's life, in a statement to the author, has verified the fact that the "kidnapped" child remained throughout life a favorite of Harriet Tubman; Mrs. Carter verifies that this woman bore a marked resemblance to Harriet, and photographs of the "favorite" do indicate this. Mrs. Carter states that this woman knew the life of Harriet better, probably, than any other person. Mrs. Brickler says that her mother died about ten years ago. The only point in Mrs. Brickler's story that might be questioned is the reference to one of Harriet's brothers as an ex-slave. Nowhere else has it been stated that Harriet had any brothers who were not slaves. Even so, it is possible that one of them might have bought his time or in some other way been manumitted.

CHAPTER VIII

[1] *Scenes in the Life of Harriet Tubman,* pp. 25-26.
[2] Sarah H. Bradford, *Harriet, the Moses of Her People,* chapter of additional incidents, pp. 133-153, passim.
[3] Sarah H. Bradford, *Scenes in the Life of Harriet Tubman,* p. 17.
[4] Richard Randall, "Fighting Songs of the Unemployed," *The Sunday Worker Progressive Weekly,* September 3, 1939, p. 2.
[5] Letters to the author, dated July 25 and July 26, 1939.
[6] William Still, *The Underground Rail Road,* p. 272.
[7] *Ibid.* William Still says that the direct reason for Bailey's flogging a few weeks earlier was a result of an altercation between Josiah and another slave. Sarah Bradford says that the beating came when Josiah was purchased by a new master, William C. Hughlett. This master immediately whipped Josiah, much as he would a new dog, to show him who was master. Whatever the reason for the flogging, Bailey decided to leave.
[8] Sarah H. Bradford, *Scenes in the Life of Harriet Tubman,* pp. 29-33.
[9] *Ibid.*
[10] John Lovell, Jr., "Social Implications of the Negro Spiritual," *Journal of Negro Education,* October, 1939.

CHAPTER IX

[1] *Frederick Douglass' Paper*, statement on Sept. 12, 1856.

[2] The *Frederick Douglass' Paper*, from 1856 on, reveals the intimate connection of Douglass and his followers to the growing Republican organization. In the Reconstruction period Douglass' allegiance to the Republican movement became orthodox, no doubt resulting from the efforts of this party in pushing through the Thirteenth, Fourteenth and Fifteenth Amendments. On May 30, 1872, Douglass wrote an editorial in *The New National Era*, a Negro newspaper, which concluded with the words, "The Republican Party is the true workingman's party of the country." The liberator, in this period, went into Negro labor organizations, trade unions, conferences and conventions, and always politicalized as a Republican, winning inestimable influence among the Negroes for this group. Charles H. Wesley in his *Negro Labor in the United States* (1927) devotes a chapter to "Early Organization of Negro Labor" wherein the important role of Douglass as a Republican is seen. Douglass' relationship to the Republican Party and the Negro influence he marshaled for this party is worth a special study. To this day Douglass' influence on the national vote, through the Republican vote, is a mighty and continuing factor in American life.

CHAPTER X

[1] *Auburn Citizen*, June 11, 1914, p. 5, col. 2. Mrs. Telford says that Harriet's parents were immediately settled there, but actually they did not stay in Auburn until the winter or spring of 1858. Mrs. Telford also says that at about that time Harriet made her first trip to Boston in the course of raising funds to pay for the new house, but Harriet had been there repeatedly for several years, according to the most reliable evidence.

[2] William Still, *The Underground Rail Road*, pp. 72-73.

[3] *Ibid.*, p. 74.

[4] *Ibid.*, p. 638.

[5] *Ibid.*, p. 639.

[6] *Ibid.*, p. 74.

[7] *Ibid.*, p. 247.

[8] *Ibid.*, p. 247. William Still goes on to say, "The Spring previous, she had paid a visit to the very neighborhood in which "Sam" lived, expressly to lead her own brothers out of "Egypt." She succeeded. To "Sam" this was cheering and glorious news, and he made up his mind that before a great while, Indian Creek should have one less slave and that Canada should have one more citizen." Harriet must have told young Green of some other Underground success, for she did not rescue her brothers until late in 1854.

[9] Boston *Commonwealth*, July 17, 1863, passim.

[10] *Scenes in the Life of Harriet Tubman*, pp. 109-111.

[11] *Ibid.*, pp. 52-53.

[12] William Still, *The Underground Rail Road*, p. 396.

[13] John Bell Robinson, *Pictures of Slavery and Freedom*, pp. 322-327.

CHAPTER XI

[1] *The Liberator*, July 8, 1859; also *The National Anti-Slavery Standard* (New York), Saturday, July 16, 1859.

[2] Frank C. Drake article, *The New York Herald*, September 22, 1907, passim.

[3] *Scenes in the Life of Harriet Tubman*, p. 25.

[4] William Still, *The Underground Rail Road*, p. 99.

[5] *Ibid.* The drawing was by a craftsman named Osler and it appears opposite page 102 of the Still book. Once in the North the Cambridge slaves were separated and settled in various places. Most of them went on to towns in Canada West; but at this time the anti-slavery sentiment in the free states was recrudescing, the defiance of the Fugitive Slave Act was becoming more overt, and many towns in the free states began to house and protect fugitives. At least one of the latest Cambridge party, a man named Nat Ambie, was settled in Seward's and Harriet's town. She, likely, was instrumental in finding shelter for him here. Nat was described by historian Still as "no ordinary man . . . and of more than ordinary intellectual capacities." p. 103.

[6] *Ibid.*, p. 109.

[7] *The National Anti-Slavery Standard*, Saturday, August 21, 1858, reprinted from *The Cambridge* (Md.) *Democrat* of August 10, 1858, article entitled "The Slaveholders of Maryland."

[8] *Ibid.*

[9] Carter G. Woodson, *The Negro in Our History*, p. 250.

[10] *The National Anti-Slavery Standard*, November 13, 1858.

[11] Report of Senator Pearce of Maryland, as the Report and Resolutions adopted by the Convention, *Anglo-African Magazine*, p. 320.

[12] *Anglo-African Magazine*, p. 316.

[13] *Scenes in the Life of Harriet Tubman*, pp. 35-6.

[14] *The National Anti-Slavery Standard*, Saturday, November 30, 1867.

[15] Item appears directly below editorials.

[16] *Scenes in the Life of Harriet Tubman*, p. 52.

[17] William Still *The Underground Rail Road*, p. 638.

[18] James Redpath, "Life of Captain John Brown," p. 64.

[19] Mary Thacher Higginson, *Letters and Journals of Thomas Wentworth Higginson* 1846-1906, p. 81.

[20] *The Liberator*, July 8, 1858; Convention reported by James M. W. Yerrington.

[21] Thomas Wentworth Higginson, *Cheerful Yesterdays*, p. ?.

[22] *The Liberator*, July 8, 1858.

[23] *Scenes in the Life of Harriet Tubman*, p. 7.

[24] *The Liberator*, Friday, August 26, 1859, article entitled "New England Colored Citizens' Convention."

ADDITIONAL NOTES TO PART TWO

How did Sarah Bradford and the others who consulted with her at the time that Harriet's story was written, in 1869, arrive at the computation of nineteen excursions into the slave land? Franklin B. Sanborn's record of the five earliest trips, from 1849 to 1852, unquestionably formed the first base of the estimate. Then Harriet's statement that she made eleven trips from Canada, but that she kept no accounting of other journeys, entered into the total. Thus, if Harriet made her first four sallies from one of the free states, and the next eleven from Canada West, this would reach fifteen. Since Harriet established her home in Auburn sometime in 1857 or 1858, there would remain, to be accounted for, about four additional trips from that town for the period on through December of 1860. (One or two of these remain to be described.) The William Still records have indicated at least one trip in the closing period; Franklin B. Sanborn described what he believed to have been Harriet's final campaign in 1860, and Colonel Higginson referred, in 1859, to Harriet's intention of "going again." About four trips would be a correct estimate, it seems, from the time of her Auburn residence through 1860. This would bring the total of campaigns to nineteen.

Actual dated journeys in the Sanborn, Still, Bradford and other accounts total only ten; but as has been observed, innumerable episodes, some of which occurred on the dated campaigns, and others belonging to a half dozen or so of voyages to which no actual date can be ascribed, bring the evidence of conductions, if not up to nineteen, then somewhere between the Sarah Bradford figure and the known dated journeys. All writers since Sarah Bradford have accepted the nineteen computations, but possibly few if any have attempted verification of the figure. There is no reason why a conservative estimate of fifteen excursions should not be acceptable. We can well afford to reduce the Bradford total to fifteen, and allow for some overlapping of records, and concede that there have been, as the cook says of the brew of coffee, a few spoonfuls for the pot. Actually, though, there is no reason, in view of Mrs. Bradford's careful check on Harriet's story (and multi-varied confirmation of both Harriet and Sarah Bradford) to question the total of nineteen. Then, as observed in the body of the story, even if there were only a dozen campaigns, it would not lessen the stature of the accomplishment; it would still be a dozen war-like marches into the camp of a desperate and vigilant enemy. If Harriet had not absconded with about 300 slaves, as is likely, and ran off with only 200, it would still be an economic blow to the slave power worth $200,000. Finally, it is when we try to estimate Harriet's total Underground effect, stimulating as she did other hundreds, perhaps five hundred, perhaps a thousand, to escape, and contributing above all others to a State-wide panic, that we run into much larger figures, much more significant end-results, and a much more likely estimate of her real contribution.

Mrs. Sarah H. Bradford published a second volume, *Harriet, the Moses of Her People*, in 1886, (George R. Lockwood & Son, New York). It was a revised version of the first, *Scenes in the Life of Harriet Tubman*, but it remained essentially the same story as the *Scenes*. It was more literary than the first book, the author apologizing for the haste with which the first "life of Harriet" was written. It contained, however, not more than a half dozen new incidents, none of exceptional significance. The main campaigns were recorded in the *Scenes* and these were reprinted, almost word for word, in the 1886 book.

Mrs. Bradford stated (on page 28 of the 1886 edition) that upon Harriet's first escape, she and three of her brothers set out, that they returned, and that she went on alone. This differed from the version of Harriet's escape as described in the *Scenes*. In the latter Harriet was said to have been brought back by her brothers.

The 1886 edition told a story (pp. 54-56) of Harriet and a company of slaves, including two "well-drugged infants," hiding in a swamp when they were threatened with capture. A Quaker knowing of the swamp, and learning their plight, came to the place where they were hiding, and aided their escape onto the next town by means of supplying a horse and wagon and provisions. Another story, (p. 92) described Harriet's visit at the home of the Reverend Henry Highland Garnett, a Negro Abolitionist, who lived in New York. Harriet arose one morning, inspired, and greeted Garnett by saying, "My people are free! My people are free!" The colored minister took her to task for her enthusiasm and optimism, and she retorted, "I tell you, sir, you'll see it soon. My people are free! My people are free!" On another flight (pp. 57-61), she aided a Mulatto girl named Tillie. This girl was waiting on the southeastern shore of the Chesapeake Bay for Harriet to come along. When she arrived with a company of fugitives, Tillie begged to be taken as far as Baltimore where she would be protected by friends. So vehement was her appeal that Harriet veered the course of the trip and took Tillie to Baltimore. They went by boat, met with difficulties, but by means of false passes finally arrived in Baltimore. The Unitarian minister, James Freeman Clarke, has also spoken of this episode.

PART III — CHAPTER XII

[1] Lillie B. Chace Wyman, *The New England Magazine*, March, 1896, vol. XIV, No. 1, pp. 110-118, passim.
[2] Boston *Commonwealth*, July, 1863, passim.
[3] Lillie B. Chace Wyman article, passim.
[4] *Ibid*.
[5] Franklin B. Sanborn, *The Life and Letters of John Brown*, p. 452.
[6] Richard J. Hinton, *John Brown and His Men*, p. 34.
[7] *John Brown's Diary*, in the Boston Public Library.
[8] Lillie B. Chace Wyman article, passim.
[9] William Ellery Channing, "John Brown," a poem, pp. 7-11.
[10] It has not been possible to verify this point.
[11] Fred Landon, "Canadian Negroes and the John Brown Raid," *Journal of Negro History*, Vol. VI, April, 1921.

CHAPTER XIII

[1] The Boston *Commonwealth*, July 17, 1863, passim.
[2] *Scenes in the Life of Harriet Tubman*, p. 6.
[3] Oswald Garrison Villard, *John Brown*, p. 396.
[4] Franklin B. Sanborn, *Life and Letters of John Brown*, p. 468.
[5] Report of the Senate Committee Investigating the Harper's Ferry Invasion, p. 69.
[6] Letter of Sanborn to John Brown (indorsed in Brown's hand), in the *Report of the Senate Committee Investigating the Harper's Ferry Raid*, pp. 67-8.
[7] *The New York Herald*, October 25, 1859.
[8] The Boston *Commonwealth*, July 17, 1863, passim.

[9] W. E. B. Du Bois, *John Brown*, p. 251.

ADDITIONAL NOTE TO PART THREE

Another colored woman entered the picture of the John Brown invasion at the time of the Chatham Convention in 1858. Mrs. Mary Ellen Pleasant, a West Coast business figure of some wealth, claimed to have presented the Old Man with $30,000. It has been proved that Mrs. Pleasant sailed to the East from California in the Spring of 1858, that she was in Chatham at about the time of the Convention, or soon afterward, and that she bought property in that town in 1858; but the size of her contribution to the campaign has been questioned. If Brown ever received such a fund there is no way of accounting how he used it, and it is doubtful whether he did receive it; but some financial aid he certainly received from Mrs. Pleasant. Complete information on Mary Ellen Pleasant's connection with John Brown may be found in the Boyd B. Stutler Collection. Another source is an article, "She Was A Friend of John Brown," by Earl Conrad, *Negro Digest*, November, 1940.

PART IV — CHAPTER XIV

[1] *Scenes in the Life of Harriet Tubman*, p. 86.
[2] *The Troy Whig*, April 27, 1860, passim.
[3] William Henry may have been Harriet Tubman's own brother, for according to her grand-niece, Mrs. Alice H. Brickler, of Wilberforce, Ohio, Harriet had a brother named William Henry who lived with her at least during the latter years of her life. The relative she called upon in Troy could have been this brother. William Henry has been referred to earlier as the one whose sweetheart escaped by disguising herself in men's clothes.
[4] *The Troy Whig*, April 27, 1860, passim.
[5] Statement of Martin Townsend in *Scenes in the Life of Harriet Tubman*, pp. 102-3.
[6] *The Troy Whig*, April 27, 1860, passim.
[7] According to *The Troy Arena*, another local newspaper whose dispatches were reprinted in *Frederick Douglass' Paper* of May 11, 1860, the only reason why many were not seriously wounded or killed by the law's gunfire was due to the poor aim of the authorities.
[8] Hayner's *Troy and Rensselaer County, New York, A History*, volume 2, p. 677.

ADDITIONAL NOTE TO CHAPTER XIV

In *The Fugitive Slave Law and Its Victims*, a pamphlet published in 1861, Harriet's role in the Nalle case is noted. In part, this account reads: "In this rescue, a colored woman was prominent, very active and persevering until success crowned their efforts—a woman known extensively among the colored people as 'Moses,' because she has led so many of their number out of worse than Egyptian slavery into the good land of freedom." (*Anti-Slavery Tract No. 15, New Series*. New York, published by the American Anti-Slavery Society, 1861, pp. 134-5.)

CHAPTER XV

[1] John Smith, *True Relations*, passim.
[2] Elizabeth Cady Stanton: "Address before American Anti-Slavery Society," Cooper Institute, New York, May 12, 1863, from *National Anti-Slavery Standard*, Saturday, April 4, 1863.
[3] *The Boston Commonwealth*, July 17, 1863, passim.
[4] *Scenes in the Life of Harriet Tubman*, pp. 54-5.
[5] The Boston *Commonwealth*, July 17, 1863, passim.
[6] *Ibid.*
[7] *Ibid.*
[8] *The Liberator*, Boston, June 8, 1860.
[9] The *Liberator*, July 6, 1860. Also *Official History of Woman Suffrage*, vol. 1, p. 276.
[10] Robert W. Taylor, *Harriet Tubman, the Heroine in Ebony*.
[11] The *Liberator*, July 6, 1860.
[12] John Bell Robinson, *Pictures of Slavery and Anti-Slavery*, pp. 330-31.

PART V — CHAPTER XVI

[1] See Tatlock statement, Tubman collection.

[2] The Boston *Commonwealth*, July 17, 1863, passim.

[3] William Still, *The Underground Rail Road*, p. 531.

[4] William Still said, however, that Stephen Ennets had been the slave of a man named John Kaiger, and that this master would not allow Stephen to live with his wife. The wife, Maria, lived eight miles away, and was "owned" by a man named Algier Pearcy. She wished to deliver her children from a life of service to this man. "Harriet Tubman being well acquainted in their neighborhood, and knowing of their situation, and having confidence that they would prove true, as passengers on the Underground Rail Road, engaged to pilot them within reach of Wilmington, at least to Thomas Garrett's. Thus the father and mother, with their children and a young man named John, found aid and comfort on their way, with Harriet for their 'Moses.' A poor woman escaping from Baltimore in a delicate state, happened to meet Harriet's party at the station, and was forwarded on with them. They were cheered with clothing, food, and material aid, and sped on to Canada."

[5] The Boston *Commonwealth*, July 18, 1863, passim.

[6] *The Frederick Douglass' Paper*, June 1861, from a speech delivered on Sunday, April 27, at the Zion Church, Rochester, N. Y.

[7] The Boston *Commonwealth*, July 17, 1863, passim.

[8] William Wells Brown, *The Rising Son; or the Antecedents and Advancement of the Colored People*, pp. 536-9, passim.

[9] The Boston *Commonwealth*, July 17, 1863.

[10] Elizabeth Hyde Botume, *First Days Amongst the Contrabands*, p. 16.

[11] *Letters of Lydia Maria Child*, pp. 159-61.

[12] *The Liberator*, February 12, 1862, p. 3, col. 3.

[13] Charles P. Wood manuscript, filed under Pension Certificate No. 415, 288, House of Representatives, in the name of Nelson Davis, the husband of Harriet.

CHAPTER XVII

[1] General Hunter letter, written February 19, 1863, in the Charles P. Wood manuscript.

[2] *Scenes in the Life of Harriet Tubman*, pp. 42-3.

[3] Charles P. Wood manuscript.

[4] *Ibid.*

[5] The Boston *Commonwealth*, July 17, 1863, passim.

[6] *Scenes in the Life of Harriet Tubman*, p. 37.

[7] *Ibid.*

[8] *Ibid.*, p. 69.

[9] *Ibid.*, p. 38.

[10] *Ibid.*, pp. 37-8.

[11] Higginson Collection, Widener College, Harvard University.

[12] In a General Affidavit, made out by Harriet, on January 1, 1898, attesting to the truth of the Charles P. Wood history. The Affidavit is on file with the Charles P. Wood manuscript.

[13] Correspondence with Mabel Runnette, Librarian, Beaufort Township Library, August 1, 1939, referring to Hariet's scouts. "As for the people whose names you mentioned, yes, we know that they were of the colored race. Their names are known here."

[14] General Affidavit, made out by Harriet, before mentioned.

[15] William Wells Brown, *The Rising Son; or The Antecedents and Advancement of the Colored Race*, pp. 536-9.

CHAPTER XVIII

[1] The *Commonwealth*, Boston, July 10, 1863, volume 1, Number 45.

[2] The *Principia*, p. 1139, column 3.

[3] *Official History of the War of the Rebellion*, Series 1, volume xiv, p. 308.

[4] *Scenes in the Life of Harriet Tubman*, p. 39.

[5] *Official History of the War of the Rebellion*, Series 1, vol. xiv, p. 306.
[6] *Ibid., Report of Captain John F. Lay Investigating the Combahee Raid*, p. 298.
[7] *Ibid.*, passim.
[8] *Ibid.*
[9] *Ibid.*
[10] *Ibid.*
[11] *Scenes in the Life of Harriet Tubman*, pp. 39-40.
[12] *Ibid.*
[13] *Ibid.*
[14] *Official History of the War of the Rebellion*, Series 1, vol. xiv, p. 305.
[15] *Ibid.*, p. 463.
[16] Luis F. Emilio, *A Brave Black Regiment*, pp. 36-7.
[17] Elizabeth Hyde Botume, *First Days Amongst the Contrabands*, pp. 50-1.
[18] William Wells Brown, *The Rising Son, or the Antecedents and Advancements of the Colored People*, pp. 536-9, passim.
[19] The *Commonwealth, Boston*, July 17, 1863, passim. Although Harriet declared that she had been away nearly two years, it was not more than a year and a half absence. It doubtless seemed longer due to the fatiguing occupation and the constant hazard.
[20] *Ibid.*

CHAPTER XIX

[1] Charles P. Wood manuscript.
[2] *The Auburn Citizen*, Tuesday, March 11, 1913, p. 5.
[3] Minna M. Schmidt, *400 Outstanding Women of the World and Costumology of Their Times*, pp. 397-8.
[4] Charles P. Wood manuscript.
[5] *The Auburn Citizen*, Tuesday, March 11, 1913, p. 5.
[6] *Ibid.*
[7] Harriet's statement to Hildegarde Hoyt Swift, author of *The Railroad to Freedom*, repeated to the present writer. Also described in Mrs. Swift's book.
[8] Albert Bushnell Hart, *Slavery and Abolition*, volume xvi of *The American Nation: A History*, p. 209.
[9] "Address of M. D. Conway," B. B. *Stutler Collection*, vol. ix (*John Brown Pamphlets*).
[10] Tatlock statement.
[11] Charles P. Wood mss.
[12] Frank C. Drake, *The New York Herald*, Sept. 22, 1907, passim.
[13] *Scenes in the Life of Harriet Tubman*, p. 3.
[14] *The Commonwealth*, (Boston), Friday, August 17, 1864.
[15] Rosa Belle Holt, "A Heroine in Ebony," *The Chautauquan*, vol. xxiii, July, 1896, pp. 459-462.
[16] Frank A. Rollins, *Life of Major Martin R. Delany*, p. 168.
[17] *Ibid.*, p. 182.
[18] Charles P. Wood mss., and also correspondence with P. M. Hamer, Archivist of National Archives, Washington, D. C., on Aug. 16, 1939.
[19] Charles P. Wood mss.
[20] *Ibid.*
[21] *Ibid.*
[22] *Ibid.*
[23] T. W. Higginson, *Army Life in a Black Regiment*, pp. 262-263.
[24] *Scenes in the Life of Harriet Tubman*, p. 46.

PART VI — CHAPTER XX

[1] *Scenes in the Life of Harriet Tubman*, p. 2.
[2] Chadwick, John White, *A Life for Liberty*, pp. 207-208.
[3] *Scenes in the Life of Harriet Tubman*, pp. 3-4.
[4] Chadwick, John White, *A Life for Liberty*, p. 205.
[5] *Scenes in the Life of Harriet Tubman*, p. 67.

[6] Also partly reprinted in *Scenes in the Life of Harriet Tubman*, pp. 22-23.

[7] *Scenes in the Life of Harriet Tubman*, p. 111.

[8] Charles P. Wood manuscript.

[9] *Ibid.*

[10] Sarah Bradford, in writing her book, did not take the word of Harriet Tubman. She checked up on every story that Harriet related and used only that material which she could verify through the written correspondence of others, or the printed page. It was a sound approach. Mrs. Bradford said, on page 47 of her *Scenes in the Life of Harriet Tubman*, that Mr. Charles P. Wood was to write for that book an account of Harriet's war services, but the Wood record was not published in that or any of the subsequent Bradford books. Mr. Wood did write a history of Harriet's war service on June 1, 1868, but it was used as evidence in Harriet's claim for a pension. As a result, when the Bradford biography appeared it gave only scant attention to the war period.

[11] *Scenes in the Life of Harriet Tubman*, p. 78.

[12] *Ibid.*, p. 112.

CHAPTER XXI

[1] Frank C. Drake article, *New York Herald*, September 22, 1907.

[2] Mrs. Florence E. Carter statement.

[3] News item in an unidentified Auburn newspaper, dated March 19, 1869.

[4] Bradford, Sarah H.: *Harriet, the Moses of Her People*, supplementary chapter, passim.

[5] *The Auburn Daily Bulletin*, Monday, October 6, 1873.

[6] *The Auburn Citizen*, March 11, 1913, p. 5.

[7] *The Auburn Daily Bulletin*, Monday, October 6, 1873.

[8] *Ibid.*

[9] *Congressional Record*, 43rd Congress, 1st Session, p. 2618.

[10] H. R. No. 3786, 53rd Congress, 1st Session.

[11] *Harriet, the Moses of Her People*, supplementary chapter, passim.

[12] *Ibid.*

[13] Tatlock statement.

[14] *Harriet, the Moses of Her People*, supplementary chapter, passim.

[15] Tatlock statement.

[16] Statement of Mrs. Frances Smith, matron in the Tubman Home, to the author.

[17] *The Auburn Citizen*, Tuesday, March 11, 1913, p. 5, passim.

[18] Henry Johnson, in a statement to the author, at his home, 27 Parker Street, Auburn, N. Y.

[19] Mrs. Florence E. Carter statement.

[20] *Harriet, the Moses of Her People*, supplementary chapter, passim.

[21] It is possible that Susan B. Anthony knew little of Harriet's service in the Department of the South and in the hospitals of the Washington region, for subsequently, when Miss Anthony, Elizabeth Cady Stanton and Ida Husted Harper wrote the *Official History of Woman's Suffrage* they made only small mention of Harriet's abolition and military record, although they incorporated in their history the achievements of most other pre-eminent American women in whatever fields.

[22] *Harriet, the Moses of Her People*, supplementary chapter, passim.

[23] *The Woman's Journal*, Saturday, April 17, 1897, column 2.

[24] Clarke, James B.: *An Hour with Harriet Tubman*, passim. The contact of Harriet and the British Queen has been verified by others then and now living, including Mrs. Tatlock, Mrs. Carter and Mrs. Carroll Johnson, of 64 Garrow Street, Auburn, N. Y.

[25] Shaw, Anna Howard: *The Story of a Pioneer*, pp. 240-241.

[26] In the Susan B. Anthony Collection, Library of Congress, Washington, D. C.

[27] Clarke, James B.: *An Hour with Harriet Tubman*, passim.

CHAPTER XXII

[1] Volume xxiii, July 1896, pp. 459-462.

[2] Correspondence in the Pension Claim of Harriet Tubman, filed under the name of Nelson Davis, No. 415,288, Veterans' Division, House of Representatives, Washington, D. C.

[3] *Ibid.*

[4] H. R. 4982, pp. 4542, 5062; *Congressional Record Index,* 1899, 55th Session of Congress.

[5] No. 1619, Harriet Tubman Davis, 55th Congress, 3d Session.

[6] *Harriet, the Moses of Her People,* supplementary chapter, passim.

[7] Statement of Mrs. Frances Smith, in Tubman collection.

[8] *The Auburn Citizen,* Tuesday, March 11, 1913, p. 5.

[9] Correspondence with Mrs. Fannie Lonon, president of the Harriet Tubman House, 25 Holyoke Street, Boston, Mass., on September 8, 1939.

[10] Statement of Mrs. H. D. Noble, of Auburn, N. Y., on July 13, 1939.

[11] Correspondence with Mrs. Emily Hopkins Drake, on August 24, 1939.

[12] *An Hour with Harriet Tubman,* passim.

[13] Correspondence with Mrs. Alice Brickler.

[14] *The Auburn Citizen,* Monday, March 17, 1913.

[15] Filed at Cayuga County Courthouse, Auburn, N. Y.

[16] *The Auburn Citizen,* March 14, 1913, p. 5.

[17] *Ibid.,* March 11, 1913, p. 5.

[18] *Ibid.*

[19] *The Auburn Citizen,* Thursday, June 11, 1914.

[20] *The Auburn Citizen,* Saturday, June 13, 1914.

[21] *Ibid.*

INDEX

A

Active Committee, 40.
Adamses (John Quincy Adams family), 213.
Adirondacks, 212.
Africa, 4, 34, 47, 64.
African Methodist Church, 27.
African Methodist Episcopal Church in Central and Western New York, 211.
African Methodist Episcopal Zion Church, Auburn, 221.
African Methodist Episcopal Zion Church, Rochester, 61.
Age of Reason, 132.
Agnew, Allen, 54.
Aireys, 194.
Alabama, 56.
Albany, 56, 59, 99.
Albany County, 136.
Alcotts (Bronson Alcott family), 141, 213.
Aldridge, Ira, 28.
Allen, Richard, 27.
American Party, The, 149.
American Revolution, 27.
Amistad case, 28–29, 34.
Anderson, Osborne Perry, 126.
Andrew, Governor, 158–159, 175.
Anthony, Susan B., 25, 60–61, 144, 146, 192, 197–200, 213–216.
Anti-Slavery Record, The, 28.
Anti-Slavery Society, 27, 59.
Anti-Slavery Society of Canada, 105.
Anti-Slavery Society of Edinburgh, 106.
Appalachian Route, 56.
Appeal, David Walker's, 27.
Ashanti, 5.
Atlanta, 202.

Atlantic (government transport), 158.
Attucks, Crispus, 27.
Auburn, 60, 74, 89, 91, 94, 115, 120-121, 129-130, 158, 177, 182, 191, 204, 206, 208-212, 214-216, 218, 220-222, 224-226.
Auburn Citizen, The, 226.
Auburn City Hospital, 223.
Auburn Daily Bulletin, The, 208.
Auburn Union, The, 129.
Ayllon, Vasque de, 170.

B

Bailey, Josiah, 78–83.
Bailey, William, 79.
Baird, Mrs. A., 184.
Baltimore, 7, 27, 42, 102–104, 153.
Baltimore American, The, 194, 196.
Baltimore Sun, The, 195.
Barnard, Simon, 58.
Barnard, William, 58.
Barnes, Surgeon General, 187.
Beaufort, 155, 158, 160-161, 163-167, 169, 174, 176, 209.
Beauregard, General G. P. T., 174.
Beechers (Henry Ward Beecher Family), 213.
Bell, John, 149.
Beman, A. G., 89.
Bibb, Mary, 25.
Big Buckwater River, 6.
Blackbird, 57.
Blackwell, Alice Stone, 78.
Blake, Mott, 166.
Blake Plantation, 173.
Blatch, Harriet Stanton, 66.
Booth, John Wilkes, 198.
Boston, 29, 60, 71–72, 100, 110, 114, 120–121, 123, 125, 127, 131–132, 139–148, 150, 156,

BOOKS BY EARL CONRAD

GENERAL HARRIET TUBMAN, Biography

JIM CROW AMERICA, Criticism

SCOTTSBORO BOY (with Haywood Patterson), Autobiography

ROCK BOTTOM, Novel

MR. SEWARD FOR THE DEFENSE, Novel

THE PREMIER, Novel

GULF STREAM NORTH, Novel

THE GOVERNOR AND HIS LADY, Novel

THE PUBLIC SCANDAL, Criticism

NEWS OF THE NATION (Co-Author), History

HORSE TRADER, Memoir

CRANE EDEN, Novel

THE INVENTION OF THE NEGRO, Historical Theory

THE DaVINCI MACHINE, TALES OF THE POPULATION EXPLOSION, Fantasy Short Stories

MY WICKED, WICKED WAYS (for and with Errol Flynn), Autobiography

BILLY ROSE: MANHATTEN PRIMITIVE, Biography

EL CRISTO DE MONTSERRAT, Novella

TYPOO, A Modern Novel

BATTLE NEW YORK: MURAL OF THE METROPOLIS, Poetry

EVERYTHING AND NOTHING: THE DOROTHY DANDRIDGE TRAGEDY (for and with Dorothy Dandrige), Autobiography

THE TUMBLIN WORLD OF TOM MacWHORTY, Poetry

CLUB, Novel

THE RED, WHITE AND BLUES: A Play in Two Acts

ERROL FLYNN: A MEMOIR